1980s Project Studies/Council on Foreign Relations

STUDIES AVAILABLE

NUCLEAR WEAPONS AND WORLD POLITICS:
Alternatives for the Future
Studies by David C. Gompert, Michael Mandelbaum, Richard L. Garwin, and John H. Barton

CHINA'S FUTURE:
Foreign Policy and Economic Development in the Post-Mao Era
Studies by Allen S. Whiting and by Robert F. Dernberger

ALTERNATIVES TO MONETARY DISORDER
Studies by Fred Hirsch and Michael W. Doyle and by Edward L. Morse

NUCLEAR PROLIFERATION:
Motivations, Capabilities, and Strategies for Control
Studies by Ted Greenwood and by Harold A. Feiveson and Theodore B. Taylor

INTERNATIONAL DISASTER RELIEF:
Toward a Responsive System
Stephen Green

STUDIES FORTHCOMING

Some 20 additional volumes of the 1980s Project will be appearing in the course of the next year or two. Most will contain independent but related studies concerning issues of potentially great importance in the next decade and beyond, such as resource management, terrorism, relations between the developing and developed societies, and the world market in conventional arms, among many others. Additionally, a number of volumes will be devoted to particular regions of the world, concentrating especially on political and economic development trends outside the industrialized West.

Nuclear Weapons and
World Politics

Nuclear Weapons and World Politics

ALTERNATIVES FOR THE FUTURE

DAVID C. GOMPERT

MICHAEL MANDELBAUM

RICHARD L. GARWIN

JOHN H. BARTON

Appendix by Franklin C. Miller

1980s Project/Council on Foreign Relations

McGRAW-HILL BOOK COMPANY
New York   St. Louis   San Francisco
Auckland   Bogotá   Düsseldorf   Johannesburg   London   Madrid
Mexico   Montreal   New Delhi   Panama   Paris   São Paulo
Singapore   Sydney   Tokyo   Toronto

The Council on Foreign Relations, Inc., is a nonprofit and nonpartisan organization devoted to promoting improved understanding of international affairs through the free exchange of ideas. Its membership of about 1,700 persons throughout the United States is made up of individuals with special interest and experience in international affairs. The Council has no affiliation with and receives no funding from the United States government.

The Council publishes the quarterly journal *Foreign Affairs* and, from time to time, books and monographs that in the judgment of the Council's Committee on Studies are responsible treatments of significant international topics worthy of presentation to the public. The 1980s Project is a research effort of the Council; as such, 1980s Project Studies have been similarly reviewed through procedures of the Committee on Studies. As in the case of all Council publications, statements of fact and expressions of opinion contained in 1980s Project Studies are the sole responsibility of their authors.

The editor of this book was Alexander R. Vershbow for the Council on Foreign Relations. Thomas Quinn and Michael Hennelly were the editors for McGraw-Hill Book Company. Christopher Simon was the designer; Teresa Leaden supervised the production. This book was set in Times Roman by Creative Book Services, Inc.

Printed and bound by R. R. Donnelley & Sons.

Library of Congress Cataloging in Publication Data

Main entry under title:

Nuclear weapons and world politics.

(1980s project/Council on Foreign Relations)
Includes index.
1. Atomic weapons and disarmament—Address,
essays, lectures. 2. Atomic weapons—Inter-
national Cooperation—Addresses, essays, lectures.
I. Gompert, David C. II. Series: Council on
Foreign Relations. 1980s project/Council on
Foreign Relations.
JX1974.7.N85   327'.174   77-8695
ISBN 0-07-023713-1
ISBN 0-07-023714-X pbk.

2 3 4 5 6 7 8 9 R R D R R D 7 0 9 8

Contents

Foreword: The 1980s Project

Decisions regarding nuclear weapons—their development, their deployment, and the circumstances in which they might be used—are traditionally the province of a very few leaders, supported by cadres of expert advisors, in a very few countries. Yet there are no decisions whose outcomes have a more profound effect upon the entire fabric of international life. The studies in this volume explore the issues raised by those decisions. They concern the roles that nuclear weapons might—and should—play in international relations during the decade of the 1980s and beyond.

These works are part of a stream of studies to be produced in the course of the 1980s Project of the Council on Foreign Relations. Each 1980s Project study analyzes an issue or set of issues that is likely to be of international concern during the next 10 to 20 years. The ambitious purpose of the 1980s Project is to examine important political and economic problems not only individually but in relationship to one another. Some studies or books produced by the Project will primarily emphasize the interrelationship of issues. In the case of other, more specifically focused studies, a considerable effort has been made to write, review, and criticize them in the context of more general Project work. Each Project study is thus capable of standing on its own; at the same time it has been shaped by a broader perspective.

The 1980s Project had its origins in the widely held recognition that many of the assumptions, policies, and institutions that have

ix

characterized international relations during the past 30 years are inadequate to the demands of today and the foreseeable demands of the period between now and 1990 or so. Over the course of the next decade, substantial adaptation of institutions and behavior will be needed to respond to the changed circumstances of the 1980s and beyond. The Project seeks to identify those future conditions and the kinds of adaptation they might require. It is not the Project's purpose to arrive at a single or exclusive set of goals. Nor does it focus upon the foreign policy or national interests of the United States alone. Instead, it seeks to identify goals that are compatible with the perceived interests of most states, despite differences in ideology and in level of economic development.

The published products of the Project are aimed at a broad readership, including policy makers and potential policy makers and those who would influence the policy-making process, but are confined to no single nation or region. The authors of Project studies were therefore asked to remain mindful of interests broader than those of any one society and to take fully into account the likely realities of domestic politics in the principal societies involved. All those who have worked in the Project, however, have tried not to be captives of the status quo; they have sought to question the inevitability of existing patterns of thought and behavior that restrain desirable change and to look for ways in which those patterns might in time be altered or their consequences mitigated.

The 1980s Project is at once a series of separate attacks upon a number of urgent and potentially urgent international problems and also a collective effort, involving a substantial number of persons in the United States and abroad, to bring those separate approaches to bear upon one another and to suggest the kinds of choices that might be made among them. The Project involves more than 300 participants. A small central staff and a steering Coordinating Group have worked to define the questions and to assess the compatibility of policy prescriptions. Nearly 100 authors, from more than a dozen countries, have been at work on separate studies. Ten working groups of specialists and generalists have been convened to subject the Project's studies to critical scrutiny and to help in the process of identifying interrelationships among them.

The 1980s Project is the largest single research and studies effort the Council on Foreign Relations has undertaken in its 55-year history, comparable in conception only to a major study of the postwar world, the War and Peace Studies, undertaken by the Council during the Second World War. At that time, the impetus to the effort was the discontinuity caused by worldwide conflict and the visible and inescapable need to rethink, replace, and supplement many of the features of the international system that had prevailed before the war. The discontinuities in today's world are less obvious and, even when occasionally quite visible—as in the abandonment of gold convertibility and fixed monetary parities—only briefly command the spotlight of public attention. That new institutions and patterns of behavior are needed in many areas is widely acknowledged, but the sense of need is less urgent—existing institutions have not for the most part dramatically failed and collapsed. The tendency, therefore, is to make do with outmoded arrangements and to improvise rather than to undertake a basic analysis of the problems that lie before us and of the demands that those problems will place upon all nations.

The 1980s Project is based upon the belief that serious effort and integrated forethought can contribute—indeed, are indispensable—to progress in the next decade toward a more humane, peaceful, productive, and just world. And it rests upon the hope that participants in its deliberations and readers of Project publications—whether or not they agree with an author's point of view—may be helped to think more informedly about the opportunities and the dangers that lie ahead and the consequences of various possible courses of future action.

The 1980s Project has been made possible by generous grants from the Ford Foundation, the Lilly Endowment, the Andrew W. Mellon Foundation, the Rockefeller Foundation, and the German Marshall Fund of the United States. Neither the Council on Foreign Relations nor any of those foundations is responsible for statements of fact and expressions of opinion contained in publications of the 1980s Project; they are the sole responsibility of the individual authors under whose names they appear. But the Council on Foreign Relations and the staff of the 1980s Project take great pleasure in placing those publications before a wide readership both in the United States and abroad.

Edward L. Morse and Richard H. Ullman

1980s PROJECT WORKING GROUP

During 1975 and 1976, ten Working Groups met to explore major international issues and to subject initial drafts of 1980s Project studies to critical review. Those who chaired Project Working Groups were:

Cyrus R. Vance, Working Group on Nuclear Weapons and Other Weapons of Mass Destruction

Leslie H. Gelb, Working Group on Armed Conflict

Roger Fisher, Working Group on Transnational Violence and Subversion

Rev. Theodore M. Hesburgh, Working Group on Human Rights

Joseph S. Nye, Jr., Working Group on the Political Economy of North-South Relations

Harold Van B. Cleveland, Working Group on Macroeconomic Policies and International Monetary Relations

Lawrence C. McQuade, Working Group on Principles of International Trade

William Diebold, Jr., Working Group on Multinational Enterprises

Eugene B. Skolnikoff, Working Group on the Environment, the Global Commons, and Economic Growth

Miriam Camps, Working Group on Industrial Policy

1980s PROJECT STAFF

Persons who have held senior professional positions on the staff of the 1980s Project for all or part of its duration are:

Miriam Camps	*Catherine Gwin*
William Diebold, Jr.	*Roger D. Hansen*
Tom J. Farer	*Edward L. Morse*
David C. Gompert	*Richard H. Ullman*

Richard H. Ullman was Director of the 1980s Project from its inception in 1974 until July 1977, when he became Chairman of the Project Coordinating Group. At that time, Edward L. Morse became Executive Director of the Project.

PROJECT COORDINATING GROUP

The Coordinating Group of the 1980s Project has had a central advisory role in the work of the Project. Its members as of December 31, 1976, were:

COMMITTEE ON STUDIES

The Committee on Studies of the Board of Directors of the Council on Foreign Relations is the governing body of the 1980s Project. The Committee's members as of December 31, 1976, were:

Approaching the Nuclear Future

David C. Gompert

For 30 years nuclear weapons have represented the ultimate in both technological achievement and political challenge. Failure properly to manage change in the qualities and numbers of nuclear weapons, as in the political relationships and institutions that provide for their control, could exact a sudden penalty of human suffering far surpassing the consequences of failure in any other field of endeavor, a penalty that would nullify traditional notions of victory and defeat. In looking toward the 1980s and beyond, we can expect that further technical development of nuclear weaponry will continue to attract, if not excite, the most advanced scientific ingenuity our world has to offer. The details of this process will be critical. Yet raw political wisdom or its absence will largely decide the course and consequences of technical change. The study of the control of nuclear weapons, then, must be a study of both the fine points of destructive technology and the fundamentals of political choice. This volume offers insights at both levels through close examination, over a broad conceptual range, of ways of dealing with the problems nuclear weapons will pose for international peace and progress.

Concern with nuclear weapons has, understandably, been dominated by the question of how to avoid cataclysmic war. Throughout the next decade, as today, this ultimate fear will be

NOTE: For a concise introduction to nuclear weapons concepts, terminology, existing nuclear arsenals, and recent arms control measures, the reader is directed to the Appendix of this volume.

1

somewhat eased by the wide recognition that the dimensions of unlimited nuclear war would be so grossly disproportionate to even the most severe disputes arising from competition among nations that no leader of sound mind would start or openly threaten such a conflict. But as long as untold destructive power is poised within minutes of detonation, we cannot rely solely on a presumption of rational calculation and behavior. Thus, beyond the question of how further to reduce the already slim danger of premeditated nuclear attack is the problem of how to avert conditions in which —out of miscalculation, panic, or even ultraprudence—either Soviet or American leaders conclude in the heat of a crisis that the odds of war are high enough and the advantages of striking first clear enough to warrant launching a preemptive attack. As we face the next decade, we must also ask what is the desired relationship between the Soviet-American nuclear balance and the new foci of nuclear danger resulting from proliferation: Should (can) nuclear peace be made divisible? And we must continue to address the crucial, practical problem of whether and how to depend on nuclear weapons and the fear of nuclear war to help suppress subnuclear forms of international conflict.[1]

The significance of nuclear weapons is not confined to these central questions of global war and peace. However faint the danger of holocaust, nuclear forces, policies, plans, and rhetoric can affect—pervasively, if subtly—hierarchy and interaction among nations, perceptions of constraint and opportunity among leaders, and feelings of well-being or fear among peoples. For instance:

---

[1]The West currently links nuclear weapons to conventional security through its *flexible response* strategy in Europe. Flexible response calls for a controlled escalation (from conventional defense to the use of tactical nuclear weapons to forward-based strategic weapons to intercontinental strategic weapons) as necessary to defeat a Soviet conventional offensive in Central Europe. Enunciation of the intention to conform to this strategy, along with the physical posture to do so, forms the basis of NATO deterrence of Soviet aggression. Additionally, theater nuclear weapons occupy an important place in the American strategy for deterring or resisting conventional aggression in the Far East, notably on the Korean peninsula. As well, the presence of nuclear weapons on American (and Soviet) warships serves to instill restraint in the engagement of naval units.

- Nuclear weapons can earn influence for those countries that ostensibly commit them to bolster the security of other countries. The very presence of American nuclear weapons in Europe and the Far East helps confirm perhaps otherwise dubious defense assurances that evoke deference to Washington on issues of trade, monetary affairs, UN voting, and the like.

- Quite apart from the military implications of success or failure in efforts to control nuclear arms competition, the direction and pace of such endeavors heavily influence the basic political relationship between those who are competing and negotiating. If the Soviet-American Strategic Arms Limitation Talks (SALT) have not been the leading edge of détente—and most would contend that they have been—they have at least given substance to what might otherwise have been a fleeting experiment in noble intentions. Conversely, failure to maintain demonstrable progress in SALT may signify if not reinforce the malaise of détente.

- Owing to the belief that constructing nuclear weapons is proof of national scientific excellence and industrial depth, the possession of a nuclear arsenal—and improvements in its size and quality—inflates the general estimation of the possessor in the eyes of other capitals and societies. China has become no richer, its scientists no brighter, by conducting nuclear tests; but in the currency of international respect, its stock as a world power has appreciated considerably since its first such test in 1964.

- Nuclear weapons can increase the national *hubris* and self-confidence of the possessor, thus emboldening its general international behavior. France's nuclear force, though minute compared with those of the two superpowers, restored a measure of French self-respect in the wake of imperial losses and fed the élan with which Charles de Gaulle maneuvered politically between Washington and Moscow in the 1960s.

- In the future as in the past, the development and maintenance of nuclear weapons will consume enormous human and financial resources. Annual worldwide investment in nuclear weaponry

3

will probably continue to exceed the level of resources needed to eliminate acute malnutrition on a global scale. To take a more practical example, it might be argued that American conventional military strength will continue to suffer due to budgetary competition with nuclear forces.

- "Mutual deterrence"—or, more graphically, Mutual Assured Destruction (MAD)[2]—has come to be widely accepted as the key to survival in the nuclear age. But the mentality that has formed around this concept, with its emphasis on "credibility" and "retaliation" and "will," may affect the judgments and warp the policies of the national leaders who have custody of the arsenals of mass destruction. To be credible in threatening certain and devastating reprisal for nuclear attack is to contribute responsibly to the preservation of civilization; to batter a weak and temporary adversary for the sake of appearing credible is a morbid misapplication of a strategic concept that is best made an exception and not a rule.[3]

- In the long run, the existence of nuclear weapons could fundamentally alter government-citizen relationships. If, over time, the need of governments to field expensive deterrent forces is not appreciated by citizens who no longer sense a real nuclear

[2]MAD (the appropriateness of the acronym has received sufficient comment elsewhere) is the relationship whereby both the United States and the Soviet Union possess the ability and espouse the determination to inflict "assured destruction" upon the other in response to a nuclear attack, thereby ensuring that such an attack never occurs. Since about 1974, when Secretary of Defense Schlesinger began openly to signal American interest in forces and war plans designed to limit nuclear war by retaliating against Soviet forces rather than Soviet citizens, a debate has raged in the United States as to whether or not to abandon MAD in favor of a more flexible and selective targeting doctrine. On the Soviet side, while the political leadership and the academic community has emphasized mutual deterrence as the basis for force planning and doctrine, the military establishment has continued to stress the importance of being prepared actually to fight a nuclear war.

[3]In *The Time of Illusion,* Alfred A. Knopf, New York, 1976, Jonathan Schell explores the effects of contemporary strategic thinking—notably, "deterrence theory" —on American politics and foreign policy over the past decade or so, especially in connection with the Vietnam War.

threat, popular support for the maintenance of forces could fade—and governments might feel themselves compelled to provide for deterrence without the consent of the governed.

Because of the apparent weight of nuclear weapons in world security and world politics, the thought of dramatic change in the management of these arms summons no less anxiety than the expectation that present conditions will persist. The current situation (in which available explosive power equals roughly 7,000 times the explosive power released in all of World War II) is absurd but stable.[4] The impulse to perfect stability is at least as strong as the impulse to escape absurdity. Attention to esoteric detail (such as how quiet, and therefore how safe from detection and destruction, missile-bearing submarines are) is both an imperative of prudent management and an impediment to the contemplation of fundamentally different nuclear futures. Those impressed with the gravity of practical strategic questions and the risks involved in departures from familiar conditions brand as naïve, if not irresponsible, those whose thoughts are on sweeping change. Those who believe that survival requires radical change—ultimately, if not urgently—despair of the experts' penchant for debating details and fine-tuning war scenarios.

The approach of the 1980s Project to the question of how to manage nuclear weapons was designed to avoid two pitfalls: preoccupation with the particulars of force posture and arms control issues at the expense of conceiving more basic alternatives to present conditions; and bold but vague prescriptions for dramatic change that leave unattended the specific policy issues most likely, in fact, to form the next decade's nuclear agenda. The approach around which this volume is organized—in which four distinct nuclear "regimes" are discussed—permits intensive inquiry into each of a diverse set of conceptions of the role and control of nuclear weapons in the decades to come. Each of this

---

[4]*Stable* strategic conditions are those in which the certainty of devastating retaliation precludes any advantage to the side that initiates a nuclear attack (*crisis stability*) and in which expectable additions to or improvements in the forces of one side will not significantly affect the overall balance of forces (*arms race stability*). It is generally accepted that these conditions prevail today.

volume's four principal authors was called upon not just to assess one such broad conception, but in fact to advocate a particular design and to indicate the steps needed to implement that design.

Simply put, *a nuclear regime may be thought of as a system of international obligations (formal accords, tacit commitments, and informal understandings), national force structures (how many and what kinds of weapons), and doctrines (when, where, why, how, and which nuclear weapons ought to be used) that together govern the role of nuclear weapons in war, peace, and diplomacy*. Each regime is based on a set of values and goals and on certain premises about the dangers and virtues of nuclear weapons. Each is shaped by certain expectations about the political and technological future. A preference for one regime over others should be based not only upon sympathy with its underlying values, but also upon satisfaction that the specified characteristics of the regime would in fact help deliver those values. Even then, doubts about the feasibility of bringing about desired conditions may cause one to lean toward a more realistic, if less satisfying, alternative, perhaps in the belief that the second best is a logical and necessary rung on the ladder toward the best.

The discipline, for each of the authors and now the readers, of having to think through the internal consistency of a single vision of how to manage nuclear arms and strategic relationships was an important aim in our decision to take the regime approach. The pursuit of contradictory objectives is the mother of policy failure. For instance, one might favor having those states with nuclear weapons pledge never to be the first to use them, yet at the same time be averse to the removal of all American tactical nuclear weapons from Europe lest such a step weaken Western confidence and encourage Soviet conventional military pressure. Espousal of both these policies would either undermine the value of the tactical nuclear weapons in deterring conventional aggression, vitiate the "no-first-use" pledge, or both.

Existing arms control literature is a cornucopia of concepts, critiques, and proposals; too often, at least of late, there has been little attempt to tie separate strands together, to scrutinize particular objectives in light of other objectives, and to develop out of a welter of prescriptions a coherent sense of direction. Admittedly, the regimes presented in this volume are abstractions; they have a certain tidiness, a snug fit of all the pieces, that cannot be expected in the complex and protean conditions of the real world. But the value of the regime approach is that it requires that proposals be set and judged in a broad context, that assumptions be spelled out, and that priorities be established among competing goals.

A sense of direction about the nuclear future must emanate from a basic philosophy about the meaning of nuclear weapons and how to govern them. (It is not my purpose here to represent the views of the authors of the various regimes presented in this volume, but rather to suggest how I would interpret each regime and distinguish it in the abstract from the others.) In its pure form, the *First Regime* (in essence, the current regime projected into the future) rests on the premise that the nuclear weapons of the United States and the Soviet Union, however they offend our intuitive sense of safety and proportionality, have in fact fostered—if not forced—moderation and stability in international politics. This regime advocates, and sees good prospects for, a continuation of the "system" that has prevailed for at least the last 10 years, a system that has stood the tests of time and tension. The *Second Regime* (an ensemble of arms control prescriptions) is derived from the belief that nuclear weapons are an inescapable burden and that our efforts should be devoted to reducing dependence on them in the conduct of world politics and the maintenance of international security. It would quite explicitly entrust nuclear weapons with one and only one purpose: to deter the use of other nuclear weapons. The availability or use of nuclear weapons for other purposes would be sharply constrained by an assortment of unilateral and multilateral measures. The *Third Regime* (a "denuclearized" world) does not accept the fate of an eternal nuclear predicament. It sees nuclear weapons not as a manageable burden but as an intolerable menace and therefore seeks to ban them. The nuclear system seems stable now, but certain stresses and contradictions may eventually lead to collapse and calamity. This expectation and the belief that it is morally corrosive for peace and stable world politics to depend in perpetuity upon the capacity and expressed willingness of leaders

7

to destroy one another's societies underscore the need to conceive of workable and enforceable arrangements for the abolition of nationally held nuclear weapons. Finally, the *Fourth Regime* (one of "strategic deterioration") anticipates a number of plausible developments in technology and politics over the next 10 to 15 years that could undermine strategic stability, shake world politics, and perhaps increase the chances of nuclear conflict. Specifically, it confronts several adverse possibilities: extensive nuclear proliferation, technological disequilibria, and nuclear imbalance between the United States and the Soviet Union. It looks less at how we can improve conditions than at how we might attenuate the perils of a forbidding nuclear future. In a sense, the implicit link between the Third (millennial) Regime and the Fourth (pessimistic) Regime closes the circle, for movement from present conditions to a denuclearized world might be politically possible only if catalyzed by a resurgence of nuclear danger.

Each of the four regimes presented in this volume is the specific creation of its author. Michael Mandelbaum provides us with his conception of the First Regime; Richard Garwin designs a Second Regime; John Barton sketches two possible Third Regimes—that is, two different visions of a denuclearized world—and suggests how world politics might be steered toward eventual achievement of the more desirable of the two visions; I explain how strategic conditions might get worse and how, in a Fourth Regime, the nations of the world might cope with such deterioration.

As the reader has learned from Richard Ullman's Foreword, the 1980s Project has tried to generate practical ideas about improving international life. In light of this objective, the essays in this volume require some explanation, for each deviates in its own way from the model.

The First Regime does not advocate *change* but rather a perpetuation of this status quo, with some refinements. But its inclusion here is crucial. Its exposition by Michael Mandelbaum provides a useful reference for thinking about the alternatives. More importantly, the First Regime deserves a defense not because inertia might inflict it upon us but because it has merits that are rarely articulated—except in a most piecemeal fashion—much less projected into the future.

The 1980s Project concentrates on *international* goals rather than on American national aims and policy choices. And while the other essays in this volume are not "American-centric," the Second Regime's author, Richard Garwin, has elected to cast his arguments mainly in terms of the actions and interests of the United States rather than from an international perspective. The exception seems warranted. Garwin believes that the United States can bring about many desirable conditions unilaterally—in some instances without a need for reciprocity by other actors and in other instances with reciprocity desirable but not essential. In still other respects, Garwin quite explicitly calls for international action to facilitate the emergence of his Second Regime. But since he argues that altered American policies would largely suffice, it is appropriate for him to make the case that such policy change is in fact in the American as well as in the "global" interest.

The 1980s Project emphasizes *achievable* solutions to international problems. So why does it bother to examine nuclear disarmament—a plainly infeasible goal for the 1980s? First, as the reader of John Barton's essay on the Third Regime will see, thinking about the nature of, paths toward, and obstacles to a world without nuclear weapons compels one to reckon with basic questions of political choice, world order, and the meaning of nuclear weapons—questions that might otherwise escape notice. Second, if denuclearization is to be a goal for a more distant future, the next decade could be a period in which certain processes leading toward that goal can be put in train and, of course, in which the interposition of new obstacles must be avoided. If, for example, the difficulty of proscribing nuclear weapons increases as a function of the number of nations that have nuclear weapons, some progress toward the Third Regime in the next decade might be imperative, lest proliferation render eventual denuclearization utterly impossible. Third, since nuclear disarmament is so widely accepted in the abstract as a fundamental goal, it is only prudent to ask more systematically whether such a condition is in fact desirable—or at least what its benefits and draw-

9

backs might be. Last, if the desirability of denuclearization depends upon what form it takes (its institutions, its safeguards, its attendant changes in politics and attitudes), we had better know with as much precision as possible toward what sort of nuclearized world we should steer.

Finally, if the 1980s Project is meant to stimulate ideas about making international conditions *better,* why does this volume contain an analysis of how conditions might get worse and what responses are in order if they do? The importance of considering a troubled and troublesome Fourth Regime lies in the fact that even as we contemplate new ways of dealing with the problems posed by nuclear weapons, the problems themselves are changing. Our present situation prompts us to conceive of measures to impede the development of destabilizing nuclear technologies, to prevent strategic imbalance, and to stem the tide of nuclear proliferation. But a nuclear regime designed to deal with these problems may be neither appropriate nor adaptable if technology brings instability, if the central balance is upset by asymmetrical growth in Soviet and American strategic capabilities, or if the spread of nuclear skills, materials, and inducements soon (i.e., within a decade) produces a new crop of nuclear states. The Fourth Regime explicitly recognizes the changing nature of the strategic agenda. The policies and programs it suggests aim at making international conditions better than they would be if new problems evoke out-of-date solutions or no solutions at all.

Starting from the same conceptual reference points, another foursome of analysts would have come up with a different collection of blueprints for the various regimes. One individual's view of how the current (or First) regime should be preserved and improved, with its basic premises and parameters kept intact, might differ markedly in its particulars from that which another First Regime proponent would advocate. Similarly, no two analysts would write identical prescriptions for ridding the world of nuclear weapons (the Third Regime). The range of specific possibilities would seem even more vast in the cases of the Second and Fourth Regimes. Whereas the designs of a First and a Third Regime are largely prejudged by their assumptions and purposes, the design of a particular Second Regime is constrained only by the requirement that it involve significantly reduced dependence on nuclear weapons in politics and security, while the details of a Fourth Regime require only the general presupposition that strategic conditions will deteriorate.

The full value of the regime approach is realized only if comparisons are made among alternatives along several dimensions of practical policy concern. What do each of these sets of premises imply for such familiar issues as the size of nuclear arsenals, the doctrines that govern their deployment and use, the conventions and institutions that might provide some measure of international control, and the acquisition of nuclear weapons by an increasing number of nations?[5] Beyond these analytical questions, comparison is also essential for judging the worth of each regime. How achievable is each, how durable—that is, how invulnerable to future erosion by the currents of competitive politics and technological change, and how flexible in the event that certain internal features of the regime prove easier to attain and sustain than others? How would each regime meet untoward contingencies—growing distrust, confrontation, war? How would each affect the tone and temper of international politics and the prospects for progress on a variety of other "issue fronts"?

I attempt to furnish some answers in the last essay of this volume. In the meantime, the reader ought to reflect on these questions while examining and comparing the alternatives the volume presents.

[5]Another 1980s Project book, *Nuclear Proliferation: Motivations, Capabilities, and Strategies for Control,* deals more directly and comprehensively with the issue of proliferation.

International Stability and Nuclear Order: The First Nuclear Regime

Michael Mandelbaum

ONE

The Current Regime

The world has learned to live with the bomb. Over three decades a nuclear regime has come into existence. It consists of a set of practices and assumptions by which the terrifying weapons of mass destruction created by twentieth-century science have been absorbed into the age-old game of international politics. Some of the tenets of the current regime are written down in treaties and formal agreements; others are tacitly understood customs. The regime is a combination of technology and politics; both have driven its development. As scientists and engineers have discovered how to put greater and greater physical power into human hands, political and military leaders have turned this technology into immensely powerful weapons aimed against their adversaries. But they have also striven to keep that power from destroying the societies it is supposed to serve and protect. Since 1945, nuclear weapons technology has resembled a giant plant springing from the ground and shooting toward the sky, like Jack's beanstalk in the fairy tale. The current nuclear regime is the political framework that has successfully kept the plant from toppling over.

This regime has three principal pillars. The first is *anarchy*.[1] The system of independent nation-states that appeared in Europe in the seventeenth century now covers all the planet, and this

---

[1]The term *anarchy* means the absence of a central governing authority. It does not necessarily imply lawlessness or chaos.

15

international system has no institutional equivalent to the government of the state in domestic politics. There is no supranational authority with a legitimate monopoly of force to guide and regulate international affairs and to enforce international law. Each member of this anarchic system retains a full complement of sovereign prerogatives, among which a central one is the right to resort to force in whatever way it chooses. Each nation-state has not only the right to make war but also the incentive to be ready to do so, for all other states retain the same right and set their own rules regarding how and when to do so. The principal nuclear states of the current regime not only have few formal restraints on the use of their arsenals, they have declared that they will actually use nuclear weapons under certain circumstances. Thus the present nuclear regime is part of an international system in which weapons, including nuclear weapons, persist, and in which the use of force, even nuclear force, is neither illegal nor unthinkable.

The present regime rests on a second pillar—nuclear *equilibrium* between the two principal nuclear powers, the United States and the Soviet Union. Although their two arsenals do not correspond in every detail, they are equal in the most important category of comparison, the capacity for "assured destruction." Each has a nuclear arsenal that is potent and resilient enough to deal a death blow to the other's society even after absorbing a full-scale attack. Neither can count on disabling the other, even with an all-out surprise attack. The result has been a standoff: the two stalks of the nuclear plant brace one another; the certainty of annihilation has "deterred" each superpower from attacking the other.

The current regime's third pillar is *hierarchy,* the uneven, rank-ordered distribution of nuclear might. Of the present nuclear powers, the United States and the Soviet Union own by far the most significant arsenals. The vocabulary of politics has drawn on other fields to describe this state of affairs. From the argot of advertising has come the label "superpower," which the two both wear with a mixture of pride and anxiety.[2] Physics has contrib-

---

[2] The Soviets do not actually use the term "superpower" in official statements.

16

uted the term "bipolar" to describe how the superpowers act as distinct centers in the international system around which lesser states cluster. But their relationship with each other is best characterized by the economic term "duopoly": like two giant firms that dominate a single market, they have common and distinctive rights and privileges that they exercise competitively but that they also collude with each other to maintain.

The United States and the Soviet Union do not share an exclusive franchise on nuclear weapons. Three other states have manufactured them, and one additional nation—India—has set off a nuclear explosion, which is tantamount to testing a bomb. But the French and British nuclear stockpiles are relatively small, and the political and geographic circumstances of the two states make their weapons, for most purposes, part of the American strategic force, despite gestures of independence by the French. China is most emphatically part of neither the Soviet nor the American camp, but the Chinese arsenal has not had a profound effect on the international system's nuclear arrangements because it is dwarfed and held in check by the two giant forces. Although the regime is not a strictly bipolar one—the Chinese nuclear force has undoubtedly influenced Soviet and perhaps American foreign policy and defense planning—the United States and the Soviet Union remain, overwhelmingly, the two most important nuclear nations.

The current nuclear regime has three closely related achievements to its credit. First, there has been no nuclear war since 1945. Since the end of World War II nuclear explosions have taken place for experimental purposes only, far from the cities, factories, and military bases that would become their targets in a real conflict. Second, within the sphere of greatest interest to the United States and the Soviet Union, which covers the most heavily industrialized parts of the world—Europe, North America, and Japan—there has been no war at all, even of a non-nuclear character, in over three decades. In the first half of the twentieth century, by contrast, this "industrial circumference" was ravaged by two of the bloodiest conflicts in history.

The third achievement of the current regime is the way in which nuclear weapons have altered the tides of international politics.

17

Within the industrial circumference the current nuclear regime has dampened political conflict. There have been sharp disagreements between the United States and the Soviet Union, but the leaders of these two nations have managed these disagreements with sobriety and caution, taking great care to limit as far as possible the political conflicts that have grown out of them. On occasions, disagreements between the two have threatened to spill over into fighting—such as over Berlin several times and when the Soviet Union placed nuclear-capable missiles in Cuba in 1962—but crises of such gravity have been relatively rare, and when they have erupted the two sides have resolved them without war. Each superpower has tacitly granted the other a free hand within its own geographic sphere of influence, as when Soviet forces crushed political uprisings in Hungary in 1956 and Czechoslovakia in 1968 and when American troops intervened in the Dominican Republic in 1965.

For most of its recorded history Europe has been a turbulent place. Wars and revolutions have broken out frequently. Political communities have risen and fallen, borders have moved, regimes have changed, and large-scale violence has often accompanied these events. But since 1950 Europe has been relatively tranquil, largely because of the feared connection between political upheaval and nuclear weapons. Revolution and territorial expansion can lead to war, and—it has been feared for over a quarter-century—once a European war begins, it will become nuclear war. The best insurance against the use of nuclear weapons, it has been widely accepted, is to avoid using any weapons at all on a large scale. European history since 1945 has not been frozen, but its course has been steadied by nuclear weapons, and it has thus been peaceful.

Within the industrial circumference as a whole, the United States and the Soviet Union have concluded that nuclear weapons are too dangerous to permit unfettered political conflict. However, outside this perimeter the reverse has been true. Political conflict has been too common, too acute, and too difficult for the superpowers to control for there to be a significant role for nuclear weapons in peace and war. The dissolution of the great colonial empires has spawned disputes and wars over who was to control the successor states, where their borders were to be drawn, and what the relationship among the diverse groups within them was to be. But, at least since the Soviet Union became a full-fledged nuclear power, nuclear weapons have not been caught up in the political turbulence outside the industrial circumference, even where one of the superpowers was involved—with the exception of the Korean peninsula. In the Vietnamese War the United States did not use, or apparently seriously contemplate using, nuclear weapons. Politics outside the industrial circumference has remained apart from nuclear weapons for a number of reasons. Most obviously, it has chiefly involved states that have not had nuclear weapons. And the mutual restraint of the United States and the Soviet Union engendered by nuclear weapons has carried over into the two nations' behavior in these regions: each has had to take care not to provoke a crisis with the other by its actions in the Middle East, in Africa, and in Southeast Asia; neither has wanted to allow their competition in these regions to take on a nuclear character. Moreover, the political ends that the great nuclear powers seek outside their own particular spheres are of neither the sort nor the severity to justify the involvement of nuclear arms. So the current nuclear regime has had the effect of moderating politics among nations within the industrial circumference and keeping weapons of mass destruction apart from the often immoderate and bloody relations among states outside it.[3]

The existence of a connection between the current nuclear regime and the relative political stability of the postwar world cannot be proven. It is possible that the "achievements" of the regime would have come to pass even if human beings had never split the atom. It can be argued that once Europe was divided and the United States and the Soviet Union faced each other heavily

---

[3]This particular distinction is drawn from Stanley Hoffmann, "Nuclear Proliferation and World Politics," in Alastair Buchan (ed.), *A World of Nuclear Powers?* Prentice-Hall, Englewood Cliffs, N.J., 1966, p. 100. The United States has indicated that it might well defend South Korea and Taiwan with nuclear weapons. These two countries have acquired manufacturing industries in the last quarter-century. They have therefore earned at least corresponding membership in the industrial circumference.

armed, they would have found a way to coexist peacefully even without nuclear weapons: weariness with fighting, the considerable destructive power of non-nuclear armaments, and a rough military balance between the two camps would have prevented another great war. It is impossible either to prove or to disprove this contention, for the history of the last 30 years cannot be rerun leaving out nuclear weapons. But it is plain that those three decades have brought with them opportunities for war between the United States and the Soviet Union. And in wrestling with the problems that gave rise to those opportunities, the leaders of the two nations have borne in mind the nuclear devastation that mishandling them could bring about. The destructive power of the non-nuclear weapons that had become available by the end of World War II would have made national leaders reluctant to go to war again. The harnessing of nuclear energy for military purposes dramatically increased that destructive power and so, it is reasonable to assume, stiffened that reluctance. If the examples of Bastogne and Dresden made World War III an extremely unattractive prospect, the vivid images of Hiroshima and Nagasaki made it a horrifying one—and have kept it so as the other battles of World War II have faded from memory.

Leaving aside the question of the existence of nuclear weapons, it might be argued that the particular nuclear regime that has evolved since 1945 has not been crucial in maintaining the political calm within the industrial circumference. Perhaps an alternative regime would have performed as well or better. It is conceivable, for example, that the third pillar of the regime—hierarchy—has had nothing to do with this stability, that *any* distribution of nuclear might would have ensured it. The distinct prospect that many more nations than now own them will have nuclear weapons during the 1980s, and especially during the 1990s, means that this proposition may be tested in the years ahead; it is by no means certain that it will be proven true. It is finally possible to concede the importance of nuclear weapons and of their hierarchical distribution for international tranquility but to doubt that the current regime's second pillar—equilibrium—has contributed to it; it could be argued that a nuclear arsenal of nearly any size and composition would have deterred each superpower once the other had one. This contention is the heart of the "minimum deterrence" school of nuclear strategy and it is the governing assumption of the French and, perhaps, the Chinese nuclear forces. But against this school stand those who argue that gross differences in the size of the Soviet and American arsenals would be bound to influence global relations between the two states, even if those differences did not give either a "first-strike" capacity.

What precisely the world would be like without nuclear weapons, nuclear equilibrium, or nuclear hierarchy cannot be deduced. What can be said of the second and third pillars of the current regime is that, like nuclear weapons themselves, they have at least reinforced impulses for stability that would have existed without them but that might not have been strong enough alone to contain the disruptive forces in world politics. So the relationship between the current nuclear regime and international stability is probable, if not provable. And in that relationship lies the regime's value and the reason for preserving it into the 1980s and beyond. The First Nuclear Regime is the current regime, projected and protected, with its three pillars intact. The three pillars are not certain of surviving through the 1980s in the same form as they exist in the 1970s. Nuclear politics—the discussion and disposition of questions involving nuclear weapons—will revolve around the respective fates of these pillars in the next 15 years and afterward.

TWO

Anarchy

The anarchic nature of the international system will persist through the 1980s. The system of independent states that made its first recorded appearance in ancient Greece, that came to prevail in Europe in the seventeenth century, and that has spread over the world in the latter half of the twentieth will endure. For the states of the world to be fused into a single unit, for some supranational body to emerge to govern them, nuclear issues—and all of international politics—would have to change dramatically. But this is unlikely in the extreme to occur. The various proposals and high hopes for world government and the vicissitudes of history that have spawned them have never managed to bring such a global order into existence, and there is no reason to suppose that these ideas will be implemented in the future. Anarchy, thus, is not so much a pillar of the present system, in the sense that equilibrium and hierarchy are, as it is the foundation of the First or any other foreseeable nuclear regime.[4]

In the absence of a world state that would do away with the international anarchy altogether, people and nations have attempted to tame it through the creation of international law. There is no authority to enforce the law of nations, but states often obey it nonetheless, and it does provide guidelines for their behavior. The anarchy of the First Regime could conceivably be modified in

[4]With the exception of the Third Regime. See the essay by John Barton later in this volume.

the 1980s by an expansion of international law to include certain nuclear rules of engagement. Whereas the United States and the Soviet Union now publicly reserve the right to use their nuclear weapons when, where, and how they choose, they could undertake to observe certain limits on these freedoms. The likeliest limits are of two sorts.

"NO-FIRST-USE" OF NUCLEAR WEAPONS

The declared policy of both great powers is ambivalent toward the use of nuclear weapons. The "strategic" arsenals of each—the ballistic missiles launched from land and from submarines and the bombers capable of attacking the homeland of the other—are plainly intended to strike second, in response to a nuclear assault by the other. Their design and deployment patterns reflect this intention, and the United States, at least, has made it clear that this is their purpose. The reciprocal deterrent balance between the two nuclear giants therefore rests upon a de facto mutual "no-first-use" understanding with regard to their strategic weapons.

But each side has also deployed a large number of "theater" or "tactical" nuclear weapons of lesser range and destructive yield, most of which face each other across the line that divides Europe. Neither power has so explicitly designated these armaments as "second-strike"-weapons. Both have, in fact, refused to rule out being the first to employ them in a conventional conflict in which the tide of battle was running against them. They both say they will not start a war, but neither will abjure the right to turn a war into a nuclear war once it has been begun—presumably by the other side. Thus it has been widely assumed that any war in Europe that begins as a "conventional" fight will, unless quickly terminated, ultimately become nuclear.

It is within the power of either or both the United States and the Soviet Union to remove the ambiguity in their stated policies by officially declaring, as the People's Republic of China has done, that they will not be the first to use nuclear weapons—strategic or tactical—under any circumstances. This step has been urged upon both of them from time to time. The main purpose of a no-first-use declaration is consistent with a principal objective of the First Nuclear Regime: to minimize the chances of a nuclear shot being fired in anger. And such a declaration could serve other First Regime goals as well. It could discourage the spread of nuclear weapons to states that do not now have them by helping to assuage one fear that must influence the decision to "go nuclear"; a non-nuclear state would have a pledge that nuclear arms would never be used against it. A no-first-use declaration could also make for smoother relations among the great powers—particularly between the Soviet Union and China, whose thousand-mile border ranks near the top of the list of troubled areas where nuclear war could be ignited in the next decade.[5]

But such a pledge would not be without drawbacks. Its main advantage would, in fact, be its chief shortcoming. A no-first-use declaration would be aimed at severing the connection between non-nuclear and nuclear warfare, but preserving that connection is an important part of the First Nuclear Regime. The strength of this connection, or its perceived strength, has helped preserve peace in the industrial circumference; the fear that conventional war would turn into nuclear war has kept political conflict in check. To sever the linkage between conventional and nuclear war would risk weakening the deterrent against non-nuclear conflict and turning Europe once again into a cockpit of political contention and organized violence. It is even possible that decoupling nuclear and conventional war would increase the danger that the worst would occur: restraint on both sides could be so undercut that war broke out, with the no-first-use pledge abandoned in the heat of battle and nuclear weapons brought into play.

There is no way of knowing whether a no-first-use avowal would bring disaster in this way. What is certain is that as long as nuclear weapons exist, the policies of states possessing them will have a double edge. The owners of nuclear weapons will always be reluctant to use them, especially when the foe is another nuclear state. But war brings with it extremes of behavior—

[5] See Richard H. Ullman, "No First Use of Nuclear Weapons," *Foreign Affairs,* vol. 50, no. 4, July 1972, pp. 669–683.

confusion, panic, and miscalculation as well as extraordinary courage and self-sacrifice—such that neither side could be certain that, once war erupted, the other would not bring its nuclear arsenal into play no matter what commitments had been undertaken beforehand. As long as Soviet and American tactical nuclear weapons remain on station in Europe—the United States also deploys such weapons in South Korea—poised for use in war that might begin as conventional, the possibility of one side violating a no-first-use agreement will be great. The removal of the tactical nuclear weapons from the European theater might give such a pledge the credibility that it would not otherwise have, but even then the two strategic arsenals would loom, ready for firing from long range to stave off a conventional victory by the other side's forces. And insofar as the withdrawal of tactical nuclear weapons gave credibility to a no-first-use pledge, there would be a heightened danger that the brake on non-nuclear aggression provided by the First Regime's linking of conventional and nuclear war would be released.

The present declared position of each great power is that while it does not promise to resort to nuclear weapons if the tide of battle in Europe runs against it, neither does it consciously renounce that course of action. The resultant unpredictability makes both sides exceedingly wary of getting into any kind of war with the other. A no-first-use agreement might reduce the cautiousness of the two superpowers and thus weaken the stability of the First Regime.

LIMITED RETALIATION

Both the United States and the Soviet Union have resolved to respond to a nuclear assault by the other with a nuclear salvo of their own. It is this resolve that deters an initial attack. And it has been assumed that in each case the retaliatory blow would be massive—each side would lay waste to as many of the other's cities and as much of its industry as it could. This policy of "mass destruction" has come under some criticism in American strategic circles on two counts. The first is that it is morally wrong to rest the nation's security upon the threat to annihilate millions of people. The second is that it is a strategic blunder to do so. It would, according to this second criticism, be irrational to do what the doctrine of deterrence threatens to do after a first strike had been launched; that is, it would be foolish—an act of spite and revenge, not of policy—to lash out indiscriminately at Soviet or American cities in response to a nuclear attack. Each great power needs to be able to do more than merely hurl the full force of its nuclear arsenal at the other in response to an attack. Each needs strategic versatility in case deterrence does fail, to try to limit as far as possible the damage that a nuclear exchange causes. And each needs versatility to prevent such an exchange from taking place at all. For if one side believes that the opponent's sole deterrent threat, that of mass destruction, is an irrational one, it may calculate that its adversary would never carry it out and proceed accordingly.

Partly in response to these concerns, former American Secretary of Defense James Schlesinger announced a modification of the American plans for nuclear retaliation in 1974. The United States, he said, would be able to reply to a Soviet assault by firing upon anywhere from a few targets to many targets in the Soviet Union and by concentrating the nuclear response on military facilities or areas where the damage to civilian lives and property would be far less than if the American warheads were aimed directly at Soviet cities. Schlesinger's policy of "limited retaliation" or "limited counterforce" did not represent a complete shift in American nuclear arrangements: American missiles had always been aimed at "military" as well as "civilian" targets, and they could be fired selectively. Nor was it purely a doctrinal matter: he asked Congress for new weapons to carry it out. But it was announced as an important change in the nation's strategic principles. It was hailed by some as both a more humane way of fighting a nuclear war and a more effective means of deterring one. And it was disparaged by others as making nuclear war more likely by making it appear less destructive (as well as by stimulating the competitive development of the kind of high-accuracy, high-yield weaponry that could improve the prospects for a successful first strike).

But the praise and the condemnations of the Schlesinger amendments to the American strategic canon were both overdrawn. What is most important about his declarations is that they, and similar shifts in stated strategic policy that may be made in the 1980s, will have little effect on the prospects for war and peace. They leave the nuclear regime unchanged.

A declared policy of limited retaliation is not necessarily more humane than one of massive response because there is no assurance that a nuclear exchange, once begun, can be kept limited. The Soviets have said that they do not expect that it will be. And precisely because it cannot guarantee to keep nuclear warfare within bounds, limited retaliation does not increase such warfare's attractiveness or plausibility in the eyes of national leaders. Finally, limited retaliation does not seem crucial in keeping one side from trespassing upon the highest interests of the other. It is impossible to say with certainty what prevents one side from attacking the other; deterrence exists wholly in the minds of those who are deterred. But for the two nuclear giants, the uncertainty concerning the nature of the other side's retaliation policy that is often identified as the flaw in American doctrine works as much in favor of deterrence as against it. The Soviets cannot be certain that a non-nuclear attack on one of America's European allies or a limited nuclear strike on an American city would call forth a nuclear barrage in retaliation, but neither can they be certain that they would not. The Soviets—and the Americans—have been sufficiently uncertain about their ability to escape with impunity that they have avoided giving serious offense to the other, with a few notable exceptions, for three decades. One of the purposes of international law is to endow relations among states with a measure of predictability. But unpredictability about when and how nuclear weapons might be used has served the cause of stability thus far in the nuclear era. Nuclear rules of engagement might damage the current regime by weakening stability.

However, it is equally possible that no-first-use, limited retaliation, or any other changes in strategic doctrine in the 1980s will *not* significantly affect the stability of the current nuclear regime as long as its physical properties persist. In the first years of the nuclear age, doctrine had enormous importance: the weapons were new, there were few of them, they seemed to have several possible purposes, and relations between the United States and the Soviet Union were tense and uncertain; each side needed to know what the other intended to do with its weapons. Now the habits of 30 years give part of the answer to that question, and the high force levels each has achieved supply the other part. Because each side has so many nuclear weapons, neither can attack the other and escape terrible retaliatory damage. Because each side has so many nuclear weapons, neither can be confident that the other will refrain from using its stockpile once war breaks out.

The deployment of nuclear armaments, far more than the doctrines governing them, will affect the nuclear regime in the 1980s. No matter what Soviet and American leaders say about their nuclear plans, the presumption will remain strong on both sides that neither will initiate strategic nuclear war, that a conventional war between them in Europe would likely become nuclear, and that a nuclear exchange between the two superpowers would not be, in any meaningful sense of the term, "limited." The blessings of stability that the current regime has brought depend for their continuation more upon how the two huge arsenals compare with each other than on what their masters say they will do with them. Of course, doctrine can affect deployment. But defense planners and political leaders on both sides will be guided more by what they see than by what they hear. The future of the regime rests less upon the fate of its first pillar, anarchy, than upon that of its second, equilibrium.

THREE

Equilibrium

The heart of the First Nuclear Regime, the strategic balance between the United States and the Soviet Union, has attracted more attention, consumed more resources, and provoked wider concern than any other nuclear issue in the last three decades. The central component of this second pillar is the series of agreements the United States and the Soviet Union have concluded at the Strategic Arms Limitation Talks (SALT): a treaty and an interim agreement in 1972 (SALT I) and a protocol signed at Vladivostok in late 1974 giving the outlines of a future accord (SALT II) that is still not completed. Together they codify the three principal elements of the equilibrium between the strategic nuclear forces of the United States and the Soviet Union.

The first element is the doctrine of mutual assured destruction (MAD). In the 1972 SALT I agreements, each superpower abjured extensive networks of missile defenses, thereby promising, in effect, to leave its cities exposed to the rockets of the other. By agreeing to curtail the deployment of antiballistic missile (ABM) systems, each effectively committed itself not to strike first by giving the other the assurance of being able, if necessary, to wreak vast destruction in retaliation.

The SALT agreements have also ratified a second important element of nuclear equilibrium, high force levels, by leaving each side with an enormous strategic arsenal. The 1974 Vladivostok protocol permitted each as many as 2,400 "launchers" of nuclear explosives—long-range bombers, submarines, and land-based

31

missiles—and both had approximately that many.[6] Of these, 1,320 could be fitted with multiple warheads.[7] These totals far exceed the firepower necessary to visit immense, "unacceptable" destruction on the two societies. The bomb that struck Hiroshima had an explosive force of about 20,000 tons (20 kilotons) of TNT; both sides now have thousands of bombs that are many times more powerful than that.

SALT has also codified a third characteristic of the nuclear balance between the United States and the Soviet Union—equality. Numerical equality in strategic weapons delivery systems is a hallmark of the 1974 protocol. Not only can each rain down "unacceptable" damage upon the other even after absorbing an initial blow; not only does each have a nuclear stockpile capable of inflicting far more than unacceptable damage; now the sizes of those stockpiles and hence the degrees of destruction they can produce are, by agreement, roughly equal.

These three elements—MAD, huge forces, equality—are like layers wrapped around each other, the outer layers reinforcing the inner ones. Mutual assured destruction is the core of the equilibrium between the United States and the Soviet Union. Even without either high force levels or numerical equality, a handful of submarines armed with nuclear-tipped missiles would give one side or the other an "assured destruction" capacity. But the two outer layers are not without consequence. High force levels anchor the strategic balance by giving each side insurance against changes in the other's arsenal. They also ensure the continuation of hierarchy—the regime's third pillar. And they may help to extend to the fringes of the industrial circumference the caution with which the two great powers treat each other in Europe; conceivably one or the other might behave more recklessly outside Europe if only a small strategic force threatened

[6]By the best unofficial estimate the United States had, in mid-1975, 2,142 launchers and in mid-1976, 2,097. The Soviet Union had 2,537 in 1975 and 2,507 in 1976. *The Military Balance, 1976–1977,* International Institute for Strategic Studies, London, 1977, p. 75.

[7]In 1976 the United States had deployed 1,046 launchers with multiple independently targetable reentry vehicles (MIRVs), and the Soviet MIRV program had just begun. Ibid., pp. 3, 73.

it. Equality is a less important layer than the other two and could be removed without seriously weakening the pillar. But the equality between the two arsenals which the SALT accords have mandated helps both governments resist domestic pressures for more—and more sophisticated—weapons. And it serves as a reassuring symbol to each great power of the other's benign intentions and commitment to restraint. The equilibrium between the United States and the Soviet Union might hold steady on the basis of mutual assured destruction regardless of the relative dimensions of their strategic arsenals, but the three layers together make nuclear equilibrium a stout and sturdy pillar of the current regime. What changes might buttress or erode it in the 1980s?

TECHNOLOGY

Nuclear technology has been depicted as a plant that has been growing precipitously, almost miraculously, since 1945. Nuclear weapons are, of course, the works of human beings. But the metaphor is apt because for 30 years their development has been so swift and so persistent that it seems almost a force of nature, beyond human control. The plant will continue to grow through the 1980s, but more slowly than it has in the past. Technical progress is likely to go on, and new weapons and improvements in existing weapons will appear. But these will not have consequences as profound for the relationship between the United States and the Soviet Union as did the advances of the first two decades of the nuclear age. The new weapons that scientists and engineers are designing are making, and are likely to continue to make, an increasingly faint imprint upon the nuclear regime as a whole.

This is so in the first place because the monumental technical developments of the nuclear age have all had the effect of tilting the military balance between offense and defense decisively in favor of offense. These developments came in three categories: those that dramatically expanded the military power a nation had at its disposal—the fission and fusion bombs; those that assured the United States and the Soviet Union a plentiful supply of those bombs—the high force levels and multiplicity of launch platforms both have developed; and those that enhanced the capacity of the two great powers to deliver the bombs on target—here the intercontinental ballistic missile was decisive. Together these three sorts of advances gave the two nations that mastered them the unchallengeable power to destroy any adversary. Both the United States and the Soviet Union were well on the way to having that power by 1955, both had it by 1965, and each had virtually given up all practical hope of denying it to the other by 1975. Predictable developments in nuclear weaponry will further refine the offensive capacities of each side, but when each can already destroy the other several times over, more destructive power will have little impact.

However, there are two sorts of technical advances that could be made in the 1980s which might affect the strategic relationship between the two superpowers. One would be the perfection of a way to defend against a nuclear attack. The other would be the improvement of the techniques of attack to the point where they threaten not just the cities but the weapons of the other side, the weapons upon which deterrence depends.

Defense   An advance in the art of defense comparable to the quantum leaps in offensive proficiency of the past three decades would drastically alter the world's nuclear balance. Effective defense would shake the second pillar of the current regime—strategic equilibrium between the United States and the Soviet Union—by eliminating its central element, the mutual threat of assured destruction. Defense has been a dream of strategic planners almost since the dawn of the nuclear age. Both great powers have thrown up networks of defense against attacking airplanes. Both have experimented with ABMs but have agreed to abandon most of their ABMs in 1972, in no small measure because neither saw much promise of success in their experiments. Knocking down an incoming missile with an interceptor vehicle is a complicated undertaking. In the early 1960s President Kennedy described it as tantamount to hitting a bullet with another bullet.

But the idea of defending against nuclear attack remains compelling, and likely technical progress in the 1980s may increase the chances that one or the other superpower will eventually be able to defend itself successfully, if not in the 1980s perhaps in the 1990s. Laser technology gives some promise of making it possible to disable incoming missiles. Missile defense with lasers would more closely resemble shooting clay pigeons than firing one bullet at another—it would be difficult, but not hopelessly difficult. There are, however, large problems with even the most sophisticated laser defense system. Enormous amounts of energy would be required to operate one. The laser is a line-of-sight weapon, and *terminal lasers* (those aimed from the territory of the defending nation) could be "blinded" by nuclear explosions in the atmosphere that would serve as a kind of smoke screen for incoming missiles. Lasers might also be mounted on satellites in orbit outside the earth's atmosphere; but satellite lasers, like terminal ones, would violate the 1972 SALT treaty. And, like a terminal laser ABM system, satellite lasers would need to perform almost perfectly to pass muster. In the nuclear age a system of defenses against missile attack would have to achieve an extraordinary, unrealistically high level of performance to protect the defending society against catastrophic damage from superpower attack. If a nation were attacked with 100 thermonuclear warheads, an attack of relatively modest scale considering the arsenals on both sides, and if it managed to deflect or destroy 95 of them—an impressive performance by the standards of all the antiaircraft systems that have so far been designed—the 5 that struck their targets would almost certainly cause unparalleled devastation. An American ABM system that so thwarted a Soviet attack that only Philadelphia, Louisville, Omaha, and San Diego—to choose some cities at random—were destroyed would not have prevented an utter catastrophe. And not even the most sophisticated laser system that will be feasible in the 1980s could be certain of protecting every population center against a more concerted attack.

Civil Defense   A nation can also seek to protect itself against nuclear attack by guarding against the effects of attacking warheads once they strike their targets. This involves building reinforced structures, preferably underground, where people can take shelter. An effective program of passive civil defense would have to provide space for a substantial fraction of the population; it would have to stock these shelters with enough food, water, and medicine to last for days and perhaps weeks; and it would have to rehearse the citizenry in the procedures for getting to the shelters quickly, since the time between warning and attack might well be short. Should either the United States or the Soviet Union adopt such a program, it has been argued, the strategic balance between them could be upset by giving one a chance to emerge from a nuclear exchange less gravely wounded than the other.

The United States has had a civil defense program since the early 1950s, although it has always been a modest one. By the early 1960s the American government had decided that it was feasible to try to guard against only the "secondary" effects of a nuclear assault, chiefly radioactive fallout, rather than against the "primary" effects of the explosions. But presidential requests for funds to construct fallout shelters received little support from the public or from Congress. Civil defense was unattractive because it intruded too starkly on the everyday lives of Americans, because it reminded them too vividly of the perils of the nuclear age, and because the civil defense programs the government recommended seemed increasingly futile in the face of expanding Soviet strategic power.

The Soviet Union has a more extensive civil defense program than does the United States, which may in large part be the result of the psychological legacy of 1941. The Soviet leaders historically have attempted to disperse their industries and their people throughout the vast expanse of their territory. While the Soviets spend more and are able to mobilize their citizens more readily than their chief rival, no large-scale run-throughs of civil defense procedures have been observed there. A large civil defense program, like a working ABM system, could in theory undercut the core of the nuclear equilibrium—MAD—by giving one side or the other the capacity to survive a nuclear exchange. But unlike the ABM, it seems futile to seek to limit civil defense programs by treaty. The problems of definition and monitoring are complicated and would probably not be manageable; in any case, the Soviets might well not even consider negotiating on this sensitive issue because of the lingering trauma of World War II.

In any case, no treaty is now necessary. There is no evidence that the Soviets now have a good enough civil defense program to tip the strategic balance in their favor, and it is far from clear that they could develop one even if they tried. People and factories are closely clustered together within Soviet cities, and the United States has enough nuclear warheads to target all of the principal ones many times over. Even with a full-blown program, the Soviet Union could not expect to escape severe damage from a massive American attack. The two arsenals are large enough to thwart any effort to limit damage. Finally, even a limited attack—and there is no guarantee that that is the kind either side would mount—would still leave its survivors with the problem of coping with the secondary effects of the war, such as fallout, atmospheric damage, and poisoned food and water supplies. No country, even one that has devoted time and resources to civil defense, will do well in the next war if that war includes a nuclear exchange. And no leader will gear policies to the expectation that his or her nation will do well.

Counterforce　Nuclear offense can in theory play a defensive role. An offensive force so potent that it can knock out the offensive weapons of the other side is tantamount to an effective defense against attack. A successful "counterforce" attack is one that cripples the adversary's striking forces, leaving it helpless to retaliate and prey to a succeeding assault on its cities. Advances in two areas of counterforce technology can be expected to play a part in the strategic calculations of the United States and the Soviet Union in the 1980s.

The first is the area of antisubmarine warfare (ASW). ASW involves both finding and destroying or at least disabling submarines. The technical capacities of both superpowers to do both can be expected to improve in the next decade. Sonar systems for tracking underwater vessels will gain in precision. The trailing ships will likely find ways to keep themselves unknown to their prey. Special "hunter-killer" submarines with the mission of dogging and destroying missile-bearing submarines may be built. But for one of the superpowers to pose a serious threat to the entire submarine fleet of the other, it would need an enormously sophisticated, highly reliable, and closely coordinated system that would be of substantial cost in national resources. And like a satellite-based laser ABM system, even assuming that one of the nuclear superpowers can equip itself with such a system, it would likely not be in place until the 1990s.[8] Unlike an ABM system, an efficient ASW capacity would not give a nation an impregnable defense by itself since it would not deflect the adversary's land-based missiles.

The other important area of counterforce technology in which advances will have a more immediate impact on the strategic calculations of the United States and the Soviet Union is that of improvements in the accuracy of offensive weapons. New guidance mechanisms that can survey the terrain being covered and make course corrections in flight will be attached to both intercontinental ballistic missiles and cruise missiles—the latter being tiny, unmanned airplanes that can fly close to the ground to avoid detection by radar and can maneuver delicately to home in on a target. Missile accuracy is measured in terms of the *circular error probable,* the radius of the circle around the target within which half the warheads aimed at it are likely to fall. By the end of the 1980s that radius may well be as small as one-tenth of a mile—or less. While very little accuracy is needed to destroy cities, accuracies of that magnitude could give the attacker an excellent chance of knocking out a large fraction of the opponent's weapons, especially the ballistic missiles sheathed in reinforced underground silos.

But even with the furthest imaginable refinements in offensive accuracy and ASW techniques during the 1980s, neither superpower can hope to destroy all of its rival's offensive forces. These forces are now and—assuming the First Nuclear Regime remains in place—will then be so numerous and so diversified that some are bound to survive any attack, no matter how fierce. Even if one side could knock out all the land-based missiles of the other, just a few of those carried by submarines could still mount an annihilating attack in return. Moreover, both sides can take countermeasures to protect their sea- and land-based strategic forces.

[8]See Kosta Tsipis, Anne H. Cahn, and Bernard T. Feld (eds.), *The Future of the Sea-Based Deterrent,* The MIT Press, Cambridge, Mass., 1973.

They can reduce the noise their submarines make to complicate the task of tracking them. They can give them the means to fire their missiles at longer ranges, move faster, and stay submerged longer than is now possible; these changes, too, would lessen their vulnerability. And both the United States and the Soviet Union can guard their land-based missiles by sinking them deeper underground, by throwing up special defenses around them to ward off cruise missiles, and—although this would make arms control negotiations more difficult—by deploying more missiles and by making them mobile through deployment on roving railroad cars and large trucks.

Thus the technical advances in nuclear weaponry that will take place through the 1980s will not shatter the core of the equilibrium between the United States and the Soviet Union, the second pillar of the current nuclear regime. That core is the ability of each state to respond to an attack with a devastating retaliatory blow, and both will have it in 1989 as they do in 1977. Moreover, the durability of the core will be protected by the second "layer" of nuclear equilibrium, very large nuclear arsenals on both sides. Force levels, like wages, seem to be rigid downward; they might, by agreement, come down somewhat in the 1980s, but not very far and not because of technical advances. And because they protect the equilibrium between the United States and the Soviet Union, high force levels are not only likely, they are desirable elements of the First Regime.

But it cannot be said that the technological changes in strategic hardware that the coming decade will see will have no effect whatsoever on the current regime. These changes could do away with the third layer of nuclear equilibrium, equality. For example, one side might develop a weapon that the other side does not have. Or improvements in accuracy, while not eliminating the assured destruction capacity of both sides, might erode it for one or the other of them. By the end of the 1980s either or both the Soviet Union and the United States might be able to pulverize a larger fraction of the other's offensive force than is now possible. If the Soviet Union builds the mightiest missile force the 1974 Vladivostok guidelines permit and the United States also stays within the bounds that that protocol lays down, a large part of the American land-based force could become vulnerable to a Soviet strike because of the greater size and "throw-weight" of Soviet intercontinental ballistic missiles (ICBMs). This is presently the worry of some of the observers and guardians of American nuclear matters.[9] The Soviets, too, could find their strategic arsenal at greater risk in the late 1980s than it has been in the mid-1970s if the United States should use its comparative advantage in nuclear research and development to outdistance them in ASW and to deploy even more accurate ballistic and cruise missiles. When he announced the new American targeting policies, Secretary of Defense Schlesinger also requested funds from Congress for more accurate and powerful warheads to place on American missiles, to make the Soviet missile fleet as vulnerable as he and others fear the American one may become.[10] Therefore, while neither the United States nor the Soviet Union will have or be close to having the capacity for making a thoroughgoing first strike in 1989, either might find its second-strike capacity diminished by the counterforce weapons of the other. What would be the consequences of such asymmetries?

POLITICAL CONSEQUENCES OF
STRATEGIC INEQUALITIES

Of the three layers of the equilibrium pillar of the current regime—MAD, high force levels, and equality—the third could most easily be eroded in the 1980s. The consequences of such erosion are extraordinarily difficult to foresee. They depend, in the first instance, upon just what sort of inequalities arise. Additions to one arsenal that threaten the retaliatory capacity of the other will obviously have more serious repercussions than those that do not. But even when the dimensions of the asymmetries are known, their implications will remain problematical. There are

[9]The largest Soviet missiles are larger, and can therefore carry more warheads (or more "deliverable megatonnage"), than American missiles. See Paul Nitze, "Assuring Strategic Stability in an Era of Détente," *Foreign Affairs*, vol. 54, no. 2, January 1976, and "Deterring Our Deterrent," *Foreign Policy*, no. 25, Winter 1976–77.

[10]For an analysis of how the Soviet nuclear arsenal might be put in jeopardy, see David C. Gompert's essay, "Strategic Deterioration," in this volume.

different indices by which the two forces can be compared, and the United States may lead the Soviet Union by some and trail by others. Comparing the two arsenals numerically may not be the best way to determine their relative strategic value, but it is a convenient approach. The erosion of numerical equality would mean the loss of a useful benchmark by which each side can judge the strength and intentions of its adversary. This erosion might conceivably lead to heightened suspicions, an escalation of the arms race, and a greater risk of Soviet-American confrontation in the international arena.

And just as importantly, strategic inequalities could affect the relationship of the central nuclear balance to the rest of international politics. The effects of inequalities would depend upon how the United States and the Soviet Union—and third countries—perceived the military balance between them and how these perceptions affected their foreign policies. Even if the inequalities were inconsequential in strictly strategic terms, if they were *perceived* as significant they could unsettle the international system. It is the psychological effect of movement away from equality more than the strategic significance of the developing inequalities themselves which can, it has been argued, damage the prestige and influence of the country that is "left behind."

Because inequalities could easily appear, because their effects are hard to estimate, and because these effects could, some believe, disturb the equilibrium between the United States and the Soviet Union, they are likely to be controversial in the 1980s. So it is worth considering what might conceivably happen should one of the great powers find itself in a position to demolish a large fraction of the other's striking force.

The Dissolution of Alliances   It is within the realm of possibility that strategic inequality—specifically, the increased vulnerability of either American or Soviet forces—could affect the structure of the postwar international system in the next decade. As the arsenal of the United States or the Soviet Union becomes more and more exposed to attack, its alliance partners might drift away from the North Atlantic Treaty Organization and (admittedly less plausibly) from the Warsaw Pact. France's foreign policy in the 1960s might be considered a precedent. The French contended that the growth of Soviet power devalued the American commitment to the security of Western Europe and that they therefore needed their own nuclear force.

However, this is an exceptionally unlikely future. Most junior members of the two great alliances would not wish to exchange one senior partner for the other and, in any case, would not be able politically to float freely between them. Building indigenous nuclear forces could well reduce security by alarming neighboring states. In estimating the reliability of their protectors they will use other indices besides the relative sizes of the two principal strategic forces: expressions of the will to defend them will continue to count for as much as keeping up with every new development in nuclear hardware that the other superpower puts on display. And the French case does not necessarily foretell the demise of the Western system of alliances. France had other motives for making her nuclear decision besides suspicion of American resolve. And the French have remained active members of the Western alliance; in fact, as the Soviet nuclear stockpile has drawn even with the American one, France has, if anything, moved closer to the United States.

The other principal alliance seems likely to remain equally sturdy no matter how the two superpowers compare in nuclear hardware in the 1980s. The great schism it underwent, the parting of China and the Soviet Union, may have been precipitated in part by the Soviet reluctance to press its challenge to the capitalist world hard enough to suit the Chinese, a reluctance nourished by American nuclear might. But the rift had many other, deeper causes, and as the Soviets have overcome the strategic disadvantage under which they labored, the Chinese have shown no sign of returning to the fold. And if the Soviet Union's East European partners stray in the 1980s (which is scarcely likely given the Soviets' substantial non-nuclear power and their demonstrated willingness to use it to discourage ventures in political independence), this will not be because much of the Soviet missile force can, in theory, be smashed by an American surprise attack.

Aggressive Behavior by One of the Superpowers   Encouraged by an advantage in strategic hardware that while falling short of a first-strike capacity is nonetheless large and visible, the United States or the Soviet Union might begin to throw its political weight around in international affairs, abandoning the cautious diplomacy that has been one of the current regime's accomplishments. Either might poach blatantly in the other's sphere of influence: the United States might, for example, send troops to Yugoslavia or arms to Rumania; the Soviets could work openly with a partly communist Italian government to sever that nation's ties with NATO.

The first two decades of the nuclear age, when the United States enjoyed distinct nuclear superiority over the Soviet Union, offer a test case of sorts for this state of affairs. If the United States drew any political benefit from its early advantage, it is hard to see what it was. In the spirited controversy among historians about "atomic diplomacy," there are those "revisionists" who decry the fact that the leaders of the United States tried to use the bomb as a diplomatic lever against the Soviet Union to force the Soviets to accept the American vision of the postwar world, as well as those who regret that these leaders did not try hard enough. But there is nobody who claims that they succeeded.

Of course, the first years of the nuclear age are not an altogether satisfactory basis for appraising the effects of strategic inequality. Despite its nuclear inferiority, the Soviet Union was never without the means to damage the interests of the United States: the Soviet Army held Western Europe hostage and so prompted American nuclear restraint. Moreover, it may be argued that the United States was a peaceful power in 1945 with no intention of overturning by force the international system that arose out of the wreckage of World War II, whereas the Soviets would not be so gentle if they ever enjoyed the same kind of advantage. Finally, for much of the period the United States did not know how far it was ahead of the Soviet Union in nuclear weaponry. For part of it the Americans actually thought that they were lagging behind. In fact, in the first two decades of the nuclear age the foreign policy of the Soviet Union tended to be more aggressive than that of the United States, especially between 1945 and 1949, when Stalin gathered Eastern Europe into the Soviet orbit, and from 1959 to

1962, when Khrushchev boasted of Soviet nuclear might and gave the world some anxious moments by his actions in Berlin and Cuba. So the political consequences of nuclear inequality in the past do not give many clues to what it may portend in the future. But at the least they do *not* suggest that inequality poses a serious threat to the stability of the current nuclear regime. And such inequalities as are possible in the 1980s will be less pronounced than those of the late 1940s and 1950s.

Crisis Stability While the normal workings of international politics might go on as before in a world of nuclear inequality between the United States and the Soviet Union, in a moment of tension and challenge either or both might behave less prudently than they would if their nuclear arsenals matched each other precisely. Inequality might aggravate crises. Here speculation is particularly difficult, for a crisis is, almost by definition, a time when people and nations do not behave as they ordinarily do, when customary conduct is suspended and sound judgment sometimes left behind.

A crisis might erupt in an international system in which one side had more weapons and a greater destructive capacity than the other, such as in the Cuban missile crisis of 1962. The United States then held a long lead in nuclear hardware, and the outcome of the crisis seems, on the face of it, to have been a resounding American victory. It was one of the rare occasions in the nuclear age when one great power used threats to force the other to do something—to remove missiles already in place—rather than merely to refrain from doing something. It was an example of successful "compellence" as distinct from deterrence.

But the Cuban missile crisis, like the Bible and the works of Lenin, can be cited to prove anything. The "lessons" to be drawn from it are far from fully obvious. First, it was not an unalloyed triumph for the United States: a flurry of negotiations took place between the two sides, out of which the Americans gave a pledge not to invade Cuba and tacitly promised to withdraw some missiles from Turkey in exchange for the Soviet retreat. The record of the crisis does not show any confidence among American officials that a nuclear exchange would have left the United States in a favorable position. And insofar as the missile crisis ended in an

American victory, this was not necessarily due to the strategic balance at the moment: the United States had much more non-nuclear military force in the Caribbean than the Soviets, and this may have been decisive. The missile crisis may demonstrate, finally, not the political productivity of marginal advantages in nuclear weaponry but the tendency of each superpower to act more firmly than the other within its own sphere of direct concern.

Conclusion Strategic equality between the United States and the Soviet Union in the 1980s is preferable to inequality between them. If their arsenals match one another, each side will harbor fewer doubts that the other is seeking to undermine the basic conditions of strategic stability (the most important of which is the invulnerability of retaliatory forces) or that it is attempting to garner greater political influence in the global arena through nuclear superiority. The impact of foreseeable strategic inequalities upon international politics in the 1980s cannot be foretold with certainty. But there are at least three reasons for doubting that conceivable inequalities will have any appreciable effect at all.

The first is that the strategic forces of the United States and the Soviet Union will continue to be very large. The larger they are, the greater will be the assurance that a powerful part of them can survive any attack. And the larger they are, the less difference inequalities in appearance, as distinct from strategic capability, will make. Two of the layers of the equilibrium pillar of the current regime—assured destruction and high force levels—will be in place through the 1980s. Neither side will look or act puny, no matter how muscular the other is. Any serious political consequences of strategic inequality would probably raise the danger of war and, when war looms, calculations about the damage that each side can inflict upon the other come into play. In the 1980s these calculations will not encourage adventurism within the industrial circumference. At the brink of war a Soviet or American leader would think less about the 80 percent of the opposing missile force he might be able to put out of commission than about the 20 percent that would remain to pulverize the country.

Second, the nuclear inequalities of the past did not have significant political consequences. The historical record is not an infallible guide to the future, but it is a source of evidence in thinking about it; and such evidence as there is does not offer much support for the view that differences between the two principal nuclear forces will crack the major alliances of the international system, convert either great power into the international equivalent of a reckless driver, or turn a crisis into a nuclear disaster.

The third and final reason is that the political usefulness of *all* military might has tended to decline in the past three decades (although nowhere is it without any use). Nuclear force has had a particularly limited utility. It has had, as noted, a sobering influence, injecting a concentrated dose of caution into the international conduct of the great powers—caution that would not be abandoned with the achievement of marginal superiority. Moreover, the growth of the Soviet and American nuclear arsenals has reached a point of diminishing returns. There is not much that can be done with 11,000 nuclear weapons that cannot be done with 10,000.

But if the fruits of technological progress in nuclear weaponry seem to offer no cause for alarm, this does not mean that nobody will be alarmed by them. National leaders are likely to continue to believe, or at least to act as if they believe, that nuclear inequalities do matter. The government of neither superpower is likely to allow the other to increase and refine its arsenal without responding in some way. The Soviets, it is true, have some experience in living on the short side of inequalities more pronounced than any that the next decade will see. But the Soviets do seem to place a high value on precisely what is at stake here— appearances. And if they became accustomed to nuclear inferiority in the past, they apparently did not enjoy it, since they made such an effort to achieve parity over the last decade.

American officials are, if anything, more likely than their Soviet counterparts to wish to avoid trailing conspicuously behind their chief rivals in strategic might. They have always operated on the theory that it is better to be safe than sorry: Where the life of the nation is at stake it is better to have a weapon, even if there is no demonstrable need for it, on the off chance that such a need might turn up. Also, the strategic balance is prone to getting tangled up in American electoral politics: in the election years of 1960, 1968, and 1976 candidates for the position of Commander-in-Chief have proclaimed that the nation needed more nuclear hardware to be safe from its enemies. Finally, the ongoing enterprises of research and development make tempting refinements in weaponry available to American—and Soviet—leaders. It is difficult simply to brush these aside, especially because there are in the United States, and perhaps in the Soviet Union, people in positions of authority and influence who have political and economic interests in the vitality and growth of the nuclear plant. And so it will keep on growing, each of its stems straining against the other. In the 1980s neither the United States nor the Soviet Union will be able to disarm the other; that is, there will be "first-strike stability." Neither is likely to be able to convert any differences between its strategic arsenal and the arsenal of its adversary into political advantage; thus there will, in all probability, be "crisis stability," if only because this turns out, in practice, to be indistinguishable from first-strike stability. But each will nonetheless want to keep its nuclear stockpile even with that of the other. Without new measures to bring it about, the international system of the 1980s is not likely to enjoy "arms race stability," a slowing or termination of the competition to build more, and more sophisticated, nuclear weapons.

THE ARMS RACE IN THE 1980s

The persistence through the 1980s of competition between the United States and the Soviet Union in the development of nuclear weapons would not be a catastrophe that would send the First Regime tumbling to the ground. The high force levels and commitment to equality central to the regime make a continued arms race a far smaller threat to strategic stability than would be the case in, for example, the Second Nuclear Regime, in which force levels would be lower and could be extremely unequal. The arms race between the two superpowers will not "spin out of control" in the 1980s, plunging them into war. The arms race is, in fact, a familiar part of the nuclear age, having begun in 1945 (if not before) and having proceeded, in fits and starts, ever since then.

In the past, the two superpowers have felt more anxious about matching each other, and wider gaps have separated them, than is likely to be the case in the 1980s. In the limited sense that the common impulse to keep pace with the armaments of the other has driven the two stockpiles up to their present quantitative and technological heights, the arms race may be said to have contributed to nuclear stability, since these high force levels have reinforced the nuclear equilibrium between the United States and the Soviet Union. But the First Nuclear Regime will be sturdier and the international system as a whole more tranquil if the arms race does not carry forward into the next decade. And both the United States and the Soviet Union will be better off if neither feels impelled to add to its already abundant nuclear store.

Nuclear weapons, while not ruinously expensive, cost a great deal of money. And neither superpower is without alternative channels for investing the funds they both devote to strategic hardware. In addition, competition in armaments is a source of political friction, although it is less a source of direct conflict than a hindrance to cooperation between the Soviets and the Americans. Neither side could, in practical terms, outbuild the other to the extent that the resultant asymmetries would be of political consequence. But if either tries, the other is likely to follow suit, leaving each of them poorer, more muscular, but no more powerful in relation to the other. Restraining the arms race is therefore a worthy project.

The arms race may partly restrain itself in the 1980s. Its pace has shown signs of slowing in the last decade and may well slow further in the next. Since advances in satellite reconnaissance let each side know what the other has, since neither has as much fear of a revolutionary breakthrough in weapons technology as it did earlier, and since both rest comfortably on cushions of high force levels, neither needs to rush to replace one generation of armaments with the next with the urgency felt during the first years of the nuclear age. And as new weapons become ever more intricate and expensive, they take longer and longer to design, test, produce, and deploy. But even if it does slow down, the arms race will not on its own wind down to a dead stop. Rather, like a hardy weed, it will keep growing if left to its own devices.

The forces that fuel the arms competition between the Soviet Union and the United States will still be potent in the 1980s: the competitive dynamics of the anarchic international system will still be at work; the hope, or fear, will persist that further investment in strategic hardware will yield political dividends; research and development will go on; and the politicians, industrialists, and government officials with personal and professional stakes in the continuing manufacture of nuclear weapons—the constituent parts of the "military-industrial complex"—will still be at their desks. In the 1980s, curbing the arms race that the interaction of these forces encourages will require a conscious policy of deliberate restraint. Such a policy could combine measures involving both the United States and the Soviet Union with steps taken by each alone.

Bilateral Measures   Explicit restrictions on the deployment of nuclear weapons to which both the United States and the Soviet Union submit offer the best hope of checking the momentum of the arms race. The several SALT agreements entail such restrictions insofar as they place ceilings on important parts of the arsenals of both sides. The Vladivostok understandings safeguard the third layer of nuclear equilibrium—equality—by mandating equal force levels within certain categories of weapons on both sides.

Since it began, the SALT process has helped to retard the arms race, but it has not shut it off completely. The limits prescribed by the various agreements, both proposed and ratified, do not cover every weapon and every refinement in the two nuclear arsenals. This is true in part because innovation has outpaced negotiation: new armaments are produced faster than agreements to restrict them can be hammered out. But more is involved than the speed of military innovation. Nations, even before the nuclear age, have been reluctant to place restraints upon weapons until all their properties are known. But by that time, in the competition between the United States and the Soviet Union, one or both sides have usually begun to deploy the new armaments and feel they are too valuable to give up. More often than not, one nation deploys a new weapon before the other does; the leader is reluctant to give up the new system unilaterally, while its competitor does not want to lag behind, and so negotiating restrictions on the system becomes almost impossible.

The two arsenals, moreover, do not match weapon for weapon. Asymmetry in the composition of the two arsenals makes it hard to find mutually acceptable limits, and arms control becomes a search for a formula to equate apples and oranges. And some weapons that do match do not fit neatly into familiar categories, which also compounds the problem of fixing limits on them. The cruise missile is one such weapon: it can be fired at either strategic or tactical range and can carry either nuclear or non-nuclear warheads.

The cruise missile illustrates another problem that besets attempts to negotiate bilateral arms limitations, the problem of verification. Each side itself polices arms control agreements, primarily through satellite reconnaissance. The globe-girdling satellites that each great power has launched into outer space serve as platforms for cameras of extraordinary precision. The photographs these cameras take tell each side how many missiles the other has and thus whether it is complying with the terms of SALT. Sophisticated electronic eavesdropping equipment obtains further information about the characteristics of the adversary's weapons. But cruise missiles (and MIRVs) are smaller and less easily distinguishable than ballistic missiles and cannot be as readily counted from the sky. And they are so flexible in their design that electronic reconnaissance cannot reliably estimate their range—whether they are "tactical" or "strategic"—once deployed. In signing an agreement that encompassed cruise missiles, each side would have to accept either more intensive inspection or a greater measure of uncertainty about deployments on the other side than is presently tolerated.[11]

To resolve some of the difficulties in achieving bilateral arms control agreements, it has been suggested that the format of

[11]The MIRV problem was solved by having both sides agree to count all platforms that could be "MIRVed" as MIRVed. Such an approach could be taken for the cruise missile, but the number of potential launch platforms is much greater than was the case for MIRV and so ceilings would have to be much higher.

negotiations be altered to include more kinds of weapons. This is always, to a certain extent, attempted at the start of all arms control negotiations: the most crucial sessions are the ones that decide what is negotiable. This was true of the SALT I discussions, which concluded that an accord would not extend to so-called forward-based systems in Europe (United States aircraft for the defense of NATO that are technically capable of delivering nuclear weapons on strategic targets in the Soviet Union) but would cover both offensive and defensive systems. In general, SALT has operated on an unwritten rule that weapons that cannot, for whatever reason, readily be controlled by treaty should be excluded from negotiations. This is preferable to trying to include all weapons and thereby risking getting no accord at all.

Increasingly, retarding the Soviet-American strategic competition means arresting the advance of technology that creates more, and more sophisticated, weapons. This is a radical project in both the literal and the figurative sense of that word. It is radical in that it goes to the root of the arms race—technological progress. And it is radical in that it is ambitious, complicated, and probably unworkable. A concerted attempt to forge an agreement to stop research and development of nuclear weapons would encounter three formidable obstacles.

First, such prohibitions would run counter to the spirit of science by restricting the liberty of inquiry and exploration that lies at the heart of the scientific method. They would not, of course, ban science itself, just one area of scientific exploration, but they would still represent a departure from customary procedures. Second, research and development restrictions would be hard to enforce. To monitor research effectively would require keeping close track of the work of a hundred laboratories, knowing with some precision what individual scientists were doing, and determining what consequences their work might have. This is not readily feasible. Third, cutting off research and development would risk stifling innovations that could reinforce nuclear stability. Designers and engineers may be able to make more reliable command and control systems that would reduce the chances of an accidental missile launching, for example, or missiles that can weather heavier assaults than current models.

Controls on the testing of new armaments lie between limits on deploying weapons and prohibitions against creating them. Test restrictions would have the virtue of being relatively easy to monitor with satellite reconnaissance. A limit to the number of experimental missile launchings permitted each side would to a certain extent obstruct the development of the high-accuracy missiles that put deterrent forces at risk. Theoretically, neither side would develop and deploy new weapons that could not be fully tested. Such limits, however, would not retard the growth or the refinement of the superpowers' nuclear weapons stockpiles as effectively as would curbs on research and development. By the time a weapon is ready for testing it has already won allies both inside and outside the government and has kindled a demand for building it. Moreover, given the modular character of contemporary weapons systems, new components can be tested on already deployed systems or on stationary test stands and can be fitted to new systems later without full-scale flight testing. Still, despite their drawbacks, test limitations would have some effect on the arms race and should be sought in the 1980s.[12]

Unilateral Measures   Mutual agreements to control the arms race may prove difficult, if not impossible, to conclude. If one side sees the other's strategic stockpile rising higher than its own, what should it do? It could decide to do nothing. This approach has a certain elegance. It would cost little (but not nothing—the business of defense contractors would fall off). It would be consistent with the position that nuclear inequality would not have serious consequences for world politics. It would also be based on the view that the value of nuclear equality is outweighed by the cost of maintaining it—in resources and in heightened political tension. But it has little chance of adoption. Even those most skeptical of the value of further increases in nuclear weaponry on either side would probably not feel wholly comfortable doing

[12]For discussions of the problems of controlling technical refinements in weapons see Herbert York, ''Some Possible Measures for Slowing the Qualitative Arms Race,'' and Harvey Brooks, ''The Military Innovation System and the Qualitative Arms Race,'' in ''Arms, Defense Policy, and Arms Control,'' *Daedalus,* Summer 1975.

nothing while the other pushed resolutely forward at the frontiers of nuclear technology. The force of arguments about the insignificance of the political consequences stemming from nuclear inequalities will not, in all probability, be powerful enough to override the psychological impulses to compete that spring from domestic politics, from the character of international politics, and from the habits that three decades of nuclear politics have bred.

The method for managing the arms race that the United States is likely to practice in the years ahead is the course begun in the late 1960s. This is the policy of displaying American resolve to match all Soviet strategic initiatives by developing, authorizing, and sometimes deploying comparable armaments. The rationale for this policy is twofold: it shows the Soviets and the rest of the world, in the clearest possible way, that they cannot hope to move ahead of the United States in nuclear weaponry, and it gives the American side something to trade for Soviet concessions when negotiations to limit their arsenals take place. This approach to controlling the arms race has become known as the "bargaining chip" tactic. It carries the notion of deterrence into the making, as well as the using, of nuclear weapons in that it seeks to prevent production of new weapons by the threat of matching that production. If this deterrence tactic fails, the side that has used it has a head start toward deploying the new weapon and maintaining nuclear equality. The bargaining chip approach is an appropriate response to a Soviet Union determined to seize every advantage over the United States that it can and willing to halt its political and military sorties only when firmly blocked. And it can lay claim to some success: the American government used its nascent ABM system as a bargaining chip to obtain a SALT agreement with the Soviet Union in 1972 that encompassed both offensive and defensive systems.[13]

But the bargaining chip tactic is a two-edged sword. It has the potential to push force levels higher than they would have gone

[13]It is arguable that the American ABMs and MIRVs were developed for other reasons and justified, after the fact, as bargaining chips. The reply to this argument is that because of the time it takes to produce a strategic weapon, each side must make its fundamental decisions in anticipation of what the other will have when the weapon is available.

without it. Equality may be restored in the process, but after great cost and not necessarily without some loss of stability. Once a weapon is under development, it acquires a constituency of military, political, and industrial advocates who resist efforts at stopping its deployment no matter what the results of negotiations with the other great power may be. The American cruise missile may prove to be a bargaining chip that military planners and defense contractors will not allow to be redeemed no matter what concessions the Soviets offer in return. Alternatively, by piling up bargaining chips one side can give the other the wrong signal and encourage policies contrary to the ones it wants to promote: the owner of the bargaining chips might appear bent on escalating the arms race and seeking advantage for itself and thus cause its adversary to seek weapons that held no previous attraction for it. And if both great powers follow the bargaining chip tactic, they can find themselves caught up in what has been called the "action-reaction" cycle: one deploys a weapon out of fear of what the other will do. This produces a similar concern on the part of the other, which then feels impelled, as it did not before, to augment its own arsenal, which in turn further alarms the first party, and the pattern repeats itself.

There are measures other than the bargaining chip tactic which could help to keep the force levels on both sides steady during the 1980s. Instead of unconditionally forswearing all further weapons development, one great power might make its restraint expressly contingent upon the behavior of the other. The United States could, for instance, announce that the size of its cruise missile fleet would depend upon how many of the largest Soviet land-based missiles were equipped with MIRVs.[14] This would be a variation on the bargaining chip tactic; it would be a proposal for an arms control agreement. Instead of an offer to give up a weapon if there is cooperation, it would entail a threat to build a new weapon in the absence of cooperation. It would avoid the twin risks of the bargaining chip approach discussed above— developing new weapons that their proponents will resist giving

[14]Equating these two weapon systems has a certain logic, for each threatens the land-based offensive force of the other side. Limiting each would reinforce the deterrent capacity of each and help steady the strategic balance.

up and pushing the other side toward a more intensive arms build-up than it might have planned. There is a precedent for this approach, although not an altogether happy one. John F. Kennedy announced in the early 1960s that the United States would not test nuclear explosives in the atmosphere as long as the Soviets refrained from doing so. When the Soviets did make an atmospheric test, it became impossible for Kennedy to keep from following suit. But even if he had not made his public declaration, pressure for more American tests would have mounted; so that declaration, in retrospect, did not leave the cause of restraint worse off than if it had never been made. The high force levels that both the United States and the Soviet Union will have in the 1980s mean that neither will suffer from lagging slightly behind the other in strategic hardware. There is therefore nothing to lose and something to gain from making declarations contingent on the other side's behavior, and they are worth considering over the next decade.

And if one of the superpowers were unwilling to keep its weapons programs at a standstill while the munitions factories of the other hummed with activity, it could still help to retard the arms competition by practicing a policy of "compensation" rather than of "imitation" in turning out its new armaments. That is, it could choose to develop only those additions to its arsenal that reinforce its invulnerability to attack, rather than ones that increase the vulnerability of the opposing force. Following this rule, the United States would respond to the increasing counterforce threat posed by the large, powerful MIRVed Soviet land-based missiles not by beefing up its own missile forces to put the Soviet force at similar risk but by taking steps to reduce its own vulnerability. It could further harden the concrete cocoons in which its missile silos are buried, and it could throw up protective fences around them to disable incoming cruise missiles. This principle would have to be carried out with care, for some of its applications could undercut other parts of the First Regime.[15]

[15] For an elaboration of this general idea, see the essay by Richard L. Garwin in this volume. For an analysis of the possible consequences of a spiraling, mutual imitation process, see the essay by David C. Gompert, pp. 214–298 in this volume.

Lessening the danger to the land-based missile force by putting it on wheels and shuttling it back and forth among "shelters" scattered throughout North America, as some have proposed,[16] would so complicate the task of verifying force levels that it might bring the SALT process to a halt. Similarly, adoption of a strategy of launching the land-based missile force upon warning of an attack, before the incoming warheads struck, would diminish the force's vulnerability but would make the nuclear trigger dangerously sensitive and increase the chances of accidental war. Finally, abandonment of the principle of equality in favor of the policy of compensation could conceivably lead, in the long run—beyond the 1980s—to such major asymmetries in force levels and composition that strategic stability would be hard to evaluate with confidence.

Conclusion   By 1990 the second pillar of the current nuclear regime will still be in place; there will be nuclear equilibrium between the United States and the Soviet Union. Each will be able to devastate the other even after being devastated itself: the warheads of each will number in the thousands, putting the assured destruction capacity of each beyond doubt. What is not certain is whether the two superpowers will manage the nuclear balance in a competitive or a cooperative fashion. If they continue to compete with each other, the restraints embedded in the various SALT accords will likely be abandoned or circumvented. The weapon systems under development in the mid-1970s will become part of the strategic landscape in the 1980s. The number of land-based missiles each deploys will probably have increased somewhat, perhaps to around 1,500; many will be as large as the largest models now in existence, and most will carry MIRVs. Each side's submarines will carry more potent payloads. The United States will probably be flying a new generation of strategic bombers, and the arsenals of both great powers will include cruise missiles. Both superpowers are likely to have explored the techniques of ASW, although neither will have the undersea fleet of the other at its mercy. The First Nuclear Regime is strong enough to absorb such developments.

[16]See Paul Nitze, "Assuring Strategic Stability," op. cit.

If the United States and the Soviet Union find ways to cooperate with each other in nuclear matters through further SALT agreements, perhaps encompassing jointly ratified limits on testing, their respective force levels will be in 1990 what they were in the late 1970s. They might even be slightly lower. The offensive forces of each side will be augmented with MIRVs, but there will be few enough of them and conceivable improvements in their accuracy will be sufficiently retarded—perhaps by test limits— that they will not pose a serious counterforce threat to the other's arsenal. An understanding might even be reached that would lead to reduced investment in research and development, although neither side would vacate its laboratories or shut down its weapons factories entirely.

The differences between these two possible futures are not trivial. The first is a more expensive one than the second. The political climate of the first is one of suspicion; of the second, one of limited mutual confidence. But the heart of the current regime— equilibrium between the Soviet and American arsenals—will remain in working order in either. Both the worst version and the best version of the First Regime are equally likely to enjoy freedom from nuclear war, freedom from war of any sort within the industrial circumference, and a circumspect, cautious style of diplomacy where the interests of the two great powers are in conflict. If the nuclear plant keeps growing, it may sway back and forth in the breeze. But its stem is so sturdy that it will not break and collapse.

This does not guarantee that the 1980s will be wholly free of war and crisis. What it does mean is that the nuclear relationship between the United States and the Soviet Union will continue to discourage instability. The sources of instability lie *outside* the nuclear regime. They could conceivably be more numerous in the 1980s than they have been in the 1970s: war in Korea or the Middle East or a continuing power struggle in China might bring the United States and the Soviet Union back to where they stood in October 1962—at the brink of war. The nuclear regime cannot prevent all political explosions. What it can do and has done is encourage the superpowers to dampen the most explosive spots in the international system and to manage eruptions as prudently

57

as possible when they occur. The second and most important pillar of the First Nuclear Regime—equilibrium—will be firm enough to promote this prudence as effectively in the future as it has in the past. The endurance of the first pillar—anarchy—will reinforce this effect by preventing the taking of measures that would formally constrain the use of nuclear weapons and thereby eliminate much of the sobering influence the fear of nuclear war has had in world politics. The third pillar, hierarchy, is not so sturdy.

FOUR

Hierarchy

Hierarchy, the third pillar of the current nuclear regime, complements the second pillar, the equilibrium between the United States and the Soviet Union. Equilibrium has meant that despite temptations to use force against the other, neither great power has dared to do so. Hierarchy has meant that the superpowers' mutual nuclear restraint has been transposed to the entire international community: as long as the United States and the Soviet Union, effectively the only countries with the option of initiating nuclear war, have chosen not to do so, nobody can.

Just as the component parts of the First Nuclear Regime's second pillar, superpower equilibrium, are codified in the various SALT accords, so are the main features of the third pillar, hierarchy, built into the Non-Proliferation Treaty (NPT) that was signed in 1968 and went into effect in 1970. The signatories to the NPT that do not have nuclear weapons promise not to acquire them and, to show the world that no weapons development is in progress, they agree to open their peaceful nuclear facilities to international inspection. The nuclear weapons states that sign the NPT, for their part, pledge not to assist any non-nuclear nation in joining what has come to be known as the "club" of nuclear weapons states.

The NPT reflects two important distinctions among nations which together make up the nuclear hierarchy. The first is the obvious, fundamental, and official distinction between those states that possess nuclear weapons and those that do not. The second distinction—unofficial but no less a part of the current nuclear regime—is that which separates the two nuclear super-powers from the other nuclear weapons states. The United States and the Soviet Union were the chief architects of the NPT and have taken on the task of coaxing other nations to sign it. Their nuclear forces give them far more political power than the arsenals of the four lesser nuclear nations provide. And the superpowers have, as well, a less equivocal commitment to the nuclear hierarchy itself than do the other four. Three of the four secondary nuclear powers—France, China, and India—have had distinctly ambivalent attitudes toward it; while none have given a bomb or the means to make one to another state, all have criticized the NPT as discriminatory against small powers and none have signed it.

Like SALT and nuclear equilibrium, the NPT not only reflects the two elements of today's nuclear hierarchy, but also is aimed at confirming and perpetuating one of them—the distinction between nuclear and non-nuclear nations. But there is no guarantee that either hierarchical distinction will last through the 1980s; both might be seriously challenged in the next 15 years. The hierarchical categories are not airtight, and states could move from one to the other in the years ahead. While perhaps not physically possible within a decade, over a longer period the arsenal of one of the smaller nuclear powers could develop until it rivaled those of the two superpowers or otherwise complicated the problem of managing Soviet-American nuclear equilibrium. Or other presently non-nuclear states could join the nuclear club. Either of these two developments could erode the First Regime and jeopardize what it has thus far achieved.

GROWTH IN EXISTING NUCLEAR ARSENALS

The erosion of the Soviet-American nuclear duopoly could threaten the achievements of the current regime in two ways. The first way is political. Their margin of strategic superiority over all the other members of the international system has helped make it possible for the Americans and the Russians to manage conflicts.

If others begin to approach them in nuclear strength, they might become less able to do so—and international conflicts might thereby become less manageable. Or, the growth of other nuclear arsenals might itself be interpreted by either of them as a hostile political act and ruffle the political tranquility that the current regime has helped engender. The second way that the growth in existing nuclear arsenals of states other than the Soviet Union and the United States could damage the present regime is strategic. A third prominent nuclear arsenal could upset the present bipolar equilibrium between the two giants. A disruptive challenge to the existing duopoly in the 1980s could come from one—or both—of two sources.

The People's Republic of China In 1975, China was estimated to have 20 to 30 ballistic missiles of intermediate range (1,500–4,000 miles), 50 of medium range (500–1,500 miles), and aircraft capable of striking targets at ranges up to 4,000 miles, all of which could deliver nuclear warheads. A sort of isoceles-triangular balance among China and the two superpowers has evolved, based as much on China's potential as on its actual nuclear arsenal. Some American nuclear weapons are aimed at China and have probably had some effect on Chinese foreign policy, especially during the Korean War and the Taiwan Strait crises of the 1950s. The diplomatic overtures to China in the 1970s came about in part because American officials wanted to put relations on a firm footing before China's expanding arsenal could strike the United States. The Soviets, too, have directed a large part of their nuclear forces at their eastern neighbor. While the Chinese nuclear stockpile has probably had some effect in deterring a full-scale Soviet attack, the millions of troops China could put in the field have undoubtedly given the Russians pause as well.

The triangular balance has held fairly steady through the first half of the 1970s. But if China's nuclear stockpile grows closer in size to the United States and Soviet arsenals in the 1980s, the nuclear component of the Chinese leg of the triangle will become more important. While that could produce even greater stability than has been the case—particularly insofar as China's ability to deter the Soviets would increase—it could also increase strategic instability. Much will depend upon how the Chinese nuclear force develops. It could develop in at least two ways that could disturb the tranquility maintained by the present nuclear regime.

First, China might try to assert globally the kind of political influence that large arsenals have given the Americans and Soviets. While the Chinese have laid rhetorical claim to the leadership of the "nonaligned" and "Third World" forces in international politics, aside from involvement—for largely defensive reasons—in the Korean War and the border skirmishes with India, they have generally tended to their own affairs since 1949.[17] If they should decide to use the umbrella of an expanding nuclear force to exert the kind of influence over Southeast Asian governments that the Soviets have in Eastern Europe, in order to assist the ambitions of North Korea or to return Taiwan to the control of the mainland, they would bump up against the commitments of the superpowers, with potentially grave effects on world order and security.

The second potentially unsettling consequence of a Chinese build-up of its nuclear force would be an acceleration of the Soviet-American arms competition. As the two superpowers came to feel that their arsenals were inadequate to check both each other and the People's Republic, they might push their stockpiles higher to counter the enlarged Chinese threat. If both the Soviet Union and the United States tried to maintain numerical equality with the *combined* forces of their two adversaries just as, in the nineteenth century, the British Navy maintained a "two-power standard" of equality with the fleets of any two other nations, the arms race would spiral out of control. Or, perhaps more plausibly, one of the great powers might be moved to invest in technologies—such as ABMs, ASW, and civil defense—that it believed would afford some protection from the upstart nuclear state but would collaterally unsettle the other nuclear colossus.

How quickly and in what direction will the Chinese nuclear arsenal grow? It is impossible to be certain. Its growth slowed

[17]See Allen S. Whiting, *China Crosses the Yalu*, Macmillan, New York, 1960, and *The Chinese Calculus of Deterrence*, University of Michigan Press, Ann Arbor, 1975, for an analysis of China's essentially defensive policy.

markedly in the 1970s, which may indicate that the Chinese do not aspire to a large nuclear force. Theirs is, after all, a large, poor country with pressing civilian uses for their resources. They may feel that they cannot afford to invest very much in nuclear weaponry and so may decide upon a strategy of minimum deterrence—one requiring relatively few nuclear weapons to give a would-be aggressor pause but still providing China with the most dramatic symbol of a modern industrial state.

Moreover, the Chinese leaders may have reservations about the utility of these armaments. Mao Tse-tung from time to time disparaged the importance of nuclear weapons in comparison with the strength and will of the masses. But he may, as Soviet leaders did in the early years of the nuclear age, have been throwing up a screen of rhetoric to conceal his nation's military weakness by putting a premium on China's chief asset—people. And the next generation of Chinese leaders may be more willing to press ahead with the development of sophisticated weaponry than were Mao and his colleagues. Political turmoil and factional disputes in the upper echelons of the Communist party may have interrupted the Chinese nuclear program in the 1970s; if the next decade brings political calm, that program could surge forward.

By the end of the 1980s China could certainly have several hundred intercontinental ballistic missiles and a submarine fleet of modest size and technical capability. By the year 2000, if they were determined to have one, the Chinese could probably deploy a force comparable to present American and Soviet forces. One way to accommodate such a build-up would be to bring the People's Republic into the presently bilateral Strategic Arms Limitation Talks that are the principal formal mechanisms for regulating the current regime. But Chinese participation in these talks is, at present, problematical for several reasons.

One reason is the simple arithmetic of negotiations. A three-handed game is much more complicated than a two-sided encounter. Another reason is the poisonous condition of relations between China and the Soviet Union. Minimal rapport and mutual tolerance are the preconditions for fruitful discussions, and these do not currently exist between the two largest Communist nations. And finally, the Chinese have publicly thumbed their noses at the idea of participating in what they have charged is a superpower conspiracy to buttress positions of privilege in the international system. They would suffer some loss in prestige by reversing this stance, although in time the People's Republic may become as staunch a champion of nuclear hierarchy as the heirs of the Bolsheviks have shown themselves to be.

It is also possible that the United States and the Soviet Union will decide that the rise in Chinese striking power requires no particular response from either of them. In the 1980s, the Chinese stockpile will probably still be small enough so that the problems just discussed will not yet be urgent ones. But as China's nuclear intentions become clearer, the two great powers will have to begin to decide what to do about them, and those decisions will not be easy to make.

Perhaps the optimal course would be for the United States and Soviet Union to do nothing to hinder Chinese efforts to acquire a minimum deterrent, thereby preserving the stability of their own nuclear balance, and for Peking—with its "right" to minimal deterrence sanctioned by the two superpowers—not to build up its arsenal beyond the minimum level. This would keep hierarchy intact. Whether this is the course that all three powers will follow remains to be seen.

Western Europe　　Both Great Britain and France have modest nuclear forces. The British have four nuclear missile-firing submarines; the French, in 1976, had three such submarines, two squadrons of intermediate-range ballistic missiles, and several squadrons of aircraft capable of launching a nuclear attack on the Soviet Union. But neither country is likely to have the political inclination or the economic resources to make these forces substantially larger or independent of the United States.

If *all* the principal nations of Western Europe pooled their resources, however, they could assemble a strategic arsenal that would rival the Soviets' and the Americans'. They would have an industrial base with an output second in size to that of the United States, a plentiful supply of scientists and engineers with the requisite skills, and the nuclear stockpiles of Great Britain and France. However, the rise of European superpower would be a political earthquake at the heart of the industrial circumference whose unchanging landscape has been one of the hallmarks of the current nuclear regime.

The advent of a great European nuclear force would disrupt the international system, in the first instance, not solely because it would add another member to the nuclear club, but also because it would place nuclear weapons partly in German hands. This would make real a nightmare that has haunted the Soviet Union for 30 years and has helped to shape Soviet foreign policy since 1945. A German nuclear arsenal became a point of contention in the early 1960s when the United States proposed to set up a multilateral nuclear force (MLF) over which the Germans were to share control. The prospect of the MLF greatly agitated the Soviets, and a European Nuclear Force would no doubt be equally disquieting. It can be argued that an independent European nuclear force would be a more credible deterrent against Soviet aggression than the American nuclear umbrella. However, it would almost certainly touch off large increases in Soviet defense spending (and therefore probably United States spending also) and bring on additions to Soviet strategic forces, since the Kremlin would feel hemmed in by three hostile nuclear powers. And these responses could disturb the Soviet-American balance. The Europeans might feel safer from Soviet attack with their own fingers on the nuclear trigger, but they are safe enough now with American-controlled tactical nuclear weapons within their borders. (So discussions about withdrawing those American weapons or agreeing to constraints on their use must be sensitive to the risks of European nuclear build-up and integration.)

The United States eventually dropped the MLF proposal, and this settled the matter not only for the past 10 years but probably for the next 10 as well. Unlike the case of China's strategic force, the Soviet Union and especially the United States, with its economic and military ties to the western part of the continent, can have a considerable say in Europe's nuclear future. Their uneasiness over an independent European nuclear arsenal is one reason why there will not be one in the 1980s. The other reason is that the creation of such a unified Western European arsenal presupposes political developments that are far from likely, namely, the establishment of a united Western European political community. European unity is an old and alluring dream, but it does not seem on the point of coming true. Even as they have developed a customs union, the various states of Western Europe have jealously guarded those individual political sovereignties that they would have to surrender to build a single, integrated nuclear force. There is no reason to suppose that the political foundation of a European nuclear superpower will be firmer in the 1980s than it is today.

NUCLEAR PROLIFERATION

The nuclear hierarchy may be eroded not only by the enlargement of the lesser nuclear arsenals of today's international system but also by the acquisition of nuclear arms by nations that do not now have them. Whether proliferation threatens the relative calm that the First Regime has brought to international politics will depend upon who joins the nuclear club and how fast its membership expands. The greater the number of countries that have nuclear weapons, the greater the statistical probability that one will go off, even if only accidentally. The farther the bomb spreads from the confines of the industrial circumference, the greater are the chances that it could find its way into the hands of persons who would not show the prudence that the guardians of existing nuclear stockpiles have so far displayed. The farther they proliferate, the greater the risk that nuclear weapons will enter areas troubled by political quarrels. And as states begin constructing primitive nuclear arsenals—initially composed only of a few bombs and jet airplanes or simply passenger aircraft to deliver them—their better-armed neighbors, or even the superpowers, may feel tempted to attack them in a preemptive strike.

The rate at which the nuclear club expands may also affect whether or not the international system can digest more nuclear states without undue distress. Nuclear weapons could spread very rapidly if a modest nuclear arsenal comes to be as vivid and as obligatory a symbol of national independence and importance as a steel mill or a seat in the UN General Assembly. Such a system-wide impulse can sometimes touch the members of the international community. This happened in the 1880s, when the principal European powers engaged in a "scramble for Africa," each feeling the need to conquer as much of the continent as it could lest its rivals appropriate a larger share of it. Their African rivalry fed the tensions in Europe that exploded in 1914. Nuclear weapons could become a similar touchstone in the 1980s.

Nuclear weapons have, it is true, encouraged prudential behavior by the superpowers and political stability within the industrial circumference. Would they not also help to keep the peace in other areas? They might, if the commitment to equilibrium (and the forces to support that commitment) that underpins the Soviet-American nuclear relationship could be quickly established wherever proliferation occurs. But there is no reason to believe that nuclear weapons will everywhere be introduced in a way that makes for stable deterrence. Different kinds of arsenals and different rates of development and deployment, suspicions about the intentions of already distrusted neighbors, uncertainty about how the "nuclearization" of a region will affect the security commitments of outside powers to the states of the region—all these possible consequences of proliferation could upset already unstable political conditions.

On the other hand, the spread of nuclear weapons would be consistent with the First Regime if it created, in other parts of the world, the conditions that have brought peace to Europe. A series of regional nuclear balances similar to the one that has forced the two superpowers to compose and restrain their differences in order to avoid catastrophe could conceivably emerge in the Middle East, on the Korean peninsula, or in Latin America. Alternatively, a single nuclear power could bring peace to a corner of the world by dominating it—India in South Asia, for instance, or Iran in the Middle East.

Regional dominance by a single nuclear power is not likely, however, because the other countries of the region will almost certainly not want to be dominated and will seek their own nuclear arsenals to prevent this from happening. China's entry into the nuclear club certainly influenced India's decision to conduct a nuclear test. And that test may have set Pakistan off in quest of a bomb. The spread of "peaceful" nuclear technology is particularly dangerous insofar as it limits the chances of restraining the *rate* of nuclear weapons proliferation. As nuclear power programs grow, nations will inevitably edge closer to the capacity to make a bomb. As a state sees its neighbor creeping toward the nuclear club through the construction of a series of nuclear power plants and related facilities, it might worry that the fabrication of a bomb was only a matter of time and, reckoning that there was some profit in being the first in the region to have one, move to acquire its own.

Still, a proliferated world might not be an unbearably grim and dangerous one. Politics among nations could conceivably continue as they have in the current regime. For example, the new nuclear nations might move into the orbit of one or the other of the great powers, as have Britain and France, or be deterred by them, as China has been. The neighbors of the new nuclear state might react, if not with equanimity, at least with enough composure to avoid alarms, crises, or war; this appears to have been true in the case of India's peaceful nuclear explosion of May 1974, although the final returns are not yet in and Pakistan's interest in a spent-fuel reprocessing plant may be an ominous sign of things to come. A state might not actually fabricate a weapon despite a demonstrated or widely accepted capacity to do so, as in the present case of India and Israel; states like these, which stand with one foot inside the gates of the nuclear club and one foot outside, might make fewer, smaller waves in international politics than states that visibly equip themselves with real bombs and the means to deliver them.

The disruptive effects of proliferation might be restrained in the 1980s if the United States and the Soviet Union jointly enforced a sharp division in the international system. As the tide of proliferation swelled beyond the borders of the industrial circumference, they might move to seal it off from the rest of the world. They could cooperate in throwing up defenses to protect themselves and their allies against nuclear attack by minor powers. They could pledge to cooperate, tacitly or openly, in punishing a third party for an attack on either of them. They could resolve, formally or covertly, to abstain from all involvement in the nuclear-infested politics beyond their own spheres of direct concern. And they could agree not to permit the taking of measures in response to proliferation—such as the construction of missile defenses—that would interfere with the equilibrium between them. They could try, in sum, to protect the second pillar of the First Nuclear Regime, bipolar equilibrium, from the consequences of the deterioration of the third, hierarchy, and so retain most of the regime's benefits.

It would not be easy, however, for either of them to insulate themselves from the effects of widespread nuclear proliferation, even if it were confined to areas outside Europe, North America, and Japan. As other countries developed arsenals formidable enough to threaten the two superpowers, their own strategic relationship could be upset. Even a strong mutual commitment to the contrary might founder on mistrust. For example, if proliferation prompted either superpower or both to start deploying an ABM system, the other might regard it as potentially threatening its retaliatory capability, contrary assurances notwithstanding. Alternatively, proliferation might frighten the junior partners of the Soviet Union or, more likely, of the United States badly enough to send them into the nuclear weapons business themselves, which could in turn trigger the unraveling of the alliances that link together the superpowers and their respective partners.

It is also conceivable that the political, economic, and cultural ties that bind the Soviet Union and its allies or, again more plausibly, the United States and its allies with outlying regions, might prove strong enough to keep the two great powers deeply involved in the affairs of these regions even though that involvement was riddled with nuclear perils. It would be especially difficult for the United States to turn away from several states that lie on the border of the industrial circumference—in particular, South Korea, Taiwan, Israel, and South Africa—and are among the most likely to enter the nuclear club in the 1980s. Each of these four nations has an acute security problem, each is uncertain that the United States will protect it and that its own non-nuclear military resources will suffice to ward off its enemy, and each has the technical skills to make a bomb without great difficulty. These marginal states—marginal both geographically and politically— are the most dangerous potential proliferants in the 1980s because the introduction of nuclear weapons into their political disputes could lead to nuclear war into which one or both of the great powers could be dragged.

Hierarchy and Proliferation

Nuclear proliferation is a complicated problem. Or, more properly, it is a complicated series of problems, which are as numerous as the number of potential nuclear weapons states. It has been suggested that a fruitful way to deal with these problems would be to alter the structure of the present nuclear regime to make it less hierarchical. Two particular steps are often proposed. The first is to reduce significantly the forces of the superpowers. This, it is argued, would diminish the perceived importance of nuclear weapons and thereby make them less attractive to currently non-nuclear states. This proposal, however, rests on questionable premises. Anyone with a memory of Hiroshima or an elementary knowledge of physics understands the power that nuclear weapons can give. Indeed, paring down the two foremost arsenals would more likely *encourage* the acquisition of nuclear weapons, since members of the two major alliances might feel their senior partners less able to protect them, while fledgling nuclear powers would not have quite as far to go to become the nuclear equals of the United States and the Soviet Union.

The second proposed step to ease the pressures for the spread of nuclear weapons is to admit other nations, especially those toying with the idea of obtaining nuclear weapons, to today's principal arms control discussions. However, this has already been tried in the past without fruitful results. Numerous UN forums over the last three decades have brought the great and the small of the world community together to grapple with the problems that nuclear weapons have presented; the more nations that have participated in negotiations, the gloomier the results. Those agreements that many nations have signed, the Limited Test Ban Treaty and the Non-Proliferation Treaty, were worked out by the United States and the Soviet Union, which then coaxed and cajoled others to subscribe to them. Broadening the strictly bilateral SALT negotiations would complicate them; there would be more parties to consult before anything could be agreed to and more potential snags in the proceedings. These negotiations are difficult enough already, involving, as they do, considerable bargaining within as well as between the American and Soviet governments. Nuclear hierarchy cannot be disguised by inviting non-nuclear states to meetings of the superpowers. That hierarchy will remain a glaring feature of international politics for the foreseeable future.

Nor will proliferation be prevented by enacting nominal measures that chip away at the nuclear hierarchy. Indeed, the prospects for curbing the spread of nuclear weapons will only brighten to the extent that the principle of hierarchy is strengthened and the United States and the Soviet Union cooperate to persuade or coerce others not to obtain nuclear armaments. There are, broadly speaking, two approaches to stemming proliferation. The first is technical: keeping the wherewithal to make bombs out of the hands of non-nuclear states. The second is political: ministering to the fears and suppressing or appeasing the aspirations that propel states into the nuclear club. Soviet-American cooperation would reinforce both approaches. Together the two superpowers could regulate with some effect the flow of nuclear technology beyond the industrial circumference. And by cooperating, openly or tacitly, they could do a great deal to guarantee the security of most members of the international system, since the two great powers tend to be either the main threat or the main source of reassurance for most of them. But whether the two can work more closely together to inhibit the spread of nuclear weapons remains to be seen; the political barriers to intimate cooperation are high. And an alliance of the two to close the doors of the nuclear club might not be received with good grace by all those left standing outside. The other members of the international community would have to be persuaded that their security was not in jeopardy and that the "condominium" of the great powers encompassed only nuclear matters and nothing more.

CONCLUSION

Like the second pillar of the current nuclear regime, the equilibrium between the United States and the Soviet Union, its third pillar, hierarchy, is threatened with erosion springing from technological change and its political application in the 1980s.

There are, however, three important differences between the futures of these two bulwarks of the First Regime. First, the technological challenge in the case of hierarchy comes not from advances in the state-of-the-art of weapons design but from the diffusion of its more elementary techniques. Manufacturing a fission bomb is not a simple operation that can be performed in an average basement, but neither is it an overwhelming or mysterious technical feat. It requires scientists with an understanding of the fundamental precepts of nuclear energy, a cadre of engineers, and a supply of fissionable material. In the 1980s more and more nations will come to have all three. Proliferation, therefore, will depend more upon political decisions and less upon technological progress than will the Soviet-American arms race.

Second, proliferation is more menacing to the First Nuclear Regime than is the arms race between the two superpowers. Proliferation increases the chances that nuclear weapons will be fired in anger, whereas the spiral of the arms competition between the two great powers is not very likely to dislodge the constraints against war—the certainty of mutual assured destruction in the event of a nuclear exchange—that both have increasingly felt for three decades.

And third, proliferation will be more difficult to control than the Soviet-American arms competition, for more centers of decision are involved: governments other than those of the Soviet Union and the United States, which are the ones most deeply committed to the First Regime, will have a say in how proliferation proceeds. In the early years of the nuclear age, the two were able to exert more influence on other members of the international community than will be possible in the 1980s. Their advantages in wealth and power and their prestige—the United States was the "arsenal of democracy," the Soviet Union the "Rome of socialism"— were greater in the past than they will be in the future.

The number of independent nuclear arsenals in the international system in 1990 will ultimately be determined by political choices that cannot be clearly foreseen. That number—and the resultant likelihood of nuclear weapons being used in battle—will depend less on concerted superpower policies and more on the "climate" of international politics than has been true for the first three decades of the nuclear age. The number may not be much higher than the present six: many nations have signed the NPT and will not lightly violate it. In fact, the nuclear club may become less, not more, attractive over time. Now regarded as a breach in the dike that had been holding back the waters of proliferation, India may, by 1985, be seen as a cautionary example of the disadvantages of joining the nuclear club. If Iran and Pakistan acquire nuclear armaments in response to the May 1974 explosion, if the maintenance of respectable strategic force turns out to be an intolerable burden on India's already staggering economy, and if the rest of the world accords New Delhi no greater—and perhaps less—respect than before, India and its potential imitators may conclude that precious resources have been poured into a project that has yielded neither power, prestige, nor security.

And whatever the rate of proliferation in the 1980s, the First Regime—and its heart, the nuclear equilibrium between the United States and the Soviet Union—will help to cushion the international system from any disruptive effects proliferation may produce. The current regime has reduced the incentives for proliferation by calming ancient political disputes and by putting in the hands of each superpower a large and sturdy nuclear umbrella under which many nations can confidently take shelter. And the high force levels that are an integral part of the regime make the states of the industrial circumference, at least, far less vulnerable to proliferation elsewhere than they would be if these arsenals were much smaller or if they did not exist at all.

FIVE

A Conservative Preference

The First Nuclear Regime is the current regime, projected and protected. Its three pillars—anarchy, equilibrium, and hierarchy—have made possible the coexistence of weapons of mass destruction with the ongoing "game of nations," of which weapons of all kinds have been such a familiar part since the beginning of recorded history. If the bomb is the modern Sword of Damocles, anarchy, equilibrium, and hierarchy have been interwoven to form a thread that has kept that sword firmly suspended above the world and its day-to-day affairs. The First Regime has given the international system a measure of stability: since 1945 there has been no nuclear war and no full-fledged war of any sort within the industrial circumference. And there has been, as well, an appreciation that unrestrained political conflict can lead to nuclear war, an appreciation that has turned relations between the United States and the Soviet Union, the two greatest nuclear powers, into a mannered contest that each side wants to win but in which neither dares to exceed sharply etched limits in pursuit of victory. For three decades the nuclear superpowers have acted like boxers with brittle fists, circling each other warily, sparring gently, but fearing to deliver the knockout blow that, even if it landed, would mangle the hand of the deliverer. The claim that the First Regime has on the loyalty of the international system's members rests upon the restraint and stability that it has achieved. That claim is a strong one and deserves to be honored through the 1980s.

The First Regime's fate depends in large part upon the contest between the advance of technology, which spurs the growth of the world's nuclear arsenals, and politics, which tries to control these armories. Technology is like a plant, growing upward and outward; politics is the carpentry that aims at keeping the plant from spreading too far beyond its main stalk or from bending to one side and toppling over. The plant's upward growth—the additions to and refinements of the two most formidable nuclear stockpiles—is the nuclear arms race. Its outward spread—the diffusion of bombs to different nation-states—is proliferation. The second kind of growth will challenge the First Regime more formidably and be less amenable to management by the Regime's champions in the 1980s than will the first. Both the arms race and proliferation could be forms of "deterioration." The regime can withstand a continually escalating Soviet-American arms competition only as long as the certainty of mutual assured destruction is maintained, and it can contain considerably widespread nuclear proliferation only as long as that proliferation does not threaten the dominant position of the two superpowers in the international system, nor cause them to adopt postures that would upset the strategic balance between them. The greater the degree to which the equilibrium between the American and Soviet nuclear arsenals is upset or to which the hierarchical relationship among the two nuclear superpowers, the four smaller nuclear powers, and the nonnuclear states is altered, the further the First Regime will deteriorate and the greater will be the peril to the benefits the regime has brought.

But deterioration is not the only imaginable future for the current regime. Politics might not only keep up with the growth of technology, it might conceivably manage to get the upper hand. That is, political leaders might succeed in reducing the nuclear stockpiles. The Second and Third Regimes that are presented in this volume reflect the belief that substantial reductions of and restrictions upon the world's nuclear stores are worthy goals that would improve the world's current nuclear arrangements.

But these "improvements" would not necessarily make the world safer and might actually make it less secure than it would be under the First Regime. Improvements could come in two forms: declarations that make the use of nuclear weapons less likely and actual reductions in the nuclear arsenals nations could use if they chose to. Formal declarations, such as one abjuring the first use of nuclear weapons, will not, as noted above, carry much weight if issued by nations with huge nuclear stockpiles, for statements can easily be forgotten when war begins. And even to the extent that such declarations are convincing, they can conceivably raise the chances of non-nuclear war, upset the declarer's allies, and thereby contribute to nuclear proliferation. The United States has never made a no-first-use declaration precisely because of the fear that it would embolden the Soviets and sow doubts among America's European allies about American reliability. Instead, tactical nuclear weapons have remained deployed in Europe to deter the Soviets and to maintain the confidence of the junior members of NATO. So there is little to gain and something to lose from this first sort of improvement.

As for force reductions, the second type of improvement, the force levels of the United States and the Soviet Union are so staggeringly high that marginal reductions in them—by a few hundred missiles, say—would not greatly affect the First Regime. While the often-cited calculations about how many dozens of times each great power can destroy the other and how many pounds of TNT each has for every man, woman, and child on the face of the earth are neither precise nor particularly revealing, they do convey an impression of excess. However, the huge supplies of nuclear weapons each superpower keeps on hand are not actually excessive. High force levels are an important part of the First Regime: they maintain the nuclear hierarchy and preserve the balance between the two foremost nuclear nations. They make the stability of the regime more or less immune to those doctrinal shifts and technological inventions by the two strongest nuclear states that are likely through the 1980s. They help insulate the central nuclear balance from the disruptive effects of proliferation.

Thus the world in the 1980s will be best served by the First Nuclear Regime, a series of nuclear arrangements as close to the current ones as possible. This is a distinctly conservative preference, and the case for the First Regime is the classical conservative one. It repeats the arguments that have been advanced by the party of order against the claims of the partisans of change throughout the modern political history of the Western world. Those arguments are as follows: the First Nuclear Regime is a complicated, intricate, and delicate entity; it does not spring from a grand design or a detailed blueprint, but is the work of many hands and minds, of trial and error, of small changes. The First Regime is an expression of the wisdom of history and has earned history's approval by passing its supreme test—the test of time. The regime is like a living organism: radical surgery would more likely kill than improve it. Its parts are connected in ways not fully understood; it is not known precisely how it works, only that it works; it is best simply to try to keep it working.

Conservatism has seldom been universally popular, as is shown by the histories of even those political communities where conservative sentiment has been strongest. Visions of different, better orders always beguile some imaginations—and this will be true of the First Nuclear Regime. The regime will seem unacceptable, even intolerable, to some critics on two grounds. First, it may be objected that the First Regime will leave the world a nuclear-armed camp in which the bombs will go off one day. As long as nuclear weapons exist, humanity remains in mortal danger. A nuclear regime that is not a way station on the path to nuclear disarmament, goes this objection—and the First Regime is certainly no such thing—is not worth having.

But the nuclear-armed camp is, alas, the result of two immutable phenomena: the first pillar of the current regime, the persistence of independent nation-states with the sovereign right to use force in whatever circumstances they wish; and familiarity with the techniques for liberating the explosive power locked in the heart of the atom and for harnessing it for use in war. The armed camp is the product, to put it bluntly, of the two most powerful social forces of the twentieth century, nationalism and science. Neither will be reversed or abolished either in the 1980s or in the foreseeable future beyond. The nation-states of the world will neither soar to a plateau of brotherhood and international sovereignty nor retreat from the understanding of the natural world that they have achieved. And the consequences of attempting seriously to do so—to ban science or pool sovereignty or simply lay down all nuclear weapons—would not necessarily be happy ones. The community of nations is stuck with its nuclear predicament. It has lived with the bomb for 30 years, and it can continue to do so. In any case, it will not have the opportunity to live without it.

The other argument against the conservative spirit of the First Regime is that it does not fit the sort of international system that is likely to exist in the future. The 1980s will be a period of flux and change. It is by now a commonplace that the international politics of the future will differ significantly from those of the last 30 years. New problems will come to the fore: food, energy, and proprietary rights in the oceans will supplant, or at least join, the location of international boundaries and the political character of national governments at the top of the world's agenda. New cleavages will divide the members of the international community; the age-old contest of nations will become more complicated and spread to previously uncharted realms. The principal task in the 1980s will be to cope with this growing volume of international business.

The First Nuclear Regime will contribute to the successful management of the host of new international issues by keeping the issue of nuclear weapons separate from them. Mingling them will redound to the benefit of no one: if nuclear weapons grow in importance in international affairs, non-nuclear states will find themselves at a disadvantage. At the same time, the nuclear powers will find their arsenals blunt and unwieldy instruments for achieving many of the goals they are likely to set for themselves in the 1980s. And if nuclear matters become entangled with the budding international questions of the next decade, these will be more difficult to resolve. A spirit of egalitarianism pervades contemporary international politics, and it is likely to gather force in the 1980s. The non-nuclear states will not want to endorse the First Regime, at least not publicly, while the nuclear powers will not want it changed. A joint exercise in reevaluating the regime would lead to stalemate and acrimony. It would sap the world's limited supply of goodwill that is needed to address the international problems that are now emerging. And the world has, as well, a limited amount of attention to bestow on each of its various problems. In the words of the late Alastair Buchan,

We, the nations, are a little like the members of a committee who have been struggling hard to settle items one to three on the agenda, how to control or eliminate weapons of mass destruction, how to create easier relations between countries of opposing ideologies, how to narrow the gap between the rich and the poor countries, only to find that we must add five, six, or seven new and important items to it.[18]

That first question, how to control or eliminate weapons of mass destruction, was the foremost item on the world's agenda in 1945. The First Nuclear Regime had, by the mid-1970s, provided a settlement of sorts for it. Discarding that regime or trying to reform it will only hurt the chances of coping with all the other matters that will be part of the agenda in the 1980s.

A historical perspective is instructive. Thirty years ago the nuclear stalk dominated the garden of international politics. But over three decades, as the current nuclear regime was put into place—in part *because* it was put into place—other issues blossomed. There is coming to be more and more to international affairs than nuclear weapons and the issues they affect. The First Regime helps keep the nuclear plant upright; away from it, other flora are poking through the soil. But the nuclear plant still towers menacingly. Should it crash to the ground, it would destroy everything in its path. The First Nuclear Regime, though awkward, fragile in spots, and far from perfectly designed, remains the best possible prop for it.

[18]Alastair Buchan, *Change Without War*, St. Martin's Press, New York, 1975, pp. 18–19.

Reducing Dependence on Nuclear Weapons: A Second Nuclear Regime

Richard L. Garwin

ONE

Premises and Purposes

A Second Nuclear Regime for the 1980s and beyond would lie between the current, or First, Regime, in which nations continue to possess nuclear weapons with declared purposes for them beyond simply deterring or retaliating against nuclear attack, and a Third Nuclear Regime, in which national possession of nuclear weapons would be proscribed. Under a Second Nuclear Regime, nuclear weapons would continue to exist, but their capabilities, numbers, deployment, and roles would be more circumscribed than is the case today. The international environment would be less dependent on nuclear weapons—that is, they would have less influence on political and conventional military interaction, their role being limited to nuclear deterrence and retaliation.

As this essay will attempt to demonstrate, a Second Nuclear Regime would be superior to the best *achievable* First and Third Regimes. Therefore, progress toward this regime should be high among national priorities. It should not be taken for granted that the world will or should progress from the First through the Second to the Third Nuclear Regime. Not all change is good; not all equalization is beneficial, even for the downtrodden. It is my belief that the world will never again be free of nuclear weapons or the threat of nuclear weapons. Our central intellectual task, therefore, it to conceive of durable, stable arrangements for living with them.

THE PURPOSE OF A SECOND NUCLEAR REGIME

The complex of physical nuclear weapons capabilities and the doctrinal and declaratory posture regarding their use should do more than simply provide national security for a period of time. These capabilities and plans should be aimed at constituting a viable posture from which nuclear weapons states can do the following:

1. Take effective measures against nuclear proliferation
2. Hold expenditures on strategic military capabilities to a minimum, while still providing adequate security
3. Avoid overemphasis on strategic threats—which leads to the neglect of real and important problems that threaten the existence of national and world society—thereby permitting the removal of nuclear weapons (to some extent) from the conduct of world politics, i.e., a reduction in their value as instruments of power politics
4. Give individuals a feeling that the world of nations is understandable and controllable and that their own condition is improving
5. Provide a stable foundation from which a Third Nuclear Regime might (but need not) evolve

The choice among conceivable Second Regimes must involve "sensitivity analysis," for a superficially attractive regime whose benefits evaporate with a slight deviation from its underlying assumptions would be unacceptable. In short, perfection of detail being unlikely, a regime not dependent on perfection is to be preferred. Fallback positions must be available in case the political, technological, behavioral, and bureaucratic roots of the regime do not hold.

For the United States, the worth of a nuclear regime must be reckoned not only in the security that it provides for the present, but also in the security for the future and even more in the degree to which the regime frees material and intellectual resources for the building of society. Obviously, other nations, especially the

Soviet Union and America's NATO allies, must see a Second Regime as helpful to them (or at least not greatly inferior to the First Regime) if they are to cooperate in its introduction. However, the transition to a Second Regime will be most feasible if its positive attributes can be achieved by actions of the United States alone; for this reason the emphasis of this essay is on American initiatives. In any case, it is hard to believe that the nations of the world will oppose a shift to a strategic posture based on confidence, competence, and sufficiency from a regime so stridently portrayed as barely adequate or worse.

BASIC CHARACTERISTICS OF
A SECOND NUCLEAR REGIME

In designing a Second Nuclear Regime for the time frame of the 1980s, it is assumed that an alliance structure similar to that of the 1970s will persist, but that neither that structure nor the relative rank of nations nor the technology of war and peace will be static over the decade. It is also assumed that public officials will generally attempt to act in the national interest as they see it—specifically, that leaders of both the United States and the Soviet Union will be wise enough and strong enough to emphasize national survival over bureaucratic advantage, to recognize the possible conflict between national security and defense industry interests, and to press for national advantage but not at great risk to national survival.

Deterrence: Foundation of a Second Nuclear Regime
There is no technical solution in existence or in sight that would enable a modern society to survive a determined attack by strategic nuclear forces such as those of the United States or the Soviet Union. But fear of the destruction of American society by nuclear attack from the Soviet Union is not high among concerns of thoughtful people in the United States (and vice versa). This is not because we have an effective defense or because the Soviets wish American society well; rather, it is because the Soviet Union is *deterred* from initiating such an attack by the knowledge that it would likely be destroyed in turn. Uncomfortable as this situation

85

might seem in the abstract, it intrudes remarkably little on the consciousness of citizens or leaders.

But what role do nuclear weapons play, and what role *should* they play, in deterring the Soviet Union from lesser, non-nuclear aggression against the United States or its allies? Can the United States continue to threaten to respond to such lesser aggression with the use of nuclear weapons against the Soviet Union with full knowledge that such a response, however "graduated," would lead also to nuclear attack on the United States? If Washington perceives the *risk* to the United States of escalating to the nuclear level as less than that of accepting the consequences of subnuclear Soviet aggression, then it can rationally and credibly deter the Soviets from committing that aggression. But Moscow must recognize that Washington sees things this way if it is to be deterred. A similar criterion holds for the Soviet Union. The risks and consequences of escalation being less vis-à-vis non-nuclear states, deterrence of aggression by threats to use nuclear weapons might be considered even more effective against such nations; but this would require that a nuclear power adhere to a policy of first use of nuclear weapons against non-nuclear states, unnecessary and unseemly for a great power and therefore not an element of the recommended Second Nuclear Regime.

Even if effective methods of defending against current strategic deterrent forces—ballistic missiles, aircraft, and cruise missiles—should be developed in the 1980s, other means—ranging from quantitative expansion of current forces and penetration aids to systems, such as biological weapons, that are at present less favored—exist or could be created to destroy societies. Unleashing destructive power is becoming less and less difficult for humanity; we will have to live with and prevent the realization of this potential. In the final analysis, maintaining deterrence is feasible; not maintaining deterrence is dangerous or suicidal for both the United States and the Soviet Union. Therefore, maintaining stable mutual deterrence between the two countries at affordable cost is a reasonable objective. The Second Regime described in this essay is a prescription for life in the 1980s with strategic offensive capabilities dominant over strategic defenses, a situation that seems sure to prevail anyway. The consequences of this situation can be managed very largely by actions of the United States alone in structuring its nuclear and conventional forces, if this physical posture is accompanied by a doctrinal and declaratory posture that provides a basis for maintaining stable relationships with both allies and opponents as well as influencing others not in either category.

Lesser Dependence on Nuclear Weapons   A Second Regime is one with continued possession by relatively few nations of weapons of terrible destructive power, but with a reduction in the perceived advantage accruing to the few possessors. Under a Second Regime, the assigned tasks for nuclear weapons are limited strictly to those roles they are generally recognized as performing well, namely, deterring or retaliating against other nations' use of nuclear weapons. These attributes would contribute to popular acceptance of the regime and would allow a diversion of attention and resources to the important problems confronting individual societies and the world at large, such as the increasing cost of resources, environmental pollution, the population explosion, and the political and social instability of nations.

Under the Second Regime prescribed here, confining the possession of nuclear weapons to a few states and limiting their utility to possessors would be furthered by the adoption by all possessors of a policy of nonuse against non-nuclear-weapons states, a restriction of the role of nuclear weapons to deterrence of or response to nuclear attack, and the extension of nuclear deterrence to non-nuclear states confronted by an adversary with nuclear weapons. Taken together, doctrinal and declaratory measures of this sort would reduce the significance of nuclear weapons in world affairs and permit certain reductions in the physical capabilities of nuclear forces which would enhance the stability and, as a result, the legitimacy of the regime.[1]

While characterized by a lesser dependence on nuclear weapons than is true of the First Regime, the Second Regime prescribed here has other parameters of comparable importance,

---

[1]See pp. 113–132 for a detailed discussion of the doctrinal and declaratory elements of this Second Nuclear Regime.

among them an enhancement of the nature and level of conventional forces to bring about a reduction of the necessity of using nuclear weapons to deter or respond to low-level aggression. Also important for Western countries are a high degree of support by the electorate for the national security policy and the prevalence of hope over despair among the citizenry. Another important parameter of this Second Regime is its effect on nuclear proliferation. Burgeoning nuclear forces among the lesser nations of the world would increase the chances of nuclear weapons being stolen or seized in coups d'état, with great potential for escalation and terrorism. As a means of severely limiting the utility of nuclear weapons and providing security guarantees to non-nuclear-weapons states, the Second Regime prescribed here would command substantial world support for effective action against nuclear proliferation and thus would promote international stability.

TWO

Physical Posture for the Second Nuclear Regime

In designing a Second Nuclear Regime for the 1980s, it is impossible scientifically to determine a single optimum posture and the best means of achieving it. Unlike the First and Third Regimes, whose natures are dictated by the very circumstances and characteristics that lead us to distinguish them, there are many possible alternative Second Regimes, and each strategic analyst could design his or her own. Hence, this section will describe in some detail one particular physical combination of weapons and associated doctrinal and declaratory postures that would characterize a Second Nuclear Regime, that is, a regime in which there is less dependence upon nuclear weapons than at present.

NUCLEAR WEAPONS CONVEY AN ABILITY TO DESTROY CITIES

Nuclear weapons have an inherent minimum efficient yield: 10 to 30 kilotons for fission weapons. No great saving in cost or size can be obtained by designing weapons with a smaller explosive yield. This is the tyranny of nuclear weapons: the use of a nuclear explosive for peaceful purposes is problematical at best; its utility in killing submarines is hardly greater than that of a modern homing torpedo; and its effectiveness in attacking heavily armored vehicles in land warfare is not much greater than that of many conventional weapons. But there is absolutely no doubt of the ability of even a modest-size nuclear explosive to destroy the lives and habitat of hundreds of thousands of people in a city. While conventional high-explosive weapons for the 1980s, now entering the inventory or in development, provide greatly increased effectiveness against military targets, no such improvement inheres in the application of new technology to nuclear weapons. The comparative advantage of nuclear weapons lies in visiting destruction upon an enemy's society rather than in directly defending one's own population, territory, or military forces by destroying the enemy's forces. If nuclear weapons and the means for their delivery against enemy cities exist, then it is inconceivable that a nation will not threaten to use them *in extremis,* in order to prevent its effective annihilation. Therefore, a Second Regime would entail the continued existence of nuclear weapons among a relative few powerful nations to deter the annihilation of these nations or their allies. In other words, under a Second Regime the principle of "mutual assured destruction" (MAD) that has long served to prevent a Soviet-American nuclear exchange would be preserved.

The size of cities, their geographical configuration, and their high vulnerability relative to missile silos and military equipment in general make them very difficult to defend against nuclear attack. Cities are vulnerable to attack by nuclear weapons, whether or not those nuclear weapons were primarily designed for city attack. This will be true as long as there are nuclear weapons, and would remain true even if nuclear weapons did not exist but could be made, or if there were no nuclear delivery capabilities except makeshift ones. In recognition of this technical fact, under the Second Regime here prescribed there would be a prohibition of strategic defense[2] in order to prevent the onset of troublesome ambiguities that would compromise the assuredness of mutual destruction essential to strategic stability.

Some thinkers contend that technology might in the long run

[2]With the possible exception of a very specialized defense of hardened intercontinental ballistic missile (ICBM) silos. See pp. 97–98.

allow the defense to overwhelm the offense. But the resources needed for research and development and for modifications to existing weapons for the purpose of preserving a strategic deterrent against defensive developments are small, and the spectrum of possible deterrents, all of which a defensive force would have to be able to destroy, is enormous. Despite one's instinctive preference for defense over offense, despite the historical Soviet emphasis on defensive systems, and despite the large resources spent by Moscow over the years, no one suggests that even the extensive Soviet air defense network can prevent a majority of B-52s from completing their strategic missions. Nor has an antiballistic missile (ABM) system been conceived for city defense that could not be overwhelmed by lesser efforts of the offense. Furthermore, relations among the great powers would scarcely benefit from defensive dominance even if it became possible; the fear that the other side could execute a surprise attack without suffering retaliatory damage would heighten mutual suspicions and tensions. In all, the United States and the Soviet Union should not put large resources into development of defensive measures, although they should maintain adequate intelligence to guard against some unexpected development of defenses on the other side.

The Threat of City Attack—the Essence of Deterrence We are not concerned here with the long-standing argument between those who regard mutual assured destruction as sufficient and those who do not. We need only note that in the absence of MAD, if one of two sides possessed, either overtly or clandestinely, the ability to destroy a large number of cities of the other side when the other did not, irrespective of other relative military capabilities, it could at any time force the outcome of a dispute or a war by threatening cities or actually destroying as many as required to force surrender. A Third Regime would have to guarantee that such capabilities never fall into national hands; a Second Regime *depends for its stability* on the capability of states to so coerce others, but with this capability restrained by the possession of similar destructive capabilities by opposing states

91

and alliances.[3] Stability of a Second Regime also rests on confining the possession of large nuclear forces to relatively stable nations, willing and able to guard them adequately; it would not likely survive proliferation to a large number of smaller and less stable countries, and so nonproliferation is an important element of the Second Regime prescribed here.

Instability of a Third Regime   It is true that nuclear weapons must be teamed with delivery vehicles—ballistic or cruise missiles, aircraft, or even surface vehicles—to so coerce nations. Advocates of a Third Regime raise the false hope that a city-attack capability could be eliminated and proscribed, for they exaggerate the possibility of banning ICBMs, subjecting space launch facilities to inspection, etc. In reality, very small ICBMs weighing on the order of 10,000 pounds, with modern guidance technology and small warheads, would be adequate to provide a force capable of destroying tens of millions of people. In an allegedly "denuclearized" world, a force of a few hundred such missiles could be easily maintained clandestinely and would be safe from attack by an adversary, even if concealed in small buildings on military bases with only modest hardening of the launch system.

If, under a Third Regime, long-range bombers as well as missiles were banned, military aircraft of intermediate range with specially selected crews could be used on one-way intercontinental missions in this coercive role, carrying bombs that may have been justified as "peaceful nuclear explosives" or as warheads for use in air-defense missiles.[4] In such circumstances, the con-

---

[3]A Second Regime, however, would not be stable if nuclear weapons were designed and deployed so as to make possible the destruction of opposing strategic forces, for this would eliminate MAD. Achieving a credible first-strike counterforce capability is practically impossible, barring a major breakthrough in antisubmarine warfare that would jeopardize the near-invulnerable submarine-based missile force. But stability under the Second Regime recommended here would be enhanced by formal agreements not to build offensive systems that would imperil the deterrent forces on either side.

[4]Emphasis on intercontinental delivery reflects not only the author's American orientation but also the assumption that his Second Regime would prevent

troversy that would rage in the United States over such systems as the Soviet Backfire bomber would make the controversy of the 1970s seem minuscule by comparison.

Finally, if non-nuclear armed cruise missiles of nominal 500-mile range entered the tactical inventories of the advanced nations, the typically 1,000 to 2,000 pound high-explosive payload of these tactical missiles could be replaced by a normal nuclear warhead with a yield anywhere from ten to a few hundred kilotons, weighing as little as 200 pounds, with a consequent extension of the missiles' range to 2,000 or 3,000 miles.[5] In a Second Regime, in which both sides already had high assurance of retaining the nuclear forces necessary for mutual destruction, the clandestine addition of a few hundred or even a few thousand such strategic cruise missiles would not imperil stability. But if one side were to abjure the *capability* of striking the other side's cities, as in a Third Regime, a few hundred advanced strategic cruise missiles in one side's possession would undoubtedly determine the outcome of any contest.

In addition to on-call delivery capabilities, there has always been the possibility that nuclear weapons could be smuggled into the target country. Doing this has become enormously easier since the 1940s, as the mass of a nuclear weapon capable of destroying a city has been reduced from thousands to tens of pounds, and as restrictions on international travel have been relaxed. But in 1977, it would make little sense for the Soviet Union to try to smuggle a nuclear weapon into New York City. The benefits would be small relative to the risks of detection, simply because Moscow has a plethora of weapons capable of striking New York. However, if the United States and Soviet Union agreed to dismantle their weapons capable of striking the other's cities, a few dozen clandestine weapons in American cities would confer decisive power on the Soviet Union. Paradoxically,

---

widespread proliferation of nuclear weapons to many nations that might hold them as an assured destruction force against nearby neighbors without any need for long-range delivery systems.

[5] The savings in warhead weight would make possible a greater fuel load, thereby providing the longer range.

American internal security measures would have to be far more severe in the event of an agreement renouncing a city-attack capability than they are at present.

Thus, so long as nuclear weapons are retained for *any* purpose, it must be anticipated that an adversary will retain, clandestinely if not overtly, a city-attack capability; and the *only way* to counter a city-attack capability is to have one's own (or to rely on that of an ally or guarantor). Symmetry is not required in other areas, however. For example, a capability on one side to knock out, or "kill," the other's ICBM silos certainly need *not* be countered by a silo-killing capability on the other. This would not lead to stability but would aggravate instability. A silo-killing or "counterforce" capability would be significant only if it could destroy such a large fraction of an adversary's total assured destruction force that this force could no longer perform its retaliatory mission. As will be discussed below, there are many counters to a silo-killing threat, ranging from a launch-on-warning policy to mobile basing, shelter basing, silo defense, reliance on submarine-launched ballistic missiles and aircraft, and the like. Together with an assured destruction force of ample size, the possibility of exercising these options would enhance the stability of the Second Regime.

Unlike a silo-killing capability, because of the dominance of offense over defense, a city-attack capability cannot be eliminated although it can be neutralized by a comparable retaliatory capability. For the 1980s and beyond, any regime encompassing the retention of nuclear weapons must ensure the maintenance of a city-threatening capability on the part of major contending nuclear weapons states or leaders of blocs. As it seems impossible to control strategic *delivery vehicles* with the certainty required to assure a disarmed state that another had no strategic capability, the Second Regime prescribed here entails the preservation of mutually acceptable strategic offensive forces. This Second Regime also provides for the protection by the nuclear powers of nations that do not themselves have nuclear forces. As will be shown below, such protection would be a strong counterincentive to nuclear proliferation.

RECOMMENDED AMERICAN STRATEGIC FORCE

The benefits of the Second Regime prescribed here can be obtained to a large extent by the initiative of one side. Therefore, American views as to the desirability of this Second Regime need not depend on Soviet responses. The prescription for the United States to eschew a silo-killing force does not depend on a similar decision on the part of the Soviet Union. As stressed above, we would like *least* to have an effective counterforce capability on *both* sides; but stability could be maintained if the Soviets alone had such a force and the Americans did not (or vice versa), for there are many feasible countermeasures that the United States could take. For the United States to respond by building a similar force would only cause serious concern on the other side regarding the probability of a preemptive strike against its strategic forces, a situation that would be as intolerable for Moscow as for Washington.

Responses to a Soviet Counterforce Capability   The easiest way for the United States to offset a Soviet counterforce threat is to maintain a sufficiently large force of submarine-launched ballistic missiles and airfield-based strategic bombers so that even an extraordinarily effective surprise attack on American ICBM silos would not constitute a disarming strike and hence would not be undertaken. Furnishing strategic aircraft with a rapid-start capability so that they can be airborne on short warning and fitting them with long-range air-launched cruise missiles that can be fired at strategic targets from a thousand or more miles away will ensure the survival and effectiveness of the bomber force by minimizing its dependence on an airborne tanker fleet in carrying out long-range missions. The advanced technology for strategic cruise missiles now coming into being will allow cargo-type aircraft to replace many of the more expensive bombers altogether, since there will no longer be a need for planes that can penetrate Soviet air defenses. Deploying the 4,000-mile-range Trident I missile in place of the shorter-range Poseidon missile on Poseidon submarines will similarly reduce the vulnerability of the sea-based arm of the American deterrent.

As an alternative, or in addition to greater reliance on the bomber and submarine arms of the "triad," the United States could restructure its land-based ICBM force. A new, smaller ICBM—with a 10,000-pound launch-weight, single 50-kiloton warhead, 1/3 mile accuracy, and hard silo to suit—could be developed as an alternative to the current force of Minutemen with multiple independently targetable reentry vehicles (MIRVs), with a view to deploying thousands of them and thus making a thoroughgoing Soviet silo-killing attack more difficult. The degraded accuracy and lesser total throw-weight would not even reduce the second strike (the deterrent) capability. The stability of the Second Regime described here does not depend on the absence of MIRVs, but ensuring against the achievement of a counterforce capability by one side would be easier if, over the years, the MIRVed forces on one or both sides were replaced by a large number of small ICBMs.

A less costly (and quicker) way for the United States to respond to a Soviet counterforce threat would be to modify the Minuteman to a "smart ICBM"—one that would have, in addition to the usual flexible command and control systems, the capability of being armed or disarmed in flight. Developing such a capability and deploying it if necessary would not only deter the Soviets from carrying out a silo-killing strike, but might also discourage them from ever developing or deploying the force capable of doing so, insofar as it would permit the United States to adopt the following declared limited launch-on-reliable-detection (LORD) options:

1. *Command–arm in flight:* On reliable detection of a Soviet attack on American ICBM silos, the United States would launch approximately 50 Minutemen, unarmed, against Soviet cities, the missiles to be armed by secure, redundant radio command after 15 minutes in flight if most of the unlaunched Minutemen were indeed destroyed in the interim.

2. *Command–disarm in flight:* Under the same circumstances, Minutemen would be launched armed, to be *disarmed* by secure, redundant command if the main Minuteman force were *not* destroyed in the interim.

Under both options, the radio signals could be relayed from satellites, from special communications rockets, from aircraft, and from land sites.

The purpose of planning and developing these more flexible capabilities is to demonstrate *in advance*, to the Soviet Union and to the world, the futility of the Soviets' deploying an expensive force of silo-killing ICBMs. Such capabilities should be publicized: if Washington emphasizes in official statements that it has developed such capabilities and is able and willing to deploy them, this may reduce the necessity of actually doing so by deterring the Soviets from deploying their new ICBMs. To the extent that the Soviets are stimulated by such American developments and deployments to create their own limited launch-on-reliable-detection options, strategic stability will be further enhanced without the overall capability for destruction being increased. The two LORD options could be maintained inoperative at presidential command under normal conditions, when strategic intelligence guarantees that Soviet forces cannot possibly destroy the American strategic offensive force to a degree that would vitiate the United States' capability to inflict assured destruction in retaliation. The command–arm-in-flight option would be readied if there was a legitimate concern for force survivability, with the command–disarm-in-flight option held in reserve for use only if the Soviets appeared to have the ability to destroy the redundant radio-arming link.

Giving such a capability to Minuteman would be analogous to having, as at present, the ability to quickly launch those bombers in the Strategic Air Command (SAC) on ground alert, and in certain circumstances maintaining bombers on air alert, until a crisis situation can be clarified. The size of the Minuteman force would be reduced temporarily by five percent with the launch of 50 missiles in a false alarm situation (one ultimately not warranting a nuclear attack on the Soviet Union and so resulting in the destruction in flight of the 50 missiles); these missiles could be replaced in refurbished silos in a matter of weeks.

Still another way for the United States to respond to a Soviet silo-killing capability is the development of modest ABM defenses specifically designed for the defense of the hardened, replicated ICBM silos and capable of being deployed at a lower cost and faster pace than a Soviet silo-killing force, but *not having* a technical capability to protect industry and population. While ABM defense of cities, in view of exaggerated claims of its effectiveness, is destabilizing—in that it might be seen to threaten the other side's ability to retaliate and thus might foster suspicions of a planned first strike—ABM systems with a silo-defense-only capability, by increasing the survivability of retaliatory forces, are stabilizing. Some are even compatible with the ABM ban of SALT I. Therefore, greater research and development efforts should be devoted to them, as well as to the Minuteman in-flight command arm/disarm system.[6]

Strategic Force Size in the Second Regime   The overall force levels resulting from SALT II, while unnecessarily high, would be acceptable in the Second Regime prescribed here. There is no compelling reason to face the problems of negotiating alternative American and Soviet strategic forces that might be more suitable to the regime. Strategic stability is insensitive to minor changes in such high force levels. This is because of the declining marginal utility of additional warheads arising from the finite number of important military, industrial, and civilian targets that a force must be able to destroy with confidence. Therefore, it is important first to move away from the First Regime, with its excessive dependence on nuclear weapons, while retaining these high force levels and not to worry about negotiating more desirable force levels until *after* the lessened dependence of a Second Regime has been achieved.

THE STRATEGIC RESERVE—A BEGINNING OF REDUCTIONS   At almost all times in the past, the United States has had what has been generally recognized as a more than adequate strategic force. Yet it has almost continuously been constructing additional strategic forces with an apparent sense of urgency. This is not necessarily logically inconsistent (although it may have been in

---

[6]Three candidates for silo defense which would have no capability of defending soft, high-value targets such as cities are warhead fuse jamming, a "bed of nails" defense, and a "pebble-fan projector," all of which could disable incoming missiles before they struck their hardened targets. See my article, "Effective Military Technology for the 1980s," *International Security*, vol. 1, no. 2, Fall 1976, pp. 50–77.

certain instances): Strategic forces are built to meet the situation that may prevail when they are fully deployed—some five to ten years hence—or in response to what may be technically feasible for the other side (as was the case in American development of MIRVs designed, in part, to counter likely Soviet advances in ABM technology). In some cases, additional forces are built in recognition of the future inadequacy of current forces (as was the case when SAC bombers were supplemented by a force of Minuteman and Polaris missiles). Fragmentation of responsibility may add to the motivation to augment the forces: the development organization has little to do after one generation of forces has been deployed, since the forces are operated by another organization (the Strategic Air Command or the Navy).

After forces are deployed, the assigned job of their operators is to maintain every possible element at maximum economic readiness to meet any possible contingency. If the strategic situation then worsens considerably, in particular if there is an increase in the threat to the survivability of an element of the strategic offensive force, there are no *reserve* forces to be physically brought into being to counter the new threats. Unfortunately, this situation leads to misleading contentions by politicians and informed citizens that the entire present force is insufficient, even though the increased threat may still be *less* than the future threat that the existing force was built to counter. Indeed, so large is the American ICBM force that only about 10 percent of the warheads in the recent past were trained on assured destruction targets; thus even the destruction before launch of 90 percent of the Minutemen would leave the assured destruction capability intact if an assured-destruction-only target were used as the second aim point for each missile. Still, even though this situation is surely clear to most American leaders, allied leaders or neutrals may see the increased threat as an indication of the growing inadequacy of the entire American strategic force; modification or construction of additional forces by Washington so as to reassure these third parties may only reinforce their mistaken view by appearing to be an admission of inadequacy.

The United States evidently regards the ability to put the SAC bomber force on various levels of alert as a significant political tool. For this reason and those indicated above, it would be useful to put a substantial fraction of the ICBM and submarine-launched ballistic missile (SLBM) forces into a *strategic reserve* from which the missiles could not be fired but from which they could be brought into readiness in a matter of weeks or months. The purpose would be not to preserve them from actual attack (in which they could be more or less vulnerable than the active strategic forces) but to reduce clearly excessive force levels in an easily reversible way. For the ICBMs, some 300 silos could be covered with earth or rock to a depth of perhaps 30 feet, making them useless on a scale of days but available in the unlikely event that continued Soviet force expansion and improvement began to place the effectiveness of the front-line American deterrent in doubt. For the SLBMs, 50 percent of the Polaris, Poseidon, and future Trident submarines could be kept in port or on patrol in the southern oceans, well out of missile range of the Soviet Union. While primarily an arms control measure, the submarine strategic reserve would also further enhance SLBM survivability. Unusual communication practices could be employed so that it would be clear to the Soviet Union that these submarines were far out of firing range. Another form of strategic reserve would be an airfield-based strategic force element consisting of a combination advanced tanker/cargo/cruise-missile-launching aircraft that in normal circumstances would be used only in its first two capacities.

Assuming that domestic opposition and uneasiness could be overcome, such a posture would make it clear to the world that the United States had confidence in its strategic strength—that it had such strength in reserve, indeed in superabundance. Furthermore, the United States would have ready an immediate response to any new Soviet deployments or to ambiguities in Soviet activities, a response that would provide a visible increase in American strategic offensive force long before any new procurement could become effective. By voluntarily reducing its ready force—without appreciable cost savings—the United States would provide evidence that smaller numbers do not connote inferiority.

United States national security would not depend on the Soviet

Union's following suit by placing some of its own forces in strategic reserve, although such actions by Moscow would certainly improve the climate between the two nations. The long-term durability and stability of a Second Regime would benefit from visible signs that the Soviet Union saw its strategic forces in the same light as the United States saw its own forces. As a first step, Washington could put its MIRVs into the reserves, if indeed MIRVs are necessary only against some future ABM systems, and move a fraction of its submarines to southern ocean patrol. Unilateral measures such as these would provide a costless test of the readiness of the Soviet Union to establish its own strategic reserve.

BEYOND STRATEGIC NUCLEAR WEAPONS?

It is certain that the capability for mutual destruction is assured if nuclear delivery vehicles are unopposed. But should the United States and the Soviet Union strive to develop and erect effective defenses against the other's strategic delivery vehicles, serious problems would emerge. Other difficulties would arise from the continuation of tactical nuclear weapons and forward-based strategic systems. How these capabilities and programs would contribute to the goals of a Second Regime—security, stability, rationality, and nonproliferation—is the question to which we now turn.

Strategic Defenses   As an extreme case, one side might develop and deploy in deepest secrecy a system highly effective in defending against the strategic weapons and delivery vehicles of the other side. Such a system would be of tremendous coercive value; if it were revealed and the other side was given no choice other than to "disarm or disappear," the strategic relationship would change substantially. While it is possible that neither superpower would seek to upset the strategic balance in this way, or at least that neither would be so confident in its ability to completely repel a retaliatory strike as to exploit a defensive advantage, either or both might still wish to develop and deploy defensive systems because of the danger of nuclear accident and third-party attack. Therefore, it is necessary to determine whether defensive programs can limit such secondary risks without being perceived as leading to strategic invulnerability.

The effectiveness of an ABM system under consideration must be judged *not* in terms of its capability against current ICBMs—which are not designed to counter ABMs since none exist—but in terms of its ability to defend against an ICBM force as would evolve to penetrate the ABM cover. Analogous considerations must be taken into account in assessing air-defense and antisubmarine warfare systems. An effective defense against an opponent bent on maintaining its assured destruction capability requires guarding against every possible avenue of countermeasure and attack. By contrast, maintaining an assured destruction capability requires nothing more than having one offensive system capable of penetrating the other side's defenses. A proposed defensive system must not only be technically sound against the existing threat and extensions of it, it must also be capable of effectively defending against quite different threats. For example, targets that the other side considered secondary in the absence of defense might become its preferred choice if the primary targets were protected by a defensive system; therefore, a less "rational" selection of targets could preserve the other side's assured destruction capacity. Moreover, the other side could simply deploy additional forces as a means of saturating the ABM coverage and guarding against other possible attempts to reduce its ability to retaliate, such as counterforce and civil defense.

A complex of defensive systems that is effective against *all* types of an opponent's strategic weapons, either in existence or possible, is not technically feasible, nor will it be in the foreseeable future. The recommended Second Regime has been conceived on the assumption of the continued dominance of strategic offense and the consequent desirability of continued controls over the development of strategic defenses, as it would be fruitless for the United States and the Soviet Union to deploy partially protective defenses against one another—the rationale behind the 1972 treaty limiting ABMs.

However, against nations with much smaller strategic capabilities, Washington and Moscow might find it desirable and even possible to construct an effective defense. Although the strategic forces of both superpowers are at least as effective, if not more so, in deterring third nations as in deterring each other, second nuclear powers may well be less able to maintain control over their nuclear weapons, to prevent theft or unauthorized launch, than the superpowers are. Since such nations, in general, would not even come close to having a strategic destruction capability against the United States and the Soviet Union, defenses sufficiently effective to reduce the damage by such nations' nuclear forces would be feasible.

However, two problems would arise for both superpowers: first, how to make such a defense clearly ineffective against a retaliatory attack by the principal opponent and not provocative in the sense that it would appear to constitute a base from which effective defense against the principal opponent could subsequently be achieved; and second, how to cover the entire territory (since retargeting of even a small offensive force could otherwise restore its limited destructive capability) and defend against a mildly responsive threat, that is, one modified to help penetrate the defense system—again without threatening the principal adversary. In the case of the United States ABM system, it was argued that a "thin ABM defense against the Chinese ICBM threat"—one not providing a base for a heavy defense—could have been deployed using "perimeter acquisition radar" and Spartan missiles to shoot down a small number of incoming Chinese ICBMs as they approached United States air space. Such a thin ABM system would not require the expensive missile-site radar and short-range Sprint missiles essential to an effective anti-Soviet system and would ostensibly be ineffective against a massive Soviet attack because the radars, the "eyes of the system," could be easily exhausted or destroyed by large numbers of light, inaccurate ICBMs. However, the effectiveness of such a thin ABM system against China or other nuclear powers is dubious, as these states could saturate the perimeter acquisition radar (by the use of lightweight decoys or balloons) almost as easily as the Soviets could.

In any case, the SALT I Treaty includes an agreement by the United States and the Soviet Union not to defend their territories against the ICBM forces of other nations. In view of the overriding importance of each maintaining an assured destruction capability against its major opponent, population defense against ICBM attack by lesser powers and revision of the 1972 treaty should be sought only if the treaty is clearly ineffective against the major opponent, a condition thus far not adequately satisfied by proposed systems, including the thin anti-China ABM. However, if future analysis and experiments provide a means for defending hardened missile silos (in their assigned roles) against ICBM attack, a means not effective in defending industry and population, deployment of such defensive systems—and revisions in the ABM treaty, if necessary—would be desirable. This would enhance stability by ensuring the survivability of retaliatory forces without compromising their offensive potential.[7]

Foward-Based Systems and Tactical Nuclear Weapons
Since the 1950s and up to the present day, the United States has had strategic nuclear weapons forward-deployed on aircraft carriers, on intermediate-range ballistic missiles (IRBMs) around the perimeter of the Soviet Union, and even on nominally tactical land-based fighters in Europe and East Asia. These forward-based systems were originally intended to supplement the far more expensive United States-based strategic bomber force; their cost (for an aircraft itself or other delivery vehicle) is lower because their required range is less. Forward-deployed strategic weapons also had the virtue of shorter response time; in contrast with the 12 hours or so of travel time for bombers traveling from the United States, a forward-based aircraft takes only one hour or less to reach targets in the Soviet Union. However, with the advent of highly secure intercontinental and submarine-launched ballistic missiles, and especially with the formal prohibition of ballistic missile defense, these reasons for forward-basing of nuclear weapons no longer exist. And when the cost of bases is included, forward-based systems become expensive. In the 1970s, ICBMs have become the dominant choice over forward-based fighters, being cheaper per weapon delivered, more surviv-

[7]See pp. 97–98.

able, more reliable and having a response time of only 30 minutes.

A separate reason for deploying nuclear weapons in Europe is that of alliance strategy. Forward-based nuclear weapons deployed on allied aircraft, piloted and commanded by allied forces (subject always to release by the Commander-in-Chief of the United States), not only contribute to allied military capabilities in the field, it is argued, but also give NATO forces a ministrategic force capable of reaching Warsaw Pact capitals on two-way missions and Soviet cities on one-way missions. Furthermore, and perhaps most importantly, the use of such weapons in a truly tactical, countermilitary role can serve as a bridge to, and a guaranteed lever of, escalation to the strategic level, and hence as a deterrent to conventional Soviet aggression. America's European allies want to be very sure that if this deterrent fails the United States will come to their aid against invading Soviet or Warsaw Pact forces. The Europeans see the vulnerability of American forward-based tactical nuclear weapons as an asset, for any Warsaw Pact attack on these forces in the event of theater hostilities would force the United States itself to respond. Therefore, since an attack on Western Europe will turn into a direct Soviet-American nuclear confrontation, the Soviet bloc is deterred from making such an attack.

While this argument reveals some of the benefits of tactical nuclear weapons, it ignores their many liabilities, including the possibility of accidental or unauthorized use by local commanders, of capture by the enemy or by the host country, and of theft or terrorism. A further liability of United States tactical nuclear weapons in Europe is their significant cost in labor and materiel (on the order of 50,000 people simply to guard and maintain 7,000 weapons). Finally, having tactical nuclear weapons in Europe means the removal from conventional forces of the aircraft and other systems carrying them, for these systems' ostensibly "dual-capable" role does in fact reflect a nuclear priority. Has there been (and is there now) some way to reduce these liabilities while retaining the benefits of deterrence which these weapons confer on American allies?

In the early 1960s, the United States fitted permissive action links (PAL) to all nuclear weapons on foreign soil, thereby taking a first step in extending the degree of physical control maintained by the President and reducing the hazards of misuse or theft of a nuclear weapon by elements of the host country's armed forces, either in peace or in war.[8] But additional ways must still be found to maintain the nuclear umbrella while further reducing the costs and hazards of theater nuclear weapons.

Since the travel times to strategic targets for ICBMs fired from the United States are now less than those for tactical aircraft launched from forward bases in Europe, and since ICBMs are far less vulnerable than tactical aircraft, the desired European ministrategic force could be better implemented by sharing targeting and release authority over some of the United States–based ICBMs or SLBMs. Doing this would guarantee that the allies' strategic force had the same invulnerability and response time as that of the United States itself. Moreover, the NATO countries would appreciate the reduced cost of supporting United States forces and the quicker response and greater assurance of penetration for their ministrategic force. As far as the Soviets are concerned, the elimination of the American forward-based nuclear capability, with the exception of the SLBMs, would be seen as an improvement of their security position. But could this scheme replace the inhibitory effect of having American nuclear weapons present and vulnerable in Europe, that is, their "trip-wire" role in deterring Soviet conventional aggression?

Before the Soviet Union possessed large numbers of nuclear weapons, American tactical nuclear weapons certainly had a deterrent effect on conventional Soviet attack in Europe; given the rather hazy distinction between tactical and strategic nuclear weapons, an American "tactical" nuclear response to a Warsaw Pact offensive would have meant massive destruction for the Soviet Union or its allies. But with the advent of Soviet IRBMs targeted on Western Europe, there was no reason to believe that a

---

[8]*Permissive action links* are essentially mechanical or electronic combination locks on the nuclear weapons or warheads themselves. A separate combination for each weapon must be set in order to permit the warhead to explode upon delivery, although "master-key" combinations are feasible in principle. Some PAL devices can also provide penalties in the case of tampering, unauthorized transport, and the like.

Western nuclear response against Warsaw Pact territory would not be answered by a Soviet IRBM counterattack on NATO territory. Nor was there reason to be confident that the use of even very small, clean, and well-controlled tactical nuclear weapons by NATO only against Warsaw Pact troops in combat would not be answered by larger, dirtier, and more randomly targeted Warsaw Pact nuclear weapons. Therefore, a strictly tactical role for United States nuclear weapons in Europe might fail to credibly deter Warsaw Pact aggression. The truly effective deterrent is the threat to the Soviet and East European homelands, which can be achieved through a shared targeting and release scheme for United States ICBMs. Thus, we must examine the only other possible justification for keeping the tactical nuclear weapons in place, their military utility.

Deployed American tactical nuclear weapons include explosives delivered from aircraft, short-range missiles or hand-fired rockets, artillery shells, and preemplaced mines. It is simpler to characterize tactical nuclear weapons according to their missions: close support, interdiction, and counter-air. In evaluating their contribution to American and NATO capabilities, there is, of course, no experience in actual combat, and so analysis and war games must substitute. Although NATO commanders may not be sure of obtaining a desirable outcome without the use of tactical nuclear weapons, the introduction of such weapons on both sides, as simulated in war games, leads to widespread destruction but *not* to military victory.

In regard to the strictly military effectiveness of NATO tactical nuclear weapons, the vulnerability of the present system of basing and delivery, the poor accuracy of the longer-range weapons, and the inability to concentrate the fire of the shorter-range weapons within the small target radius associated with "tactical" missions are among the major disadvantages. The 50,000 American military personnel required to protect and care for the weapons is a serious burden. The catastrophic risks of erroneous field intelligence, incorrect targeting, and errors in aircraft navigation are nightmares for any national leader evaluating the feasibility and impact of using highly destructive theater nuclear weapons. Improved tactical nuclear weapons of the future could use the same technologies now demonstrated in conventional precision-guided munitions to increase their accuracy, thereby allowing weapon yield to be reduced to cover only the desired radius of effectiveness. But one would still be left with the problem that the area of destruction of a nuclear weapon is circular, while many targets (e.g., a tank column) are linear. If tactical nuclear weapons were costless and without alternatives, improved versions would have a place among our future armaments; however, neither of these two conditions obtains.

Developments of the last decade in precision-guided munitions and microelectronics, together with the deployment over the next few years of the Navstar navigation and guidance system[9] (which will provide American and NATO cruise missiles, cannon shells, and bombs with accuracy as great as 20 feet almost all the time, anywhere in the world), have greatly reduced the comparative utility of nuclear weapons in performing tactical missions—that is, in attacking troop concentrations, armored columns, and the like. The tactical nuclear weapon has always been a major threat to an army on its *own* territory, but since civilians far outnumber potential combatants in any region, the use of tactical nuclear weapons on American or allied territory has not been looked upon with favor. Recent technological advances have somewhat improved the capability of tactical nuclear weapons, but they have also enhanced the capability of non-nuclear weapons to the point that tactical nuclear weapons no longer have an overall advantage. Improved accuracy and flexibility of delivery vehicles, advanced homing and fusing technology, new dispenser warheads and minelets, and more capable command and control systems all improve the capability of conventional weapons far more than they improve that of nuclear weapons. Because of the greater variety of conventional weapons and the lesser inhibitions to their use compared with nuclear weapons, a well-conceived non-nuclear force is *more capable* than a tactical nuclear force. Higher-yield weapons are not tactical at all; their use will be countered or deterred by determined use of strategic

[9]*Navstar* is a set of approximately 20 satellites that will provide radio signals to delivery vehicles in flight, permitting them to determine their position with great accuracy every one-tenth second.

nuclear weapons. Therefore, to the extent that strictly *local* capabilities are desired, the non-nuclear precision-guided munitions, mines, and the like which have entered the United States inventory in recent years, and which are susceptible to further improvement, are far preferable to the maintenance of nuclear weapons by the thousands in Europe. In fact, not replacing the tactical nuclear weapons with conventional systems of this sort, while it might not be tragic in the European context, could have the unintended side effect of encouraging nuclear proliferation, for it would convey to would-be proliferants the erroneous notion that nuclear weapons are of great utility in theater warfare.

Conventional Forces

In the building, deployment, and use of conventional forces, a principal objective is that this activity not lead to nuclear war. But this objective relates only to the actual *use* of conventional forces; some consider it also desirable to maintain the appearance that the use of conventional weapons will indeed lead to nuclear war, in order to *deter* conventional warfare as well. Yet the elimination of tactical nuclear weapons, and the resultant reduction of the threat of escalation to nuclear war in local contexts, means that an element of deterrence of conventional attack will be lost. As with nuclear weapons, while a nation would prefer to prevail ideologically and politically through the deterrent effect of its existing conventional forces, both experience and analysis show that conventional forces are far more likely than nuclear forces to be used. This condition results, in part, from there being a much more gradual ladder of escalation in the case of conventional weapons (all the way from police weapons to aerial bombardment) than in the case of nuclear devices, but it also derives from the lesser utility of conventional weapons in destroying population and industry relative to their usefulness against military targets. If tactical nuclear weapons are to be eliminated—a goal of the Second Regime prescribed here—and conventional conflict still prevented, there must be compensation for the lost deterrent effect of the tactical nuclear weapons.

Offensive and defensive technology are much more evenly

matched in the case of non-nuclear forces. A single aircraft that penetrates air defenses can do many billions of dollars of damage with nuclear weapons, whereas many thousands of conventionally armed aircraft would be needed to produce the same level of destruction. But defense against aircraft delivering *nuclear* bombs is usually performed by *conventional* weapons. In fact, unlike the case of defensive nuclear weapons versus offensive nuclear weapons, defensive conventional weapons may even enjoy superiority over offensive systems under some circumstances, and this might become truer with the technology of the 1980s. Consequently, strengthened defensive capabilities for NATO's non-nuclear forces would provide a sufficient deterrent to conventional attack by Warsaw Pact forces and an adequate replacement for tactical nuclear weapons.

The United States should therefore carefully review its activities oriented toward the development of technologies with offensive superiority. Since the United States and its allies do not anticipate making use of such offensive capabilities and since they would be vulnerable if their opponents acquired such capabilities, it would be wiser to concentrate on developing systems with defensive superiority. The task is, of course, complicated by the fact that offensive-superior technology is useful even in defensive situations, as in recovering land that has been lost in a fallback after an unexpected conventional attack. Furthermore, the United States might need offensive capabilities in support of national or alliance goals outside Europe. Nonetheless, effective and invulnerable defensive forces should be the priority. In general, emphasis should be on low-cost, high-attrition systems, for these would make force effectiveness less sensitive to the opponent's defenses and countermeasures.

With respect to land forces, a major goal should be improving capabilities for emplacing mines by aircraft and cannon, as well as by armored minelayers. Guided antitank missiles that can be fired from a position displaced from that of the person guiding the missile (in order that the person's vulnerability be reduced and willingness to fire be increased) can also contribute to future ground capabilities. The ability to attack fixed and moving ground targets can be further improved by deploying surface-launched tactical cruise missiles with a range of 500 miles, so as to both reduce vulnerability of cruise missile stores and allow massing of fire across the front. Such cruise missiles with 1,000-pound warheads could be based in small numbers in each of hundreds of dispersed underground storage sites hundreds of miles within NATO countries. These cruise missiles could be designed for launching without any additional mechanisms in response to secure signals from a theater command-and-control system. They would be capable of flying to their targets with 100-foot accuracy, thanks to midcourse guidance adjustments by Navstar signals, and could be transferred into a safe, low-altitude holding pattern a few minutes from the target area for last-minute target reassignment in case targets moved or targeting priorities changed.

In the field of command, control, and communications, stress should be placed on improving helicopter-lifted theater radar systems with data links to the ground which would be capable of monitoring movement of ground columns and other moving targets and providing redundant coverage of air operations. Regarding tactical air capabilities, since most American or NATO tactical aircraft are not necessary when air-to-ground attack is carried out by cruise missiles, it is preferable to perform counterair operations over NATO territory using surface-to-air missiles (SAMs) with a range of about 100 miles, remotely directed in order to reduce launch site vulnerability and provide concentration of fire.

In sum, new technologies and the concomitant force reorganization necessary to apply them efficiently can and should provide conventional forces with much greater capabilities than they now enjoy, and with less vulnerability as well. Such refinements, rather than an erosion of United States will, should be the basis for removal of theater nuclear weapons. The deemphasis of tactical nuclear weapons, tactical aircraft, and long-range artillery in general should be no more regarded as a diminution of effectiveness or of American support than would the replacement of a 20-year-old computer system by a smaller, cheaper one capable of 10 times the performance.

Declaratory Posture for the Second Nuclear Regime

An important part of any nuclear defense posture is that which is announced about it—within a nation, to other nuclear powers, and to non-nuclear powers. Like the physical force posture, the declaratory posture influences the actions of adversaries, allies, and neutrals in building their own nuclear and non-nuclear forces as well as their willingness to use those forces. Both postures should be chosen with this in mind.

UNILATERAL POSITION

As stressed above, the physical posture for nuclear forces in this Second Regime can be largely achieved through the unilateral actions of the United States. This is equally true for the declaratory posture regarding the use of those forces.

Assured Destruction Capability   With respect to the central confrontation between the United States and the Soviet Union, Washington should be consistent in publicly declaring its readiness to respond to the use of strategic nuclear weapons by the other side with its own nuclear arsenal, either to inflict assured, massive destruction or to use its own strategic weapons more flexibly (that is, in smaller numbers). In other words, it should be made clear that any nuclear provocation will be answered by a nuclear response, that there is an inevitable, near-physical linkage between destruction of the United States and destruction of

113

the Soviet Union. Consistent with this posture, no silo-killing capability should be sought or tested, even if the Soviets deployed some elements of such a force, since the American nuclear force would be intended solely for second-strike retaliatory missions. While under the Second Regime prescribed here, a nuclear response to a non-nuclear Soviet provocation would not be explicitly ruled out, it would be reduced to an extreme option.

The Role of Uncertainty   Relying on an assured destruction capability in the 1980s raises once again the question of the proper threshold for response. While it might seem proper for Washington to destroy the Soviet Union if Moscow destroyed the 20 largest American cities, would Washington do so if Moscow leveled only the twenty-third largest? If there were a threshold below which it could be assumed that the United States would not act, would the Soviet Union not be free to threaten or exact damage below that threshold? And if once, why not again and again? There is in reality no such definite threshold; American response depends on mood, chance, and circumstances. But under the Second Regime, with tactical and forward-based nuclear weapons eliminated, the United States would have only its central, massively destructive strategic systems with which to respond. Therefore, the Soviets might become more inclined to believe that Washington—deprived of its ladder of "flexible options"—had established a higher, more precise threshold below which Soviet provocations would be tolerated. If Soviet uncertainty regarding likely American responses were reduced in this way, such provocations could become more frequent, and the increased chance that Moscow might overplay its hand—that it might underestimate Washington's willingness to use its strategic nuclear forces—could increase the likelihood of a nuclear exchange. Therefore, a means to preserve the role of uncertainty in deterring low-level nuclear provocations is an essential element of this Second Regime.

An intellectually respectable and technically feasible solution to the problem would be for Washington to announce that it had not a threshold, but a predetermined range of responses with varying probabilities, ranging from near zero for small provocations, to 50 percent at the point where most individuals would have placed an absolute threshold, and to near 100 percent in the case of total destruction of the United States. By declaring that such a range of responses exists, any American force could, in principle, serve credibly to deter a wide range of Soviet actions; American inaction after a modest provocation would convey no signal to Moscow that it would be safe to provoke again at the same, a higher, or even a lower level.

To enhance further the credibility of the American deterrent, Washington could also emphasize that it had fractional response options—that it could launch a small fraction of its forces (say, one to ten Minutemen) in response to low-level nuclear provocations—and that these options had a higher probability of being exercised than did massive response options in the event of small-scale Soviet nuclear attack. There would be greater willingness to establish and adhere to a predetermined response procedure if the maximum damage to be visited upon the enemy could be kept proportional to the provocation in this way. A declared readiness to launch less than the total strategic force, something we have been able to do in any case for as long as we have had strategic forces, would in essence provide the United States with a new variety of "flexible options" permitting a more certain (higher-probability) and proportionate response to any given provocation and consequently a more credible deterrent.[10]

Problems would arise if the Soviet provocation were non-nuclear. The Second Regime prescribed here does incorporate the principle of no-use of nuclear weapons against non-nuclear-weapons states.[11] While this principle would not in itself preclude

[10]In addition, a proportionate response capability would be more effective than a counterforce (silo-killing) capability in keeping nuclear wars limited. The former would rely on deterrence to prevent escalation even after an initial nuclear exchange, whereas the latter, while ostensibly aimed at damage limitation, would rest on a provocative threat to the invulnerability of retaliatory forces upon which stable deterrence rests. Announcing damage limitation as a goal would also imply a reluctance to use one's retaliatory forces against the other side's cities, thereby eroding the credibility of deterrence.

[11]This doctrine will be discussed below, along with the question of the desirability of a general no-first-use policy. See pp. 128–130.

the use of a nuclear weapon against the territory of the Soviet Union in response to a Soviet non-nuclear attack on Western Europe, the basic premise of a Second Regime, that the principal role of nuclear weapons is to deter the use of nuclear weapons by others, means that launching even a fraction of American nuclear forces would be an inappropriate response to Soviet conventional aggression.[12] Therefore, under this Second Regime strong non-nuclear forces to resist non-nuclear attack are prescribed. Still, to deter further the possibility of Soviet conventional attack, a strategic nuclear response to conventional attack would remain a declared option, albeit one with an extremely low assigned probability.

This approach to determining whether and how to respond to Soviet non-nuclear provocations is not vital to a Second Nuclear Regime. However, if it could be put into practice, it would help preserve the deterrent value of nuclear weapons below the level of massive strategic attack without requiring the retention of tactical nuclear weapons, the advancement of counterforce weaponry, or the abandonment of the principle of mutual assured destruction.

High-Quality Deterrence?   In recent years many voices have argued that deterrence by means of the capability for assured destruction of Soviet population and industry is somehow inadequate and that something called "high-quality deterrence" is needed. These critics are not satisfied that the United States has the capability not only to destroy the Soviet Union entirely but also to exact a destructive toll on the U.S.S.R. that would more than offset the gains from any Soviet initiative, as well as having comparable or greater net military capabilities. They stress that

[12]Some observers might argue that with the removal of American nuclear weapons from the European theater, the use of United States–based nuclear weapons in response to Soviet conventional aggression there would be an incredible threat as well as an inappropriate one, since it would be unlikely that an American President would put his own population at risk in the absence of a direct Soviet nuclear provocation. But the American population is *always* at risk of Soviet nuclear attack; what determines whether or not the Soviet Union will attack with nuclear weapons is not what the United States *has* done but what the Soviets perceive it *will do* in response.

for allies and neutrals—especially those who have no understanding of the relative importance of such force parameters as throw-weight, accuracy, number of MIRVs, and the like—the appearance of the American nuclear force is as important as its actual capabilities. As in the case of America's naval and tactical air forces, Washington has built a force of highly capable, sophisticated strategic delivery vehicles on the basis of the advice and decisions of leaders in the defense establishment, only to find many of those same individuals arguing that raw numbers in fact make the difference in perceptions, that perceptions are as important as real capabilities, and that we should therefore build these very expensive systems in numbers comparable to the numbers of less capable vehicles deployed by the Soviet Union.

Such arguments about the current or creeping inferiority of the United States vis-à-vis the Soviet Union are most frequently heard in connection with Pentagon efforts to obtain congressional approval and funding of American military forces, but the United States' declaratory posture before the world cannot be kept independent of such Congress-oriented statements. Examples abound in which American representatives have emphasized supposed inadequacies of the United States' strategic forces, an emphasis that may have the primary objective of persuading the administration, Congress, and public to increase or upgrade nuclear forces but that casts unnecessary and undesirable doubts on the ability of existing forces to deter strategic attack. For instance, behind the ABM debate of 1969, in which Pentagon officials argued that the Soviet Union's deployment of a MIRVed version of its heavy SS-9 ICBM would imperil the United States' assured destruction capability, lay the completely arbitrary and wrong-headed assumption that the small fraction (perhaps 10 percent) of American strategic warheads then targeted on Soviet population and industrial centers would not be increased if the threat to the survivability of the Minuteman force indeed developed. Instead of considering the changing of numbers on a sheet of paper to restore an adequate number of warheads to the assured destruction role in case the MIRVed SS-9 materialized, the Defense Department's response was to demand a large ABM system that in fact would have been inadequate against the threat had the Soviet Union actually moved in the claimed direction. (Indeed, the Soviets have never tested MIRVs on an SS-9 missile; they have deployed only a few MIRVed SS-18 heavy missiles.)

Actually, the denigration of "deterrence" and the call for high-quality deterrence is very much an attack on a straw man. It is neither logical nor useful to suggest that existing Minuteman and Poseidon forces do not effectively deter the Soviet Union because "these forces are capable of nothing more selective than the death of 100 million Russians." President Nixon's plea that he and later Presidents should not be left with the sole option of massive retaliation against Soviet people and industry ignored the long-existing flexibility in the capabilities of American forces. And Secretary of Defense Schlesinger's argument that ICBMs capable of knocking out hardened silos were essential to the United States' deterrent capability was an irrelevant and unresponsive answer to that ill-informed or misleading plea. While a silo-killing retaliatory strike might reduce Soviet ICBM capabilities that could otherwise be used to destroy American population and industry ("to save American lives rather than kill Soviet citizens"), having such a counterforce capability would pose a threat of preemptive strike to Soviet retaliatory forces and, therefore, undermine deterrence. Just as important, an emphasis on counterforce capabilities reduces the credibility of the American deterrent by showing a reluctance to do what is necessary to dissuade the Soviets from attacking. Whether an all-out Soviet nuclear attack on American cities comes out of the blue or is the result of Soviet escalation from lower-level American nuclear strikes, a nuclear response by the United States must be regarded as inevitable if deterrence is to work. It is harmful to suggest that a retaliatory response by the United States at that point would result only in dead Russians and not in more live Americans; such suggestions serve only to reduce unnecessarily the deterrent effect of America's nuclear weapons, as does the view that no American President could ever make the decision to use our strategic force in such a way.

By contrast, flexible targeting options are much more effective and less provocative than a silo-killing capability as a deterrent to limited nuclear attacks, and forces capable of carrying out such options have been in existence for a long time. In the absence of ABM systems (as codified by the 1972 SALT Treaty), a single Minuteman warhead (or each of every three Minuteman MIRVs, or ten Poseidon MIRVs) has guaranteed access to its targets, whether they be cities or military supply compounds, barracks, defense industries in isolated communities, and the like. To insist on the difficult—that the first targets struck be defense plants or facilities in urban areas but that damage to civilians still be kept to a minimum—would suggest to Moscow that Washington is more inhibited in the use of its strategic capabilities than is really the case. If the United States' goal is credible deterrence of Soviet attack, then it makes no economic or strategic sense to announce that American targeting plans dictate using the first missiles against the most difficult targets. Within the context of flexible response, it is just as effective for the United States to attack those defense elements that can be more easily destroyed or, if low collateral damage is an American aim, those located in nonurban areas. But a goal of low collateral damage should not limit American retaliatory options to the extent that the credibility of deterrence is eroded.

As long as strategic nuclear weapons exist in the world in the hands of nations with aggressive intent or an evangelical ideology, the survival of an independent United States will depend on those nations' knowledge that a nuclear response by the United States, if not inevitable, is at least not precluded. It would be desirable if the doctrine and force structure recommended here for the United States were also adopted by the Soviet Union, but it would not be essential. The adoption of a Second Regime posture by the United States alone would modify the expectations and therefore the probable crisis behavior of the Soviet Union even in the absence of formal Soviet acceptance of the same force structure and declaratory posture.

THE ROLE OF INTERNATIONAL AGREEMENTS

Although many of the benefits of a Second Regime to both sides can be obtained by either country's unilateral actions, the two nations are party to important bilateral and multilateral agree-

119

ments whose broadening would further contribute to the nations' future security and arms control interests. While unilateral initiatives would be sufficient for creating a stable physical and doctrinal posture for the recommended Second Regime, arms control agreements and the process of their negotiation are still important in that they can give the regime legitimacy. By providing symmetry of constraints, arms control agreements can reduce uncertainty about the other side's strategy. Formally codified restrictions may also be more effective than informal unilateral restraints in constraining political and bureaucratic pressures for more or more advanced weapons. In addition, in negotiating arms control agreements that increase the stability of the international environment, the nuclear powers set an example that can persuade other nations that their own courses of actions should be weighed (and would be weighed by others) in terms of their effect on the international system and not just on their neighbors or trading partners. There can be hazards as well as benefits to arms control agreements: some states (or bureaucratic forces within states) might seek to legitimate by agreement dangerous, costly, or irrational strategic postures; numerically symmetric constraints on forces may produce greater asymmetries in force effectiveness or vulnerability than would asymmetric limits; the process of negotiation may be exploited for domestic political gain or, alternatively, be impeded by domestic politics to a greater extent than efforts to achieve unilateral action, thereby producing either unstable agreements or no agreements at all. But if these hazards can be avoided, bilateral arms control agreements will contribute to the stability of the Second Regime here prescribed.

Current and previous Soviet-American arms control agreements include the SALT I accords of 1972—the treaty banning antiballistic missile defenses and the Interim Agreement on Strategic Offensive Arms—and their still uncompleted successor, the SALT II agreement, which is to be based on the preliminary Vladivostok agreement of 1974, setting a limit of 2,400 on the strategic weapon launchers of each side, with a sublimit of 1,320 MIRVed launchers. In 1976, the two countries signed the Threshold Test Ban Treaty, fixing a limit of 150 kilotons on the yield of underground nuclear weapons tests in designated test areas as well as on the yield of peaceful nuclear explosions (PNEs), requiring the exchange of very detailed information to permit the calibration of teleseismic equipment to verify compliance with the yield limit, and providing for on-site inspection of PNE blasts. The Threshold Test Ban is actually a bilateral extension of the multilateral Limited Test Ban Treaty of 1963, banning atmospheric tests and permitting only those underground nuclear explosions that do not release into the atmosphere radioactivity detectable beyond national frontiers.

The most important multilateral treaty other than the Limited Test Ban is the Non-Proliferation Treaty (NPT) concluded in 1968 and in force since 1971. The NPT binds signatory nuclear powers not to transfer nuclear weapons and weapons technology to other powers and binds non-nuclear signatories not to acquire nuclear weapons. The NPT also commits nuclear states to help non-nuclear adherents with the peaceful application of nuclear energy, while establishing international safeguards to detect the clandestine transfer of peaceful nuclear materials to weapons programs.[13]

The breadth and detail of these bilateral and multilateral agreements set a precedent for negotiating more substantial arms reductions. The following types of agreements would be most useful in this Second Regime.

A Ban on Silo-Killing Forces   A SALT II agreement between the United States and the Soviet Union may soon set a numerical ceiling on strategic nuclear weapons, providing a framework for subsequent reductions; it ought also to control nuclear-armed cruise missiles by restricting their deployment to aircraft, which

---

[13]Other, less significant nuclear arms control agreements include: the Antarctic Treaty of 1959, the Soviet-American "Hot Line" Agreement of 1963, the Outer Space Treaty of 1967, and the Seabed Arms Control Treaty of 1971. For a general analysis of the many different arms control accords, see *Arms Control and Disarmament Agreements*, U.S. Arms Control and Disarmament Agency, Washington, 1975.

would be counted among the 1,320 permissible MIRVed launchers.[14] Because of its high accuracy and ability to penetrate air defenses but its low speed, the long-range cruise missile is generally considered a second-strike system that would be part of the strategic retaliatory force. Although cruise missiles in themselves would not be effective silo killers if silos were well defended with short-range SAMs or other point-defense systems, it would make a mockery of the Vladivostok strategic force limits if there were no limits on the numbers of this new kind of strategic nuclear weapon. Therefore, limiting cruise missile deployments to aircraft—as a means of ensuring the offensive capability of the strategic bomber force—would be a positive first step toward a Second Regime.

It would also be desirable to seek in the SALT negotiations a political agreement expanding on the ABM treaty, by which the United States and the Soviet Union would agree neither to build nor to lay the base for any form of ballistic missile defense of their national territory. A similar treaty codifying a commitment not to build forces that threaten the survival of the other side's strategic offensive forces would provide a basis for considerable reductions in numbers of weapons on both sides and a slowing or reversal of their qualitative improvement. Appropriately structured, such a treaty could make management of the Soviet-American strategic balance more independent of vagaries in day-to-day relations between the two rivals. The following three agreements could be elements of this treaty banning counterforce systems.

---

[14]Deploying nuclear-armed sea-launched cruise missiles (SLCMs) on submarines and surface ships would provide nothing more than a marginal improvement in the strategic capabilities of the sea-based arm of the deterrent triad. Nuclear air-launched cruise missiles (ALCMs), however, would eliminate the need for costly penetrating bombers such as the B-1, since simpler standoff aircraft, including the older B-52, could launch the low-flying, hard-to-shoot down missiles against strategic targets without entering Soviet air space. Since ALCMs could be deployed in groups of 20 on B-52s and in larger numbers on converted transport planes, it is logical to include under the MIRV ceiling all cruise-missile-bearing aircraft.

,LIMITATIONS ON MISSILE TEST RATES Long-standing concerns regarding vulnerability of Minuteman to Soviet ICBM attack, the existence of the bomber and submarine elements of the strategic triad notwithstanding, have increased recently with the MIRVing of some Soviet ICBMs. A MIRVed force with sufficient accuracy and reliability could be used by either side to destroy the opponent's ICBM silos (although the missiles themselves need not wait in their silos to be destroyed), thereby raising fears of preemptive attack and forcing the adoption of potentially dangerous launch-on-warning strategies to protect vulnerable retaliatory forces.[15]

Without explicitly eliminating MIRVs, one could reduce the fear of a countersilo capability by reducing the rate of missile testing. An agreement to limit the United States and the Soviet Union to, say, ten missile tests per year would slow the development of more accurate and more reliable systems. Less able to test its new systems, each nation would have less confidence in the reliability of its individual missiles, especially since very high reliability is required for silo attack, without reducing the perceived reliability of the force for conducting a more general attack on conventional military and assured destruction targets. Such a test limitation would also retard weapons development in that it would pit demands for test firings of new weapons against the desire to use the few permitted tests to increase confidence in already deployed systems. A total prohibition of MIRV testing could also be part of an agreement limiting missile tests: a nation could retain its existing MIRVed force, but would not be permitted to test its reliability or that of improved versions and would be discouraged from making such improvements. A ban on MIRV testing could reinforce the effectiveness of a possible eventual agreement to de-MIRV existing missile forces: a MIRVed force untested for many years would hardly be as attractive as a thoroughly tested single-warhead force.

---

[15]Launch-on-warning options that would be less dangerous have been proposed on pp. 96–97. Nothing should be done to preclude the adoption of launch-on-warning strategies (when believed necessary) if these can be made as safe as possible—e.g., "launch-on-reliable detection" (LORD).

General test limitations such as these, by allaying fears of ICBM vulnerability, would lay the basis for reductions in the size of both sides' strategic forces or at least for the transfer of a portion of those forces to a strategic reserve.[16] More specific test restrictions would serve further to prevent the achievement of a silo-killing capability on either side.

A BAN ON TESTING OF LOW-DRAG OR MANEUVERING REENTRY VEHICLES Land-based ICBMs in fixed silos are vulnerable to a comparable number of ICBMs on the other side only if the latter are MIRVed (so that one ICBM can potentially destroy several ICBM silos). But MIRVs cannot do the job unless they are accurate, and sufficient accuracy in the face of variable winds and atmospheric density can be achieved only with low-drag reentry vehicles[17] or ones that can maneuver to compensate for atmospheric conditions. Therefore, prohibiting all tests of such vehicles would be useful in preventing the achievement of a silo-killing capability.

If all ICBM testing were restricted to designated reentry areas by Soviet-American agreement, it would be relatively easy to verify that no low-drag reentry vehicles were ever tested and that there was no maneuvering on the part of tested high-drag vehicles. Additional agreements could be reached, verifiable by "national technical means," to guarantee that no low-drag or maneuvering high-drag reentry vehicles were tested in other locations or without being launched out of the atmosphere, for example, by airdrop.

MIRVed forces with high-drag reentry vehicles would still retain great military utility. Their ability to penetrate possible future (clandestine) ABM systems could be assured by the use of saturation tactics and high-drag decoys. The temptation to deploy ABMs which would be created by the elimination of low-drag and maneuverable reentry vehicles could be reduced by creating provisions in the test ban treaty for storing the present low-drag

[16]See pp. 98–101.
[17]A *low-drag reentry vehicle* is one that is aerodynamically designed to penetrate the atmosphere without losing much speed and thus is not greatly influenced by winds or unexpected levels and variations of atmospheric density.

reentry vehicles rather than destroying them; these could be tested and redeployed within a year or two if the ABM treaty were abrogated.

An ancillary part of an agreement prohibiting low-drag and maneuverable reentry vehicle testing could be an extension of the SALT I ban on the upgrading of SAM systems which might give them some capability of defending against the lower, high-drag reentry vehicles. Another possible agreement might even require that the drag of reentry vehicles increase in proportion to their weight, so as to make the most powerful reentry vehicles, that is, those with the highest explosive yield, the least accurate and thus prevent their use in killing silos.

A BAN ON SLBM TESTS IN DEPRESSED TRAJECTORY By moving a ballistic missile submarine closer to its target than the maximum range of its missiles, but by firing the missiles to full velocity at a lower angle of elevation, higher average speed and shorter travel time can be obtained, although at some cost in accuracy and increased heating of the reentry vehicle. Having such a capability would enable one side to hit a large fraction of the other's strategic bombers on the ground before they could take off in response to radar warning. Therefore, such a capability would be destabilizing and should be avoided. Neither the United States nor the Soviet Union has ever tested an SLBM in a depressed trajectory mode; a ban on such testing should be formalized in an agreement to ensure the invulnerability of land-based bombers.

A Limitation on Strategic Antisubmarine Warfare Consonant with the goal of eliminating threats to the prelaunch survivability of offensive forces would be a limitation on strategic antisubmarine warfare (ASW) capabilities, deployments, and activities. Unfortunately, there is no clear distinction in means employed between antisubmarine warfare against strategic submarines and that against tactical (antiship or ASW) submarines. Consequently, some limitations on strategic antisubmarine warfare may lead an undesirable constriction of traditional naval capabilities. Nevertheless, since ensuring the invulnerability of strategic forces is essential to the security of both the United States and the

Soviet Union, implementing one of the following two proposals would be desirable. The first of the two is the more feasible and should be pursued in forthcoming rounds of SALT.

- The two superpowers could agree to ban active trailing of each other's strategic submarines (that is, the use of active sonar, lasers, and the like which would enable submarines or other vessels to tag along at close range with missile-launching submarines). Ballistic-missile-launching submarines have special hatches and other distinguishing features that can be detected by appropriate close-in sensors. Passive sonars (that is, those that do not transmit sound energy) would not be restricted, since their use in trailing can be more readily countered. The effect of such a ban would be to eliminate fear that a specially built fleet of active trailers could make a preemptive attack on the SLBM fleet—the one anti-SLBM measure that is technically feasible now.[18]

- A second way to protect the sea-based deterrent would be formally to establish sanctuaries of substantial size (several hundred miles square) in which all forms of antisubmarine warfare would be banned and the SLBM submarines left undisturbed. Limiting such regions to the Arctic Ocean, geographically close to both superpowers' homelands, could eliminate the necessity of providing guarantees of innocent passage to and from the sanctuary areas. Alternatively, agreement could be reached to ensure, in times of tension or even non-nuclear war, safe transit or unopposed escort for SLBM submarines passing through ASW barriers to the sanctuaries.

A Comprehensive Nuclear Weapons Test Ban   The dozens of underground nuclear tests conducted annually by the United

---

[18]There are, of course, numerous nontechnical counters to such ASW capabilities; for example, the missile-bearing submarine could run for miles within its own territorial waters, into which the enemy trailer would not dare penetrate. Or measures could be taken to make it very difficult for waiting trailers to acquire active sonar contact, as by having several submarines emerge from port simultaneously.

States and the Soviet Union serve, if not as the cause, at least as an excuse for complaints by non-nuclear-weapons states and for their refusal to support the nonproliferation policies of the super-powers. Soviet tests also raise concerns on the part of some observers in the United States that Moscow may be making progress in nuclear weapons that could in some way destabilize the strategic balance, and the tests thus fuel Washington's competitive response. A comprehensive test ban could in small measure reduce the impetus of the Soviet-American arms competition and could play an even more important role in enabling these two nations and their allies to take a firmer stand against the acquisition of nuclear weapons by other states.

One of the chief obstacles in recent years to a comprehensive test ban has been the enthusiasm of some Soviet technologists for peaceful nuclear explosions. They hope to use PNEs in performing the massive excavation required to reverse the flow of the Pechora River in order to provide needed irrigation water and to revitalize the Caspian Sea. Soviet enthusiasm was maintained at a time when enthusiasm and support for peaceful nuclear explosions were declining in the United States, and even as it became clear that it would be impossible to carry out extensive excavation without violating the requirements of the Limited Test Ban Treaty barring explosions that vent radioactivity into the atmosphere. But the recent signing by Moscow of the Threshold Test Ban Treaty, with its provisions limiting peaceful nuclear explosions, suggests that the Soviets are at least taking a more reasoned view of the worth of PNEs, and this development opens the way to consideration of a comprehensive test ban. No substantial delay is required or justified; accession to a comprehensive test ban by 1978 would not significantly affect the military capabilities of the United States or the Soviet Union, but it would provide a basis for both to adopt a strong nonproliferation posture, perhaps extending to the imposition of joint or parallel sanctions against states that initiate testing of nuclear explosives. The treaty could be made subject to reevaluation and possible modification 15 or 20 years after going into force, to take into account the possibility that peaceful nuclear explosions may become more feasible and beneficial in the future. Because of its utility in retarding the

Soviet-American arms race and in discouraging nuclear proliferation, a comprehensive test ban signed only by the United States, the Soviet Union, and perhaps one or two other nuclear powers would be useful even if the last nuclear weapons state refused to sign or put off its signing for, say, 10 years, during which it continued testing to "catch up" with the superpowers. Substantial efforts, however, would have to be made toward achieving universal adherence by that time if the treaty were not to break down.

No-Use against Non-Nuclear Weapons States A commitment by nuclear weapons states not to use nuclear weapons against non-nuclear-weapons states, insofar as it was regarded as binding, would discourage the acquisition of nuclear weapons by the non-nuclear states, since to acquire nuclear weapons would be to forfeit the protection of the treaty. The strength of this disincentive, of course, would be limited, depending on the degree to which non-nuclear states believed the treaty to be regarded by nuclear states simply as a convenience, to be abrogated or ignored at some future time. A formal international agreement might engender greater confidence on the part of non-nuclear states than would a unilateral declaration, but it would not remove all doubts. In addition, the strength of the disincentive would also be reduced if nations perceived the United States and other nuclear states as highly unlikely to use nuclear weapons first even against nuclear powers. While logically it might seem that a treaty on nonuse of nuclear weapons against non-nuclear-weapons states would be most effective in countering proliferation if it were accompanied by a declared policy of first use against nuclear states, such an extreme corollary would hardly entail "lesser dependence on nuclear weapons" and is therefore not part of the recommended Second Regime.

In addition to discouraging proliferation, a treaty on nonuse against non-nuclear states would also serve to reduce somewhat the likelihood of nuclear weapons being used in a regional context. Moreover, the intimidating effect of nuclear weapons vis-à-vis non-nuclear neighboring states would be reduced if the nuclear state subscribed to a strong no-use agreement.

But there are problems in defining a "non-nuclear state." One possibility is to restrict the category of non-nuclear states to those that have ratified the NPT and are not nuclear weapons states. But if the Soviet Union and its Warsaw Pact allies invaded West Germany, could NATO use nuclear weapons against these invading forces within West Germany? Could such weapons be used against the forces in East Germany or in Poland or only against forces in the Soviet Union, thereby making a Soviet-American strategic exchange more likely? Alternatively, could American nuclear weapons be used against Chinese armies in North Korea, in the context of a massive Chinese–North Korean invasion of South Korea? So that such ambiguous situations would be avoided, I advocate that the policy be one of no-use of nuclear weapons against states that do not have their own nuclear weapons and do not have others' nuclear weapons on their territory. This policy would encourage the removal of Soviet and American nuclear weapons from the territory of other states; in this regard, it is consistent with the recommended reduction of American and Allied dependence on tactical nuclear weapons.

A General No-First-Use Policy?　An international arms control agreement that would formally codify a general policy not to use nuclear weapons against any state, except in response to nuclear attack, would be less desirable under the Second Regime than the limited no-use posture just discussed. Less general forms of no-first-use agreements[19]—such as ones limited to a geographical region or to opponents also subscribing to a no-first-use policy—would also be counterproductive. The problem is not of verification; if another nation uses nuclear weapons, this will be known. But unlike many arms control agreements, abrogation or violation of a no-first-use pledge can have very serious and immediate consequences. While it may be potentially useful for a nation to subscribe to a no-first-use policy under some circumstances (specifically, for the United States to announce such

---

[19]For an analysis of several possible types of no-first-use arrangements, see Richard H. Ullman, "No First Use of Nuclear Weapons," *Foreign Affairs*, vol. 50, no. 4, July 1972, pp. 669–683.

a policy vis-à-vis China),[20] a broader, more inclusive no-first-use agreement would not have the same effect in stopping nuclear proliferation as would an accord on no-first-use with respect only to non-nuclear states, since going nuclear would no longer expose a nation to new risks. Indeed, since tactical and forward-based nuclear weapons would not be present in the prescribed Second Regime, a no-first-use policy would prevail de facto. The United States can make known its intention to use nuclear weapons only in response to others' nuclear weapons without signing a formal agreement that would eliminate first use as even an extreme option, and therefore without reducing the uncertainty regarding American strategy that deters Soviet conventional aggression in Europe.[21]

Nuclear Weapons for Use by Non-Nuclear States In 1975, Alton Frye suggested a novel approach to curbing nuclear proliferation.[22] He proposed that nuclear powers individually or jointly guarantee that in the case of nuclear attack on a non-nuclear state, this state would be given immediate access to nuclear weapons for retaliation in numbers and megatonnage comparable to those used against it. Therefore, the non-nuclear state would have no need to acquire its own nuclear weapons, for it would have the superpowers' arsenals both as a deterrent to nuclear attack by an adversary and as a retaliatory force if the surrogate deterrent failed. In requiring that non-nuclear-weapons states depend on surrogate nuclear weapons, this proposal might seem to run counter to the lesser role for nuclear weapons integral to a Second Regime. But the guarantee proposed here would be one of such a form that the state guaranteed would have little or no detailed contact with, or planning for, nuclear weapons or their delivery. The Frye proposal—by extending the superpowers' nuclear de-

[20]In this case, a bilateral no-first-use agreement could be tied to a Chinese undertaking not to deploy ICBMs or to other, more political considerations.

[21]See pp. 114–116.

[22]For a more complete exposition of his scheme, see his article, "How to Ban the Bomb: Sell It," *New York Times Magazine*, January 11, 1976, pp. 11, 76–79. (As is customary, the article's title was supplied by the magazine, not by the author.)

terrence to non-nuclear states and thereby reducing the military and power-political utility of nuclear weapons in regional contexts—would inhibit *both* the use and the spread of these weapons and would therefore be consistent with the principles of a Second Regime.

Most comments on the Frye proposal have ignored its dual utility, concentrating on its effectiveness in deterring the use of nuclear weapons rather than on its influence in preventing the acquisition of these weapons. The deterrent to the use of nuclear weapons is of course significant, in that a nuclear weapons state could no longer attack a non-nuclear state with impunity. But more important is the fact that a non-nuclear state, by acquiring nuclear weapons, would immediately lose that access to advanced retaliatory nuclear weapons which it was guaranteed before abandoning its non-nuclear status. This loss would be a very major penalty for a first peaceful nuclear explosion; the fear of losing the surrogate nuclear umbrella would undoubtedly be a stronger disincentive to the development of a nuclear explosive capability than would the high cost of a weapons program.

The Frye proposal has aroused criticism and disdain in about equal measure, and there would be obvious political and technical difficulties in implementing it, beyond the problems of defining a non-nuclear state and distinguishing among those who may have been responsible for the nuclear attack. For instance, it must be decided whether or not the non-nuclear states should provide their own delivery systems for the surrogate nuclear weapons. To have many non-nuclear states of the world testing nuclear weapons delivery systems would be only marginally compatible with the aim of lesser dependence on nuclear weapons. Possession of effective nuclear weapons delivery systems might create new incentives to acquire the weapons themselves—an outcome opposite to that sought by the Frye proposal—and should therefore be avoided.

A more attractive alternative would be for the two major nuclear weapons states to maintain some of their ICBMs in support of their guarantee to non-nuclear states and to target them according to the request of non-nuclear victims of nuclear attack. Unfortunately, highly MIRVed ICBMs would be of little utility in this role, and 10-megaton warheads seem excessive as well. Ten or twenty Minuteman I missiles (or SS-11 or SS-13 missiles on the Soviet side) could be fitted with a stock explosive of lower yield—say 10 kilotons—as such a guarantor force. In the longer term, considering the modest number of nuclear weapons likely to be needed for retaliation on behalf of non-nuclear states, it would be useful for each of the two major nuclear powers to build a force of, say, 100 small ICBMs, each weighing 10,000 pounds and carrying a single nuclear warhead with selectable yield of 10, 30, and 100 kilotons. Such forces, although on national territory, could conceivably be supervised by a transnational group; such supervision (e.g., processing of pleas for weapons to be delivered according to the pledge) would help guarantee that retaliatory nuclear weapons were released to all non-nuclear victims of nuclear attack, be they friend or foe of the provider of the nuclear weapons. These extra weapons could even replace an equal number of larger ICBMs under the SALT II ceiling, thereby achieving some modest reduction in overall nuclear force levels while providing a more practical tool for carrying out the guarantee of nuclear weapons in support of non-nuclear states attacked with nuclear weapons.

FOUR

Political and Military Utility to the United States of the Second Regime

The Second Regime just described would be a posture of restraint—one in which the United States in particular would continue to possess nuclear weapons in a dangerous world but would seek above all to nullify the importance not of its own weapons alone, but of nuclear weapons everywhere. Thus its nuclear weapons would not only protect the United States against destruction by the Soviet Union, they would also help protect other, even nonaligned, if non-nuclear, nations against nuclear attack. Continued United States retention of strategic nuclear weapons would become much more acceptable to many nations.

The recommended posture could be achieved by the United States acting alone. By limiting expenditures on its strategic force and limiting the scope of what that force need and can do, the United States would be able to avoid buying excess insurance for a very narrow aspect of its national security. Such excessive emphasis would lead to reduced security and also give the false impression to the world's less favored nations that the United States felt it had an exclusive right to protect itself against the threat of nuclear destruction. Reduced expenditures of human and material resources on strategic systems might facilitate the achievement of other American goals in both domestic and foreign policy. Even more important to the attainment of this end would be the introduction of a philosophy of purpose and a sense of proportion in the strategic sphere.

Having indicated above what nuclear and non-nuclear forces

would be required of the United States in this Second Regime and what posture should be taken regarding their use, we may ask how well it all works.

PERFORMANCE OF THE REGIME IN WESTERN CONFRONTATION AND ALLIANCE RELATIONSHIPS

In 1977, NATO military leaders seem generally persuaded that the enormous waste of resources associated with the lack of standardization in weapons production should be curtailed, that national logistic support forces should be replaced by theater forces, and that a great increase in theater force effectiveness could be achieved through new organization and a proper introduction of new technology: precision-guided munitions and perhaps cruise missiles. But little has actually been done in these crucial areas because of a lack of agreement on how to go about achieving these goals. Therefore, it is necessary to summarize here how the recommended Second Regime might work in various circumstances, in order to foster the consensus required for its implementation.

NATO remains a military alliance whose forces are intended to prevent a successful Soviet or Warsaw Pact invasion of Western Europe. During periods in which NATO's non-nuclear capabilities and readiness were not clearly adequate to repel, and therefore, deter, a Warsaw Pact invasion, NATO has relied on American-supplied tactical nuclear weapons. (Although in wartime some British and more recently some French nuclear weapons would also be employed.) While no consistent doctrine for the use of these weapons has been formulated, NATO has been reasonably confident that the losses to the Warsaw Pact resulting from the use by NATO of its theater nuclear weapons, or from the use of American forward-based and strategic nuclear forces, would far outweigh the gains to the Warsaw Pact from an invasion of NATO territory.

Although the wealth, workforce, and technology of NATO countries are adequate to support a conventional force capable of defeating Warsaw Pact forces in conventional military combat,

Western economic competition and other aspects of intra-alliance relations have led the NATO countries to prefer dependence on nuclear weapons to deter conventional aggression. But an equally effective and perhaps more credible way to deter a conventional invasion would be to show its military infeasibility; the conventional forces prescribed above would give NATO an additional layer of deterrence. A nuclear deterrent would still remain to NATO if the conventional deterrent failed, but improving NATO's ability to stop the invasion by actual use of its non-nuclear forces would make a nuclear response—the use of United States–based strategic nuclear weapons under the proposed share-release arrangements—an option of last resort rather than the only real option.

Some critics object that giving NATO a highly effective anti-tank force, one capable of stopping a Soviet invasion without the use of nuclear weapons, would lead to Soviet nuclear attack on NATO rear areas and cities. But this objection ignores the capability of the Soviet Union to take that step in any case and the fact that it is deterred from doing so (now) by the NATO ministrategic force of forward-based systems and (in the proposed Second Regime) by the United States–based strategic arsenal. To opt for a weak conventional defense so that the Soviet Union may win on the battlefield without having to resort to nuclear weapons is no solution to the problem.

The replacement of NATO's theater nuclear weapons by advanced non-nuclear forces would not be a concession to the Soviet Union or to budget cutters but a means of improving NATO's deterrent and war-fighting posture. NATO's present flexible response strategy carries with it the danger of unwanted escalation to strategic exchange—a deterrent to Soviet aggression, perhaps, but a serious problem to NATO once conventional forces were actually engaged in combat. Moreover, nuclear weapons in the European theater are vulnerable to capture or preemptive destruction and so should not be relied upon exclusively. One may well believe that the United States involvement is guaranteed more by the presence of American troops in Western Europe (which would be retained under the Second Regime) than by the possibility of Soviet capture of American tactical nuclear weapons. Finally, aircraft capable of delivering both conventional and nuclear weapons ought not be risked in their conventional role if their nuclear capability is not to be lost; the precision-guided cruise missile of 600-mile range would be a highly capable replacement for more expensive and vulnerable fighter-bombers in performing some conventional missions.

PERFORMANCE OF THE REGIME WITH RESPECT TO NON-NUCLEAR STATES

A central element of the proposed Second Regime would be the principle of no use of nuclear weapons against non-nuclear states that have no nuclear weapons on their territory. Since a nation's acquisition of nuclear weapons would entail the forfeiture of the guarantee under this principle, the regime should help prevent both the use and the acquisition of nuclear weapons in currently non-nuclear regions. And it would also prevent the nuclear involvement of the superpowers in conventional wars between their respective allies. For example, if North Korea attacked South Korea without the participation of nuclear-armed Chinese or Soviet troops, American help to South Korea would have to be limited to conventional weapons, with or without American troops. In such circumstances, it is hardly conceivable that nuclear weapons would be either necessary or useful anyway, so the recommended regime cannot be said to undermine security guarantees between nuclear and non-nuclear powers. Should the Chinese or Soviets aid the North Koreans by deploying troops with nuclear weapons on North Korean territory, the policy of no-use against non-nuclear states would no longer constrain the United States, just as the dispatching of American troops with nuclear weapons to South Korea would vitiate any Soviet no-use pledge. Even in these circumstances, the actual use of nuclear weapons by either side would probably still be deterred by a reluctance to be the first country since 1945 to use nuclear weapons and by the fear of nuclear response by nuclear powers allied with the other side. But a formal policy of no-use of nuclear weapons against states with no nuclear weapons on their territory would be a more reliable guarantee that no nuclear weapons were even introduced, much less used, in Korea.

Perhaps more interesting is the prescribed Second Regime's effectiveness in stopping the spread of nuclear weapons. Prior to testing its first nuclear weapon, a non-nuclear nation would be secure against nuclear attack by the major nuclear powers in view of their policy of no-use against non-nuclear states. It would also have available to it advanced American and Soviet nuclear weapons for retaliation to a nuclear attack on its territory by any other nuclear power if the Frye proposal were implemented and institutionalized. But if unrelieved security concerns or a desire for nuclear-weapons status impelled it to construct and test a nuclear weapon, the nation would no longer benefit from the superpowers' no-use pledge, and it would no longer have available to it on demand modern nuclear weapons for retaliation to a nuclear attack either by a neighbor or by one of the superpowers.

In other words, the country's national security would be *reduced* if it were to obtain nuclear weapons. Whether or not the protection should be restored if the country subsequently renounced its nuclear weapons would be a matter of policy choice, as would the question of whether the United States and the Soviet Union should take additional measures—such as economic or political sanctions—to ensure that proliferants suffer in peacetime as well as in wartime. In any case, the proposed Second Regime would have a strong antiproliferative impact.

FIVE

Paths to the Second Regime

Although its benefits would be enhanced by international arms limitation agreements, the prescribed Second Regime, as has been stressed above, could be achieved largely by actions of the United States (or the Soviet Union) alone. What would happen if Administration and Congress became simultaneously convinced of the desirability of such a Regime?

First, the United States would take the recommended unilateral actions, which would serve equally well in the First Regime as in the Second. Doing this would entail more rational and less wasteful attitudes toward national defense. Of immediate utility would be the introduction of elementary point defenses for the short-term protection of potentially vulnerable Minuteman ICBMs, replacement of the B-1 bomber program with deployments of cruise missiles on cargo-type aircraft giving a less vulnerable and more capable force, and cancellation of the Trident submarine program while the long-range Trident I missiles were being retrofitted onto Poseidon submarines to enlarge the older ships' operating range and, hence, reduce their vulnerability to Soviet antisubmarine warfare efforts.[23] Together, these three actions would guarantee the survivability of all three arms of the American deterrent triad even if the present escalatory trends in Soviet strategic programs accelerate. If the Soviets do, in fact,

[23]The Trident submarines (*not* the Trident missiles)—aside from their excessive cost—would not necessarily increase the invulnerability of the sea-based deterrent. Because Tridents carry 24 rather than 16 SLBMs, fewer Tridents

develop a silo-killing capability, the further unilateral American responses recommended above could be undertaken.[24]

While unilateral actions would suffice in protecting the American deterrent, the Strategic Arms Limitations Talks with the Soviet Union should still be continued, since international arms control agreements would enhance both the stability and legitimacy of the Second Regime. Republican and Democratic leaders should not allow SALT to be used as domestic political capital, but rather they should give SALT the high priority that national security concerns and limited budgetary resources warrant. Early objectives of the talks should include obtaining a formal agreement codifying the principle of not threatening the strategic offensive force of the other side and negotiating a limitation on missile test rates, with a complete ban on MIRV tests. A comprehensive nuclear test ban could also be negotiated in SALT and then made available for accession by other nations.

In Europe, American tactical nuclear weapons would be withdrawn, to be compensated for by an aggressive program of modernizing NATO's non-nuclear capabilities, with greater reliance on tactical cruise missiles, land and sea mines, theater surveillance, and advanced command and control capabilities. Strategic nuclear weapons based in the United States, with flexible targeting options and shared-release authority, would stand as last-resort support for the conventional forces in place of American tactical and forward-based nuclear weapons. Major changes in organization and staffing would be required for efficient use of the new capabilities.

---

than Poseidons could be deployed, assuming SALT ceilings on strategic weapons launchers remained in force, and the detection and destruction of a single, larger Trident by the Soviet ASW fleet would mean a 50 percent greater reduction in United States strategic forces than would the destruction of one Poseidon or Polaris.

[24]Greater reliance on the bomber and submarine-based deterrents; deployment of rapid-start capabilities for strategic bombers; deployment of in-flight command arm/disarm capabilities on Minuteman to permit a launch-on-warning strategy, replacement of the MIRVed ICBM force with a large force of smaller, single-warhead ICBMs; etc. See pp. 95–98.

Having itself decided that such a course would be preferable to a continuation of NATO's present posture, the United States would have to persuade the other members of the alliance. A concrete display of the American determination to do more than compensate with advanced conventional forces the withdrawal of its tactical nuclear weapons would be key to convincing the Western Europeans that the United States was no less committed to European security than in the past. With only promises, the Europeans might decide to depend more heavily on their own nuclear weapons to bolster deterrence against Soviet provocation. With positive evidence of continued United States commitment, the Europeans would be inclined to follow the lead of their ally in developing adequate conventional defense for NATO.

Offsetting the costs of preparing for conventional defense and another possible incentive to acceptance of the American view would be the opportunity for increased weapons development and manufacture in the individual NATO countries which a major reorganization and reequipment program would provide. Such a program could promote the long overdue standardization of weapons production within the alliance through competition for NATO-wide supply; standardization would have a purpose, rather than being a make-work scheme. A coherent American plan for a Second Regime posture may be just what is required to restore direction and military capability to NATO. Building a modern force with a new, more rational purpose would provide an opportunity to revitalize an alliance that has been suffering from political disunity, military inefficiency, and a sense of irrelevance.

Would the Soviet Union exercise similar restraint in response to American initiatives? Would it join in the proposed agreements? I believe it would, because it is in the Soviets' national security interest to do so. The Second Regime prescribed here would put an end to the situation in which the continuing display of American technical virtuosity—whereby the United States has repeatedly gained putative "advantages" in strategic capabilities (silo launch, undersea launch; multiple reentry vehicles; MIRVs; strategic cruise missiles; flexible, miniaturized digital computers for missile guidance, etc.)—has compelled the Soviets to follow suit, at a tremendous cost to the strained Soviet economy, with this imitation by the Soviets, in turn, spurring some in the United States to urge further improvements because the Soviet Union is "catching up." A consistent American policy of restraint would strengthen the hands of those in the Soviet bureaucracy arguing for a similar rationalization of Soviet strategic programs and, per-haps, of those advocating reductions in Warsaw Pact forces.[25]

But it is important that the Soviet Union join in the proposed agreements for reasons of national security and not because it is offered incentives—economic, political, or otherwise—outside SALT. No such incentives can be as persuasive as true national security interests; they only complicate the negotiating process and induce delay while one side tries to obtain more and the other to give less on these non-security-related incentives.[26]

How ought the United States respond should the Soviet Union, for reasons of its own, choose to build what are, in Washington's opinion, excessive forces? The United States government should patiently explain to its citizens, its allies, and the rest of the world that there is no way it can keep a sovereign nation from wasting its resources, that the sensible American response is simply to main-tain its own ability to fulfill the imperatives of its chosen doctrine of deterrence (which does not depend on the size of the Soviet strategic force), and that instead of a wasteful counter build-up, the United States is employing its limited resources to maintain its usable military strength, to build its society, to help and protect its allies, and to assist friendly, less-developed nations in solving their internal problems.

The only circumstances under which the United States should

[25]Admittedly, it is probably quixotic to expect Warsaw Pact reductions at a time of a conventional build-up in NATO. In any case, the Warsaw Pact forces' internal security function in Eastern Europe would likely prevent sub-stantial reductions there.

[26]In particular, the question of trade advantages and credits for the Soviet Union should not be made contingent on progress in the SALT negotiations. The Soviet Union should be treated like any other wealthy advanced nation, with commerce left to suitably regulated private business firms on the American side. United States government supervision would be required to ensure that the overt monopoly power of the unified Soviet governmental and commercial sectors was appropriately limited and that strategically sensitive goods were not exported.

abandon a Second Regime posture would be the deployment by the Soviets of ABM systems of such advanced design and in such numbers that the Soviets could repel any attack by the American strategic offensive force. But no ABM system with this capability is known or anticipated, and the 1972 ABM treaty commits the United States and the Soviet Union not to deploy such a system in any case. Moreover, even if an effective ABM technology should emerge, it would be naïve to believe that one side could maintain a monopoly on such technology. Ultimately, there is nothing in the dynamics of Soviet American relations to compel the two nations to perfect and deploy such systems, since they would destroy the stability of whatever nuclear regime prevailed without offering offsetting benefits.

BUILDING SUPPORT FOR A SECOND REGIME

Domestic Sources of Legitimacy It is almost a truism that foreign policy, diplomacy, and military activity are supported by the citizenry if they are recognized as being in the national interest. Particular policies or activities could be so recognized either directly (when they are simple and their contribution to the national defense is obvious and strong) or indirectly (through citizen support for public officials rather than for their policies *per se*). In setting a criterion for legitimacy in a democracy, one could require support for policies by:

1. Average citizens who are not well informed and who have not given much thought to the subject
2. Average citizens, if they would take the time to study the publicly available information on the subject
3. Average citizens if they were given the opportunity to study not only the publicly available information but also secret information pertinent to the decision
4. Only by those professionally trained to deal with the subject

The breadth of popular acceptance required to sustain policy varies from one political system to the next. In a democracy such as the United States, planning for and authorization of most governmental activities must have fairly broad support; a policy can be considered legitimate if it is accepted by citizens in category 2 or at least category 3. A policy approved only by those professionals in category 4 would not generally enjoy legitimacy. In more centralized, elite-dominated political systems such as those of France or the Soviet Union, support from category 4 has been regarded as a sufficient source of legitimacy.

Over the years there have been demands in the United States that the criterion for legitimacy be raised to category 1, i.e., that a policy must be supported by a majority of citizens, including the uninformed. But it is clear that a complex modern society must rely on a specialization of function, if not of training. It is not possible for every citizen, even the most dedicated and intelligent, to vote on every decision important to the nation; he or she would have no time to understand all the issues. In our representative government, citizens elect to Congress individuals who do not necessarily have the relevant background to address every issue, but who can, through an apportionment of responsibilities, concentrate on an acceptable number of issues; if these elected individuals are truly representative (even randomly chosen, acting with responsibility delegated by their constituents), then complex policies can be regarded as legitimate under category 2 or 3, depending on the degree of access to secret information given responsible Congressional committees. Thus, a representative democracy provides a mechanism to ensure that only those policies will be adopted that would enjoy the support of the majority of ordinary citizens, if they were provided with the relevant information.[27]

Global Sources of Legitimacy   Although most of the actions

---

[27]Lacking specialized training, as do the highest officials in the Executive branch, representatives benefit from access to specialists of varying views on a given policy—i.e., consultants with immediate access to classified information. The support by representatives for that policy must, of course, be based on their evaluation of the validity of statements by these specialists and technicians.

advocated here for maximizing American security can be taken by the United States unilaterally, the endurance of the proposed Second Regime depends on the actions of others, particularly with regard to nuclear proliferation. Many people and nations in the world wish the United States ill; they cannot all be won to America's ideology, let alone to America's support. But others can and will support American actions that advance the goals of order, justice, and equity of opportunity in an imperfect (but improving) world. Halting nuclear proliferation would further these goals, and it is for this reason—in addition to improving American security directly—that the prescribed regime would downgrade the importance of nuclear weapons in international life. A Second Regime would make it clearly to the advantage of non-nuclear states not to acquire nuclear weapons. Most nations would come to see the United States and the Soviet Union as antagonists whose declining stocks of nuclear weapons were a burden they bore, somewhat unwillingly, for the benefit of the rest of the world, putting their nuclear weapons at the disposal of others to deter nuclear attack, but not using them to defend against non-nuclear attack or to coerce non-nuclear nations.

It is reasonable to expect that a rational, measured American effort to delimit the role of nuclear weapons within the existing system would earn support from the majority of the nations of the world. Since it would be possible and desirable for the United States to move toward the prescribed Second Regime largely through its own actions, it would be inappropriate to make the achievement of successive SALT agreements with the Soviet Union a prerequisite to American actions to rationalize its defense programs and policies. The development and deployment of "bargaining chips" for the SALT negotiations is therefore undesirable because they can weaken American security, will increase defense costs, and may make the United States more vulnerable to manipulation by Soviet bargaining tactics in SALT. Attending to American defense needs and using the recommended Second Regime posture as a framework for modernizing and rationalizing NATO would seem to constitute a good foundation for progress in SALT, and better insurance against the failure of SALT than the threat of massive expenditures. The Soviet Union has no reason to fear such massive expenditures, because it can certainly match them, given the nature of the Soviet political system.

BASES FOR COMPARISON OF THIS SECOND REGIME WITH THE FIRST AND THIRD REGIMES

American evaluation of the desirability of alternative nuclear regimes for the 1980s should be done on the basis of the following criteria:

- The security a given regime provides to the United States (the principal agent in shaping the nuclear future)
- The stability of the regime, that is, its ability to prevent nuclear war and subnuclear conflicts that could lead to nuclear war
- The degree to which the regime slows or prevents nuclear proliferation
- The degree to which the regime advances the goals of equity of opportunity and of reward in the world
- The degree to which it preserves the benefits to all nations of certain unequal aspects of the international order
- The regime's cost to the United States
- The probability that the regime could actually be achieved, given the realities of the international system

Considerable discussion has been devoted in the text to how the prescribed Second Regime would satisfy these individual criteria, aside from those concerning the advance of equity of opportunity and of reward, and the benefits of inequality. Of course, the recommended Second Nuclear Regime would not in itself solve the problems of the presently poor nations, but it would redirect the nuclear strength of the United States and the Soviet Union toward an explicit role in protecting non-nuclear nations and away from threatening such nations. The beneficial elements of inequality of which I write are those which allow a rich nation a surplus of talent and energy, enabling it to develop technologies and products which, when sold or copied, can benefit the rest of the world, together with a surplus of wealth which can benefit other nations not by transfer for consumption but by enabling them to contribute to global well-being in a like manner. The lesser role that would be given to nuclear weapons in superpower relations would not necessarily have a direct and positive effect on superpower friendship or cooperation, but it would permit mankind to exist more confident of survival, its spirit freed for more constructive activity. A lesser role for nuclear weapons would not, however, insure that this spirit is not directed toward destructive non-nuclear military adventure and ideological crusade.

The Third Regime as presented in this volume—a regime in which nuclear weapons would be totally proscribed and denuclearization enforced by an international government—might be superior to a Second Regime in satisfying most, if not all of the above criteria, if it were achievable. But its low probability of ever being achieved—the last criterion—rule it out as a realistic goal toward which to strive in the 1980s.

The only achievable alternative to a Second Regime, aside from the undesirable strategic deterioration discussed under the title of the Fourth Regime, is the current, First Nuclear Regime. I believe this essay has shown that in terms of security, stability, cost, contribution to nonproliferation, and advancement of global equity, the proposed Second Regime would be superior to the First Regime, and the obstacles to its achievement could be surmounted.

The Proscription
of Nuclear Weapons:
A Third Nuclear Regime

John H. Barton

ONE

The Concept of
Proscribing Nuclear Weapons

This essay analyzes a world in which nuclear weapons are prohibited and is intended to complement the three essays on more likely nuclear regimes. The unlikely case of a denuclearized world deserves consideration to highlight the effects of nuclear weapons on international politics and to help define goals for arms control. Denuclearization is often an implicit goal of proposals to reform the international political order; few reform proposals, however, examine the desirability of a denuclearized world or the long-term strategy for achieving such a world. These questions are therefore emphasized in this study, which seeks to avoid reiterating the undeniable difficulties of denuclearization. The time focus of the essay necessarily reaches well past the 1980s.[1]

After reviewing the arguments favoring the proscription of nuclear weapons, the first part of the study attempts a realistic definition of such proscription for a world in which nuclear

[1] I would like to acknowledge those works on whose ideas I have relied most heavily. They are Leonard Beaton, *The Reform of Power*, Viking, New York, 1972, and Richard Barnet and Richard Falk (eds.), *Security in Disarmament*, Princeton University Press, Princeton, N.J., 1965. My analysis of the possibility of verifying denuclearization relies upon Mason Willrich (ed.), *International Safeguards and Nuclear Industry*, Johns Hopkins University Press, Baltimore, 1973, and my thoughts about the politics of internationalization draw upon parallels suggested by Charles Tilly (ed.), *The Formation of National States in Western Europe*, Princeton University Press, Princeton, N.J., 1975, and upon conversations with Ralph Goldman, who has made available unpublished materials.

technology would not be forgotten and the existence of hidden nuclear weapons inventories could not be precluded. These considerations lead to two models for a world in which nuclear weapons have been proscribed. One, the "incremental" model, would retain the nation-state system and make only those changes necessary to help nations succeed in eliminating nuclear weapons. The other, the "internationalized" model, would transfer citizen loyalties from the national order to an international order and thus transform politics in a way that leaves nuclear weapons essentially irrelevant to the conflicts that might arise.

The second part of the essay reviews various forms of military action that might still arise under the two models of a denuclearized world. It suggests the political effects of denuclearization under the two patterns and outlines more fully the institutional and political requirements for the two patterns. Although these requirements are heavily shaped by world economic and political goals, the primary emphasis in this section is upon military security issues and questions such as what the role of conventional forces would be and whether or not an international nuclear force would be needed. The section concludes with an estimate that the denuclearized incremental world is not desirable, but the internationalized version is desirable.

The third part of the essay examines the transition to the denuclearized worlds and reviews the three crucial aspects of that transition: the phasing out of superpower nuclear deterrence; the entry of developing countries and of potential challenging great powers, such as Brazil and Iran, into the structure; and the transfer of power from national governments to international bodies. Power balances for negotiating the transition for each aspect are discussed, as are potential motivating goals and alliances, and an effort is made to outline a conceivable transition sequence for each aspect. It is the nonmilitary issues—which are likely to provide the strongest motivations for change—that are emphasized in this discussion. These transitions appear to me less infeasible than I had expected; there is, however, some risk associated with the transition to an internationalized world.

The final section briefly reassembles the different aspects of the grand transition and enumerates those interim measures that could be taken over the next decade or two and might make the internationalized version of a nuclear-free world available sometime in the twenty-first century. These interim measures are likely to be desirable whether or not a denuclearized world is later sought.

WHY PROSCRIBE NUCLEAR WEAPONS?

Ever since the invention of nuclear weapons, many strategic and political thinkers have urged that these weapons be removed from national control. Undoubtedly, this attitude toward nuclear weapons rests primarily upon an emotional reaction against the magnitude and horror of the destruction produced by such weapons. This emotional reaction is a crucial political asset supporting the control of nuclear weapons. Yet even though it has created very strong inhibitions against the *use* of nuclear weapons, it has not proven strong enough to inhibit a number of nations from *possessing* them.

Arguments against the possession of nuclear weapons are therefore somewhat more subtle. Nuclear weapons have at least four effects that argue for their undesirability or their incompatibility with existing institutions. The first is that the destruction that might accompany even "limited" use of nuclear weapons is disproportionate to the goals that can be obtained through their use. The emergence of nuclear deterrence muted the fears, reflected in the initial Acheson-Lilienthal Plan, that there could be no defense against nuclear weapons. Nevertheless, the dynamics of nuclear deterrence place the lives of enormous numbers of people at risk, and the resulting responsibility—in decisions that must be taken rapidly—has impressed every American and Soviet leader. Although the Soviet-American nuclear relationship has become remarkably stable, the chances of nuclear destruction seem likely to increase as the number of nuclear weapons states rises and the potential for nuclear terrorism grows. One feels that a world structure of national defense policies that imposes such risks is fundamentally irrational.

Second, with the spread of nuclear weapons, the balance-of-power system—the classical way of controlling conflict between autonomous opposed actors—may lose its ability to maintain peace. A successful balance-of-power structure requires an ability to shift coalitions to bring a preponderance of power against a potential combatant. This underlying military requirement—that against a single nation, a coalition will deter war that one nation cannot deter—is much less likely to be satisfied when the nations are armed with nuclear weapons. Stable deterrence may be possible between two nations; but any effort to calculate first-strike- and reply-strike-force balances with varying coalition possibilities leaves one less confident that stable deterrence is possible among many nations, unless all nuclear forces are deployed unambiguously as strictly retaliatory systems or unless all proliferants are deterred by the mere possibility of nuclear war. Even if a multipolar nuclear deterrence system is possible, it is likely to be much less flexible and adaptable at the political level than is the traditional balance of power system. Deterrence has made it difficult for the United States and the Soviet Union to meet political conflict except through stalemate. If nuclear weapons spread, one naturally wonders if stable deterrence relationships—and multiple regional deterrence relationships—would produce stalemate on problems throughout the international system out of a widespread fear that altering the status quo may be more risky than accepting it. In a proliferated world, problems that might otherwise have been solved—although in some instances with subnuclear violence—might instead be frozen. Some would dissipate over time. But others might fester until unrelieved tensions burst, stable relationships broke down, and large-scale violence—now nuclear—erupted.

Third, nuclear weapons are more easily adapted to attacks upon civilians than to attacks upon military forces. This anticivilian role raises profound moral issues. It also affects the philosophical relationships between government and citizen, for in the nuclear era a government can defend its own citizens only through threats to attack other nation's citizens or through agreements with other governments, sometimes even designed to leave its own citizens vulnerable. The government's defense function is, in a sense, turned against its citizens, and part of the unity of interest between government and citizen is lost. Perhaps because national governments are now tending to find their central mission an economic one rather than a strategic one, this philosophical separation between government and citizen has not yet become politically significant, but it is hard to visualize this disparity of interest being submerged for much longer at a time when national governments are under attack on so many other grounds.

The force of the last point is intensified by a final point: nuclear weapons give national governments military power that is substantially independent of the contributions and control of the citizenry of the nations. Once the nuclear weapons are built—a process that will become increasingly cheap for all but those engaged in large-scale deterrence competitions—the contemporary government controls its nuclear power independently of the people and husbands it relatively independently of the economic and political factors that shaped conventional military capability. The point holds for all sophisticated weapons but is particularly strong for nuclear weapons, with their relative power, their low personnel requirement, and the special authority that citizens are willing to give to governments in the nuclear area. This independence from moral and institutional constraints means that nuclear forces are relatively unaffected by political changes: one can visualize American and Soviet strategic arms construction going on and on, whether or not there are actual grounds for conflict between the two nations. Military capability is not necessarily likely to be proportionate to a regime's ability to solve internal political problems: a weak government's nuclear weapons may deter about as effectively as those of a strong government.

On the domestic side, governments could thus lose both their need to maintain public support and part of their basis for public support. Although the economic function of government might remain coupled with the conventional forces that maintain internal security (and some measure of external security), the nuclear security role could become uncoupled from traditional government. Although some branches of government would continue to face traditional problems, persons who control the nuclear weapons might become little more than warlords, ensuring their own survival through the threat to use nuclear weapons but not compelled to accede to public political desires. The ultimate change in world politics arising from nuclear weapons could be as profound as the transition from feudalism to the nation-state system. In that transition, the application of gunpowder undermined the decisive military role of the mounted knight. Strength in battle was no longer determined by the loyalty of a relatively small number of knights. Instead, infantry, larger armies, and ultimately the Napoleonic nation-in-arms became crucial. Although nontechnological factors also played a major role, the effect of gunpowder was thus to support an order in which national power was dependent directly on the citizenry. This system gave military power as a reward to economic success; it tended to ensure that those governments more successful in nation building would also be more successful in war; and a central government's dependence on the citizenry sometimes favored the development of democracy. These couplings helped make the nation-state system beneficial with respect to many world goals. The parallel to today's transition is not perfect. Nuclear weapons holders might still be vulnerable to a broadly based revolution or a coup d'état, and the economic aspects of feudalism differ radically from those of nuclear weapons procurement. Nevertheless, the nuclear weapon may tend to undermine precisely those dependencies that made the nation-state system relatively beneficial.

Although the arguments just stated are far from fully probative, they suggest that the nation-state system may find it very difficult to adapt peacefully to the existence of nuclear weapons. The fact of one generation's nuclear peace between the United States and the Soviet Union does not refute this point: the arguments depend on the existence of more than two major nuclear powers and on the emergence of political and cultural responses that may require a generation or two to unfold. More broadly and more strongly, the arguments imply that any system embodying relatively free access to nuclear weapons is likely to be risky, to pose serious moral dilemmas, and to have difficulty in adapting to change without catastrophic conflict. It is therefore sensible to examine the proscription of nuclear weapons as a possible rational goal under various assumptions about the future of the nation-state system.

WHAT DOES IT MEAN TO PROSCRIBE
NUCLEAR WEAPONS?

Even the most perfect inspection system could not guarantee that there would never again be nuclear weapons in the world. The limits of possible denuclearization must therefore be defined, because these limits shape the character of military disputes in a denuclearized world.

First, ever since sometime in the 1950s, national nuclear-material production capabilities have been so large as to create uncertainties in each nation's intelligence estimate of other nations' production capabilities. Even if a denuclearization agreement were reached, these uncertainties would prevent an accurate assessment of whether those other nations had actually destroyed their nuclear stockpiles. Significant quantities of weapons or nuclear materials could thus be retained and concealed. Although the numbers that can be hidden could perhaps be calculated more precisely using data about intelligence capabilities, this study will assume that these numbers are on the order of a fraction of a percent of nuclear inventories preceding denuclearization. Based on current inventories, the numbers might be in the low hundreds of weapons for the United States and the Soviet Union and in the tens of weapons for the other nuclear powers. Long-term concealment of nuclear weapons might be more difficult than it sounds: there would probably have to be guards (although guards need not know what they were guarding), there would have to be informed military planners, and there might eventually have to be physical refurbishment of the weapons themselves. Nevertheless, such hiding could perhaps be successful for a time measured in several transitions of authority in the nation's government—from a few decades to a few generations. These weapons could be available for national use within hours; their military role would depend on the delivery vehicles available.

Second, weapons could be constructed from nuclear materials diverted from peaceful nuclear programs. (The analysis assumes that a substantial peaceful nuclear program would remain and spread through the world but be subject to reasonably stringent safeguards.) The quantities available this way—even with the

157

best safeguard systems likely to be politically possible—would again be substantial: at least tens of weapons a year from a reasonably sized national nuclear power program that included a reprocessing facility. The amount would depend on the reactor type, on the importance attached to obtaining a high-yield weapon, and on the characteristics of international safeguards and the importance attached to avoiding detection. Weapons would not, of course, be immediately available: conversion of the material into weapons would require perhaps several months to a year. Those nations with access to experts who had participated in a successful nuclear program would be able to move more quickly. Nations could also develop and maintain a small stockpile of clandestine, untested weapons in this way in anticipation of a crisis. There would always be some risk of detection, probably greater than the risk that a former nuclear nation's retained stockpile would be detected, because a new weapon-building program would involve more detectable activity.

Third, so long as there were experts who had participated in a nuclear weapons program or were able to reconstruct nuclear weapons technology, a nation could initiate a new nuclear weapons program. Depending on the details of safeguards arrangements for the international nuclear industry and on whether the nation had independent access to uranium supplies and its own reprocessing or enrichment facilities, the time lag could range from months to years and the probability of detection from moderate to quite high. Avoiding detection for long would probably be impossible with current technology; it might become possible with the advent of laser enrichment and thus enable a closed society to build weapons clandestinely. One also has to assume that any major nation could choose to rebuild nuclear weapons openly under circumstances such as a long conventional war.

Fundamentally, then, the primary meaning that can be given to denuclearization is that it could *increase the time lag* before nuclear weapons became available for use. Denuclearization would replace a deterrence at the military response level with a deterrence at some point closer to production. It would probably be several generations after the proscription of nuclear weapons before one could assume with any safety that all hidden nuclear weapons were gone. But for the current nuclear powers, the number of nuclear weapons immediately available could be drastically decreased, the meaning of "immediately" stretched from minutes to hours, and through parallel arms control measures, the speed of delivery systems perhaps decreased. Depending on new enrichment and reprocessing technologies and on international safeguards arrangements, other nations could have at most a small untested stockpile immediately available, and any nation seeking to rebuild substantial nuclear forces might have to do so openly and over a number of years.

TWO MODELS OF A WORLD IN WHICH NUCLEAR WEAPONS ARE PROSCRIBED

The overall concept of a denuclearized world must rest logically on the fact that denuclearization is possible in only the limited sense just described. For at least several generations, the denuclearized world could never be more than hours to months from a nuclearized world. Some of the political forces of a nuclearized world would therefore remain, and almost any major long-lasting war or conflict might lead to renuclearization. If the world is to remain denuclearized, then, these political forces would have to be accommodated and the long-lasting war or conflict avoided.

By far the most important question related to the design of a denuclearized world is whether the nation-state system remains. Retention of that system would be based on the possibility that national governments would find themselves forced to control and ultimately to eliminate nuclear weapons out of recognition that lasting nuclear stability cannot be assured. The difficulty is that the most relevant weakness of the nation-state system in the face of nuclear weapons is a systemic one—the danger of catastrophic war—and not one that exerts a constant and strong pressure upon each individual national government. National leaders assume that a systemic breakdown can always be averted for a few more years. Therefore, an "incremental" pattern in which the nation-state system remains—the more commonly assumed pattern for a denuclearized world—is most likely to be negotiated in the aftermath of a nuclear war or a narrow escape from such a war. It would presumably involve the minimum change necessary to cope with denuclearization.

The alternative, or "internationalized," pattern—as will be discussed in greater detail below—would arise from the accumulation of power and authority at the supranational level due to political processes quite separate from the control of nuclear weapons, from the persistence of nuclear weapons while these processes are under way, and, later on, from the possibility of renuclearization. As hypothesized above, political forces could tend to divide citizen and government and to weaken the ability of the nation-state system to respond to change. Citizens might transfer their loyalties to more responsive authorities, presumably at the international level. National governments would follow, caught in an evolutionary process over which they would have little leverage. The pressures would operate continuously and the transition would be gradual. It is not inevitable that the transition be toward international authority rather than toward regional authority or even some form of decentralized feudalism or warlordism. Although such forms are perhaps more likely to emerge, they seem so unlikely to be stable that only the global international pattern will be considered in this paper.

The traditional sovereignty of the state would necessarily be severely infringed in both cases. But political structures and alliance patterns would differ radically between the two. In the incremental model, popular concerns would continue to be expressed through national governments, and the necessary international organization would be an ally of those governments, helping them to avert wars and ultimately avoid loss of power. The pattern is analogous to that of the centralization of Prussia—an alliance between the crown and the feudal lords in which the crown gained power at the expense of the population. In the centralized world, in contrast, popular concerns would be expressed to the international organization directly or through non-national organizations. The nuclear weapon would hopefully become irrelevant to these popular concerns and to the national governments, which would eventually no more think of acquiring nuclear capabilities than do the states of the United States. The pattern is comparable to that of the centralization of England—an alliance of Parliament with the bourgeoisie in which power was centralized and democratized at the same time.

TWO

Security in a World Without Nuclear Weapons

The questions of the desirability and the central design of a denuclearized world center on the maintenance of security. Denuclearization would probably enhance the security of non-nuclear powers and might well be preferable per se to widespread proliferation. But its benefits for the nuclear nations, whose security has been relatively great since World War II and who hold a veto against at least the incremental denuclearized world, are less clear. And all nations might fear clandestine stockpiles or open rearmament. Any evaluation of a denuclearized world therefore requires careful analysis of the mechanisms for maintaining security. These mechanisms would, in general, differ between the incremental world and the internationalized world.

THE MECHANICS OF
MAINTAINING DENUCLEARIZATION

One need not pause very long on the technical issues of verification and of control of the international nuclear industry. These issues have been the bread and butter of a stream of nuclear arms control efforts from the Acheson-Lilienthal Plan to the contemporary antiproliferation debate and are relatively well understood. Careful safeguards would have to be imposed on all peaceful nuclear facilities, and the right to inspect places where clandestine stockpiles were suspected would have to be guaranteed. And as the International Atomic Energy Agency has concluded, safeguards could not be applied effectively unless there were some outside control over the design of nuclear facilities.

The primary security goal of a technical control system would be to provide assurance that the denuclearization arrangements would be respected. The problems of undetected clandestine stockpiles, of open or detected renuclearization, and of the appropriate international response in either case would be much more political than technical and will be discussed below. But the character of these political problems provides a useful organizing concept for the control system: to help lengthen the warning time between a nation's decision to renuclearize and the actual availability of militarily significant weapons. Thus, the international supervisory body might seek to locate such sensitive facilities as plutonium stockpiles and enrichment plants in places where their seizure for conversion to nuclear weapons would be relatively unlikely. Various denaturing procedures for nuclear materials might lengthen response times. Control or verification of missiles and perhaps long-range aircraft, if consistent with non-nuclear arms control arrangements, could add a few more hours to help delay the use of clandestine stockpiles that would offer the quickest form of renuclearization.

POLITICAL STABILITY AGAINST WAR IN THE INCREMENTAL WORLD

The technical procedures just described would be inadequate to meet severe challenges to denuclearization: a nation maintaining a large clandestine stockpile, a nation becoming dissatisfied with the system and directly challenging the denuclearization requirements, and nations or other political groups in such conflict as to create severe temptations toward renuclearization. These would be the fundamentally political problems of enforcement and of maintaining a relatively stable general peace.

The prevention of war is best considered by dividing forms of war initiation into two types: diplomatic and ideological. *Diplomatic war* is defined here as war decided upon or stumbled into by government leaders in pursuit of foreign policy goals, while *ideological war* is defined as war forced upon government leaders by deeply felt popular beliefs and domestic pressures. World War I, at least in its immediate triggering phase, is an example of diplomatic war; the American Civil War is the example, *par excellence*, of ideological war. Although it is obvious that most war initiations contain elements of both types, the distinction does point to two different aspects of war initiation: the diplomatic mechanism emphasizes the bargaining among sovereign leaders calculating their relative power and ability to influence one another, while the ideological mechanism emphasizes the underlying forces that are beyond the control of government leaders but shape the context in which they seek to pursue national goals.

This distinction is particularly important for the present study. Most far-reaching arms control and security proposals have assumed the effective sovereignty of national leaders and have concentrated on the prevention of diplomatic war. Yet the approach of this essay emphasizes the possibility that such sovereignty could change. Much more important is the reality that ideological war—led by new popular movements and inspired by new demands—is quite likely during the coming decades. Hence, the control of ideological war is by far the more interesting case. However, because the problems of diplomatic war are more fully understood, this study will begin with them before taking up the more complex questions of ideological war.

Diplomatic War in an Incremental World

Just as it was possible before nuclear weapons were invented, war deriving from the interplay of different nations' strategic ambitions and from miscalculations in anticipating other nations' reactions to strategic actions would remain possible in an incremental world. Such war would become more likely if escalation to the nuclear level were a more remote possibility. At the same time, such war and even its threat could create temptations toward arms competitions that could lead to retention or reconstruction of nuclear weapons.

Stability therefore would depend on keeping the risk of dip-

165

lomatic war low. A balance-of-power system based on conventional arms might arguably be possible and might be stabilized by non-nuclear arms control. (Arms control is likely to be much more effective in preventing diplomatic war than in preventing ideological war.) On the other hand, clandestine nuclear stockpiles and rapid nuclear rearmament might be perceived as decisive in a conflict. Although the potential for nuclear rearmament might create a new form of deterrence, nations would perhaps know less about other nations' nuclear capabilities than in today's world. The result could be diplomatic bargaining less stable than that in today's world, with strong temptations to violate the denuclearization agreement. The fundamental questions—whose answers require more judgment than logic—are how much arms control and what sort of international force would be adequate to provide reasonable stability, and how that level of stability would contrast with the stability that would be present in the type of nuclear world that is likely to exist in the absence of an international authority.

One approach might be to build on those political factors that have often made the balance-of-power concept relatively effective in maintaining peace. The concept might work successfully with conventional weapons; nuclear weapons are where it probably would fail. In the most successful eras of balance-of-power diplomacy, e.g., nineteenth-century Europe, several factors combined to produce success. National governments were confident masters of their foreign policy. Fairly broad consensus existed on the permissible limits of strategic behavior—on what would or would not produce a serious reaction. Weapons technology probably disfavored preemptive attack. And perhaps most important, military outcomes were relatively predictable; each nation could analyze the consequences of an action or of a war relatively accurately.

In the coming decades, with or without nuclear weapons, none of these requirements will be clearly satisfied. The leaders of the emerging great powers, such as Brazil, India, Iran, and also of such established powers as Japan, may find their strategic policies limited by domestic politics. Their intellectual viewpoints are likely to differ so drastically from those of one another and from those of the more traditional great powers that misunderstandings seem nearly inevitable. The weapons technology, the relative force levels in different nations, and the likelihood of outside military support are and will continue to be varying so rapidly that predictions of military outcomes seem likely to be wildly inaccurate. Current rates of political change in areas such as the Persian Gulf look like a recipe for another World War I.

These risks might be greatly alleviated by strengthening the factors that make balance-of-power diplomacy effective. A serious effort could be made to create contacts among the different new decisionmakers that would enable these people to understand one another and one another's domestic limitations and to develop a set of common rules that would help each to avoid inadvertently threatening those interests that another perceives as vital. A worldwide concert of Europe would be easier with today's communications technology, although it would reinforce the foreign policy mystique of national governments and might be no less antidemocratic than its nineteenth-century model. Formal or informal international organization could provide intelligence information and assistance in making military evaluations so as to reduce the chances of military miscalculation. Arms control could help shape weapons delivery systems and procurement patterns to take advantage of the potential defense dominance of the new high-accuracy weapons systems, to decrease the attractiveness of conventional preemption, and to decrease the immediate usefulness of any illegal nuclear weapons. Some arms control or asymmetrical force level adjustment is in any case essential to denuclearization because the current world depends on nuclear guarantees to stabilize such points of potential conventional force competition as Central Europe and the Far East. The possibility that hidden stocks of nuclear weapons might exist could retain the role it presumably has for Israel—to warn other states against extremes of diplomatic miscalculation that might threaten the ultimate existence of the putative stockpiler. The risk that hidden nuclear weapons would be decisive could then play the same role in discouraging overly aggressive conventional threats that the risk of nuclear escalation does today.

Thus, a balance-of-power system might be helped to operate

167

effectively in an incremental world in which nuclear weapons were proscribed while conventional forces were only weakly constrained. Building such a system, however, would require an almost universal détente, and it is hard to imagine the system surviving much serious strain. There would likely be many economic and ideological strains on the diplomatic system, some of which could be resolved through new international structures outside the security area, but others of which might lead nations to challenge the system directly or lead their neighbors to fear such a challenge. Moreover, the structure would tend to perpetuate power relationships deriving from the current nuclear era, because the possibility of a country's maintaining clandestine stockpiles or undertaking renuclearization—which would influence diplomatic bargaining—would be roughly proportional to its present-day nuclear force levels. (The political bargaining capability of France would remain greater than that of Brazil, for example, for a much longer time than without denuclearization.) Therefore, a traditional balance-of-power system would almost certainly be neither stable enough nor flexible enough in an incremental world. Both the short-term negotiability and the long-term survival of the incremental world would require creation of an intervention capability designed to meet, at a minimum, the clandestine stockpile and renuclearization problems.

The history of international intervention arrangements is not encouraging. The typical collective security sanction, as found in the original United Nations structure, amounts to a form of warfare potentially so costly to the sanctioner—whose vital national interests are usually not at stake—that the sanctionee can often discount it as irrelevant. This factor, together with the fact that in an incremental world, as today, the legitimacy of international authorities would be quite limited relative to that of national governments, suggests that intervention would have to be inexpensive and its perceived value high. For protection against renuclearization, therefore, the intervention would best be made early and, when possible, would entail a peaceful removal of only the relevant nuclear facilities of a nation believed to be reconstructing nuclear weapons. It is enrichment and reprocessing facilities and plutonium stockpiles that would have to be removed, so power supplies would not have to be interrupted. If it were almost certain that the nation was in fact building nuclear weapons and if there were resistance by the nation, one might have to consider an international disarming attack upon nuclear facilities. National or international intelligence systems could probably give enough warning so that the nuclear "sterilization" could be conducted before the offending nation obtained any usable nuclear weapons or at least before it had enough nuclear weapons to deter the international intervention. Thus, the international force would not require nuclear weapons unless the violator had a clandestine stockpile.

The problem of intervention against a clandestine stockpile would arise if a former major nuclear power defied the denuclearization agreement or if a strong conventional power threatened to use a previously clandestine stockpile to intervene in a conflict or to deter international intervention. This problem would be parallel to that of the invulnerability of the United States and the Soviet Union to sanctions under the UN system—they are too powerful to be defeated by a coalition of all other nations. Perhaps such intervention would continue to be impossible, and it might be wisest not to prepare for this situation, just as the framers of the United States Constitution chose not to resolve questions of nullification and secession; it might be impossible to negotiate a reasonable response in advance, and the problem might never arise. If a response is to be prepared, one alternative could be to maintain an international force with a number of nuclear weapons comparable to that which can be clandestinely hidden, to defend and disperse the weapons well, and to design a disarming attack using *conventional* forces, operating under the umbrella of the international nuclear deterrent. The burden of initiating nuclear escalation would thus be on the offending nation; depending on prior arms control arrangements, there might be some chance of effective intervention—assuming the clandestine weapons could be located after being announced. If they could not be located, a full-scale conventional war would be the only practical form of intervention. It is hoped, but not necessary, that the possibility of such a war and the existence of an international nuclear force in reserve would be enough to deter violation in the first place.

Alternatively, the intervention force against detected stockpiles could be non-nuclear. Its tactics would be essentially the same, but it would have to work without a deterrent umbrella and might be itself deterred. Nuclear or non-nuclear, however, the force would have to be able to assemble strong conventional capabilities.

The choice between no preparation, a non-nuclear intervention force, and a nuclear intervention force would depend on the probability of effectively deterring violations and on the ability adequately to control the international nuclear force. Nuclear weapons would probably be essential to the international force; otherwise the violator would almost certainly be appeased rather than deterred. Nuclear weapons would also give additional legitimacy to the intervention organization. Nuclear intervention forces perhaps would provide the only basis upon which non-nuclear nations would accept an incremental world model, for without such a force, the former nuclear nations would retain a permanent diplomatic advantage. Moreover, the problem of deciding when to use nuclear weapons may be relatively soluble. Intervention itself would be non-nuclear, perhaps even peaceful, and would be occasioned only upon violation of the denuclearization rules. The intervention force would use nuclear weapons only in response to a prior use of nuclear weapons. Thus, the decision to use nuclear weapons would follow relatively simple rules and depend more heavily on factual determinations than on political judgment, and the use of nuclear weapons in a strictly retaliatory mode would have relatively high innate legitimacy. This would be as favorable a decision-making situation as possible. Moreover, misuse of the nuclear weapons could be restricted through geographic dispersal of the forces among a number of nations. Thus, on balance, the intervention force probably should be supported by an international nuclear capability: while there would be a risk that clandestine stockpiles would be retained for protection against the international force, the benefits of an international nuclear deterrent to discourage nations from retaining clandestine nuclear stockpiles for blackmail purposes would appear to outweigh this risk.

Direct antinuclear intervention alone might not be enough, because conventional war could continue and could motivate reacquisition of nuclear weapons. Effective antinuclear intervention might not be possible against strong conventional powers. And to the degree that antinuclear verification and intervention arrangements were believed to be effective in eliminating clandestine stockpiles, conventional aggression and conflict might occur which otherwise would have been suppressed by the fear of hidden nuclear weapons. Moreover, demands of justice could sometimes be opposed to demands of denuclearization, decreasing the chance of effective antinuclear intervention. For example, the decision making just described would dictate intervention *against* a weak nation that had turned in desperation to nuclear weapons as a defense against a powerful aggressive nation. One would therefore be tempted—if not forced—to add a combination of arms control and a broader-purpose intervention authority to help avert conventional conflict and to protect weaker nations. The realities of collective action would again force one to settle for the weakest possible form of intervention that is still useful—perhaps that of defense. After proper decision making, an international force could offer to help defend the territory of any participant against attack. This system might be adequate to make attack pointless and therefore to prevent diplomatic war. A possible variant would be to permit forcible international seizure and destruction of conventional arms procured in violation of arms control rules. Although none of these variants need require that the international authority use nuclear weapons, they all would pose difficult political questions and require enormously difficult decision making. For example, in the defense case, the international authority might have to decide whether to defend South Africa if a rebellious faction were receiving foreign support. In the arms control case, effectiveness would probably require some imposition of arms control arrangements against the consent of some participants. One should not overestimate these difficulties. Comparable decisions are sometimes made by great powers and in the UN, but their political character is drastically different from that of the decision needed for antinuclear intervention.

The general bias of an incremental denuclearized world would be toward the powerful if there were no broader-purpose intervention force and toward the status quo if there were such a force. Security for all would probably be greater than in a heavily proliferated world, but the model leaves so little opportunity for readjustment of power relationships that it would not likely be stable for a long period. There would be great danger of a world split in which both sides would be willing to ignore the antinuclear rules.

Ideological War in an Incremental World

Ideological or popular war will be the more dangerous threat to international stability over the next several decades. Mass movements, or at least elite movements acting with mass support, are likely to come into conflict in ways that cannot be controlled by established leaders, particularly if national governments begin to lose their legitimacy. Recent examples of such conflict include the Arab-Israeli conflict, the religious conflict within Lebanon, and the Northern Ireland conflict. The era of conflict over decolonization may be nearly over, and ideological conflicts will likely change their character in developing nations as these nations enter a second generation of independence, but, nevertheless, conflicts will probably continue to arise from ethnic or religious antagonisms and from concerns about the treatment of communal groups in foreign lands. Economic conflict seems likely to encourage ideological war given the world's inequitable resource and income distribution as well as global unemployment. New transnational ideological movements analogous to communism are certainly possible.

These conflicts may often be manipulated by national leaders. They may also capture national leaders and pressure them to build military forces including nuclear weapons. Objectives can be unlimited, unlike those of diplomatic war: persons participating in ethnic and ideological conflict often dehumanize opponents, frequently place a positive value on martyrdom for the sake of the cause, and nearly always support temporary injustice for the sake of a greater future good. They are thus relatively likely to use any available nuclear weapons, even in the face of likely retaliation. The nation or international organization seeking to negotiate a compromise or maintain a temporary truce is itself likely to be seen as being compromised and to become the target of popular movements of terrorist attacks.

Arms control is not a very helpful option in preventing these conflicts, which tend to occur regardless of initial force levels. One must instead devise political ways to prevent the conflicts and, as a second step, establish security systems that discourage escalation of the conflicts to the nuclear level.

In an incremental denuclearized world, prevention of ideological war would require drastic improvement in the diplomatic and political structures through which nations adjust their objectives in deference to the political pressures upon one another. The extent of improvement would have to be enormous because ideological conflict would probably be more difficult to contain than in today's bipolar nuclear world—though probably easier to contain than in a proliferated nuclear world. In the bipolar nuclear world, the superpowers have it within their power to set limits on the scope of local conflicts, if necessary through intervention; in a proliferated world, the superpowers, out of fear of nuclear complications, would be more wary of playing a conflict-defusing or -containing role; in an incremental denuclearized world, the superpowers would find it both more difficult and less exigent to intervene to contain conflict. Nations would be so strongly tempted to build nuclear weapons out of fear of ideological war that the incremental world could be stable only if the potential for widespread ideological conflict were generally believed to be low.

Some of the conflicts could possibly be avoided by new institutions that were basically extensions of existing ones. For example, those economic issues in which cooperation would be in everyone's interest—such as many global macroeconomic problems—would be amenable to solution by more substantial efforts of international organizations. But there are issues, such as resource allocation, which might not be amenable to solution by traditional forms of multilateral diplomacy. At the least, international decision making in these areas would be much more difficult, and the right to withdraw from international organizations might have to be restricted. Truly heroic national commitments to international order would be necessary.

Ethnic and religious conflicts would present even greater difficulty because it is not clear that any form of institution can prevent them. Sometimes an international organization might help avert such conflicts by helping to rectify the conditions that give rise to disputes rather than acting only to block the outbreak of hostilities or to terminate them once begun. A regulatory power, such as an international body to protect human rights, might help control ethnic and religious conflicts. One might also establish rules against unilateral intervention by foreign nations in such conflicts. Although the *assistance* techniques and the restrictions on international subversion would infringe upon traditional national sovereignties less severely than would the *regulatory* techniques (which would infringe upon traditions of national sovereignty dating at least from Westphalia), all the techniques would require extremely difficult political decision making. Moreover, as the Ulster conflict and even the history of desegregation in the United States indicate, any enforcement efforts are difficult, even with rather great legitimacy on the side of the enforcers. Perhaps an adequately narrow definition of international powers could be negotiated, but it is hard to visualize a system of international prevention of ethnic conflict that would not be a major political step toward a centralized world model. So one's only hope for an incremental world structure is that an international world emphasizing the sort of positive assistance suggested above, with enforcement powers limited to those ethnic conflicts deemed most likely to lead to international war, might prevent conflict often enough to avoid renuclearization.

The settlement of disputes through the aid of international authorities might be possible at a later stage in the development of a specific ideological conflict. For example, an international authority could bolster national authorities by offering legal reasons to reject public demands for military action before those demands become irresistible. The techniques used by Henry Kissinger in the Middle East—combining negotiation, dispute settlement, and economic and military assistance—also suggest a useful model for international arrangements. Informal arrangements applied by the great powers could be more flexible, include offers to provide or withdraw military support, and have quite effective intelligence support. On the other hand, international arrangements might have much more legitimacy and thus could more readily impose a military solution in the extreme cases. It is still not clear, however, when outside decision making would be successful in solving disputes that could not be solved locally, particularly if the conflicts arose from public movements and the outsider's legitimacy were subject to any question.

After an ideological conflict began, intervention forces would have to be available to resolve the conflict before it lasted long enough to encourage the development of nuclear capabilities. Creation of such forces would require wide consensus among the great powers. Except to meet the secession of a substantial alliance from the entire international structure, such forces would probably be used more in a peacekeeping mode than in an enforcement mode and would certainly not require nuclear weapons. The power to impose a peacekeeping force would still have to be greater than under the current UN structure, which requires at least the coerced consent of the participants, because the international force would also have to shape the explicit posttruce status quo. Current UN peacekeeping often simply freezes the conflict, allowing it to flare up again after a period of rearmament and bitterness; the Cyprus and Middle East conflicts and the Indo-Pakistan War are obvious examples. If the goal is to be the prevention of nuclear rearmament, underlying problems must be resolved; such resolution would require some willingness to choose between different claims and to intervene in traditionally internal affairs.

Some ideological conflicts will appear as revolutions rather than as international disputes. The legitimacy of national governments may be in doubt, and new weapons, such as precision-guided missiles, may favor revolutionary forces over central governments. The global dangers resulting from ideological revolution might also be substantial: revolutionary groups might seek nuclear weapons. The government defending itself could readily argue that it needed increased forces in order to quash the rebellion. Neighboring governments, who might be aligned with one side or the other, could similarly argue a need for increased arms levels. And many governments would fear that the revolution could be exported. Thus, even a revolutionary struggle could produce temptations toward renuclearization.

One possible response could be to attempt to discourage revolutions themselves. Presumably, relatively healthy economies and substantial democratic institutions should help prevent revolutions. Many observers have argued in precisely the opposite direction, however, and much more analysis of the ways in which democratization and economic advancement affect both national and international stability is fundamental to any effort to design a new world order. Another response could be to work specifically to prevent revolutions from having nuclear effects, for example, by detaching the nuclear industry from national control and removing all dangerous nuclear materials during a revolution. Finally, efforts could be made to localize the domestic conflict to ensure that it is not spread to foreign nations. Doing this would probably require that foreign nations not be permitted to aid national or insurgent forces. International forces might seal borders or enforce an embargo; such embargoes would likely affect the outcome of the conflict because the national forces and the insurgent forces would depend differentially on arms supplies, and the abilities or decisions of the international force would differentially affect supplies to the two sides.

If the peacekeeping power in an incremental world is to have enough authority to shape truce patterns or to apply embargoes, it would have to be placed under broadened political control. Some of the developing world already regards peacekeeping as a mask for great-power intervention; greater authority would increase the force of this argument. Political control would require a carefully designed international structure for making decisions to commit and control the intervention force. It would require legal limitations on the activities of the force and the international organization. It might require the avoidance of economic dependence of the international organization on particular nations and a balance between the military capabilities of the international organization and those of particular nations. The decision making would be even more difficult than that needed for intervention to prevent conventional diplomatic warfare. Political and ideological splits would necessarily be associated with such decisions, while they might sometimes be avoided in the diplomatic-warfare context. Fortunately, the toughest decisions would be required only after a war broke out, and during war nations would likely be particularly supportive in stopping the conflict. But a substantial divergence among major powers or a deadlock in the international organization could still break the system.

The problem of dealing with nuclear terrorism would seem likely, on balance, to be little changed by the proscription of nuclear weapons. There would be fewer nuclear weapons available for theft, and security arrangements in the nuclear industry would also likely be more effective. In an incremental world, the only really new opportunity for terrorists to obtain nuclear weapons would lie in the possibility that a nation might supply weapons from a clandestine stockpile to terrorists or covert agents. But the arguments against such supply would be quite strong, resting on both inhibitions against the use of nuclear weapons and fears of the untrustworthiness of the terrorists or even of the agents. Even the use of nuclear weapons by terrorists would pose relatively few new problems. One finds it hard to visualize the need for a nuclear response against a nuclear terrorist; this threat would not require the international authority to possess nuclear weapons. The relevant defenses to terrorism would still be the traditional ones: careful police work, maximum physical security around nuclear material, and international accords to deny safe havens to terrorists. One would anticipate greater integration of counterespionage services; this might call for international agreements to protect against abusive actions by those services, although national civil liberties arrangements might suffice.

Non-nuclear terrorism could become a more serious problem in an incremental world than in today's world if, as national governments began to lose legitimacy and were perceived as weak, citizens became more prone to condone or even support terrorism. At the cost of still more interference with national structures, one might try to ensure that there were enough outlets for effective political activity to minimize the incentives toward terrorism. The more likely response would be that national governments, learning to cooperate in other areas, would cooperate against their citizens to halt terrorism by forceful means. A repressive police structure marked by substantial exchange of information and responsibility among different national police forces would be a disturbing possibility and could necessitate an international response to protect civil liberties.

The total array of intervention mechanisms that would be needed for the incremental world appears overly elaborate. The design of such mechanisms would reflect political and military balances of the time when they were created; after a decade or two these balances might change significantly enough that the intervention system would lose credibility. To renegotiate these arrangements successfully, to foresee conflicts accurately, and to resolve them early would require both good luck and continued goodwill on the part of all major powers. And it is not clear what pressures would lead nations to maintain such long-term diplomacy. The pressures and viewpoints would be substantially like those of today's world, a world that, at least in the absence of widespread proliferation, poses many of the same problems.

In the nuclear world, the effect of breakdown is war; in the incremental denuclearized world, the effect would likely be nuclear rearmament in unpredictable and asymmetrical patterns that could lead to war. In either world the amount of power to be transferred to an international authority is a matter of judgment, for no one can predict quite how much tension the system can accept. An international organization could help resolve crises, but it could also provoke crises because its power balances, reflected in voting schemes, might shift less flexibly than those reflected in conventional diplomacy.

If the incremental world worked, it could be a way station to an internationalized world, because the intervention process might help build international legitimacy and attract citizen pressure to the international organization. If it failed without war, it could be a way station to repression by a few nations able to act in concert and dominate others in the arenas of both power politics and international organization. The inflexibility of the incremental model and its risks of instability and repression leave one doubtful

178

that it would be an improvement over any but the most pessimistic projections for a nuclear world.

POLITICAL STABILITY AGAINST WAR IN THE INTERNATIONALIZED WORLD

In the internationalized world, citizen loyalties would shift substantially to an international government. The remnants of national governments would retain a role somewhere between that of the states of the United States and the national governments in the European Community. The dominant form of conflict would be, at most, a sort of ideological civil war resulting from the maneuverings of leaders divided more by class or racial group than by territorial location. Where the stability requirements of an incremental world were cast in terms of international organization and of arms control, those for an internationalized world can be cast in terms of the allocation of power between the international level and the local level and in terms of the character of the transfer of citizen loyalty.

Diplomatic War in an Internationalized World

Ideally, in an internationalized world, the defense roles of national governments would be so weakened that diplomatic warfare would become extremely distant from the normal aspiration of national governments. This is not quite so utopian as it seems. In essence, it happened to provincial rulers during the transition from feudalism to the nation-state system and to the states of the United States during the transition associated with the Civil War. Some current trends suggest movement in a parallel direction. The role of strategic calculations in diplomacy is weakening in some important areas—such as among the Western European nations. The armed forces of many developing nations are becoming police forces, defining their role as domestic rather than external defense. Most important of all, national governments are more and more defining their mission in economic rather than defense terms.

A great transfer of legitimacy from national to international authorities would be necessary to make the world so clearly internationalized that diplomatic war became unlikely. The relative legitimacy of the federal government and the states in America seemed to be creating a stable pattern in the early nineteenth century, but proved unable to avoid a conflict that had some diplomatic overtones. If the ideological conflicts had been less intense, the pattern would most likely have been stable. In general, the key criterion for stability is probably that the central government be seen as an acceptable decision maker whose decisions are likely to be effective. Citizens and local leaders must expect relatively reasonable and enforceable resolutions of conflict from the central authority and anticipate that resort to armed force would be counterproductive.

Historically, centralization has usually proceeded through military conquest and a transfer of legitimacy to the victor as the only possible guarantor of security. In the contemporary situation, such conquest is both unlikely and undesirable. A more plausible contemporary mechanism of centralization is covert conquest based on, for example, intelligence operations and economic penetration. This pattern is equally undesirable. Therefore, given that national governments are unlikely to abandon their power willingly, the mechanism prescribed in this essay is one in which legitimacy would be transferred by citizens themselves: citizens would look to the international authority rather than to national authorities for security and for some of the benefits of government. After the transfer of legitimacy, national leaders would have three types of reasons to hesitate at the use of force: their own subjective sense of the legitimacy of the international order, their expectation that international authorities would intervene decisively, and their fear that citizens would follow the international rather than the national authority.

There are a range of techniques that could help support the military power of the international authority. Presumably, some national military forces would remain during a long transition; this would probably be politically necessary and essential for responding to any resurgence of nationalism. In normal times, military forces could be commanded internationally. Military units could be recruited and located in patterns designed to discourage national identification—the transition from state militias to a unified federal force was an important aspect of nation-building in the United States. The control and financing of formal intervention could be subject to international organs directly responsible to citizens rather than to national governments. This direct relationship would give increased legitimacy to the central government and also encourage citizens to look to international organs rather than national governments for protection from abuses by the force. An empirical example is again available in American history: the substitution of direct election of Congress for election by state governments was an important aspect of the relative growth of federal legitimacy. Although many other historical forces were involved, these legitimacy-creating factors were more important than formal restrictions; state militias withered as significant strategic forces without ever being formally restricted. (The Constitution in fact prohibits such restriction.) If international legitimacy were being supported, it might not even matter if certain concessions—such as permitting national forces to be withdrawn to national command under some conditions—were made to traditional national sovereignty.

A transfer of legitimacy could nevertheless create a stable world structure only if both citizens and national leaders believed the structure to be capable of meeting the challenge of a resurgent national government. (The problem of a large-scale global division, analogous to the American Civil War, would be more a problem of ideological conflict than of diplomatic conflict and will be considered below in that context.) Nuclear terrorism or a national government that retained clandestine nuclear weapons and sought to use them on its own behalf, unsupported by popular legitimacy, would present only a weak challenge; in an internationalized world, there would be little political difference between terrorists and such a government. The stronger challenge would be that of a government that—perhaps following a revolution—reevoked nationalistic fervor among its people and, in the worst case, also retained a clandestine stockpile and recruited a new military force. An international force would clearly be necessary in this situation, and it would more likely be available in the internationalized world than in the incremental world because of the former's greater international legitimacy. In addition, in an internationalized world, the intervention force might be able to use policelike techniques as well as military techniques and perhaps benefit from some mass support within the offending nation. Furthermore, as a nation appeared likely to approach such a violation, the international authority could seek to discourage the nation by removing dangerous nuclear facilities and by exercising whatever power it had over troop locations. While still depending on the pattern of retained national conventional forces, the need for the international authority to have nuclear weapons would be much less compelling than in the incremental world.

The international authority's legitimacy would depend partly on the effectiveness of its intervention capability, which in turn would depend partly on its legitimacy: the internationalized world could work only if it were expected to work. Assuming that the necessary threshold of legitimacy had been crossed, this world would clearly provide far greater stability against diplomatic war than the incremental world or even a predictable nuclear world. Moreover, since federal systems have innate checks and balances and since the most likely internationalized world would be one in which the international forces were directly responsible to citizens, this world would likely be relatively effective in preventing the misuse of force.

Ideological War in an Internationalized World

The internationalized world may represent the end of international strategic politics, but it would certainly not represent the end of politics. Ideological conflicts would still arise and could create conflicts like the Paris Commune uprising or the recent Lebanese and Portuguese conflicts. Some of them could spread to other areas that had analogous problems or political ties with the warring groups, as racial riots tend to occur in a number of cities at the same time and as separatist movements in different parts of a nation tend to become active at roughly the same time. There could even be division within, or an effort to withdraw from, the international government, analogous to the American Civil War.

Ideological conflict might be more likely in such a world because of the weakening of the legitimacy of national governments and the greater fluidity of political relationships. These conflicts, however, would be unlikely to lead to *widespread* ideological war and particularly unlikely to lead to nuclear war. Normally, the contending factions would seek only to influence specific policies of the national and international governments rather than to achieve the more formidable and more abstract goal of transfer of sovereignty. Conflicts would be likely to reflect immediate human concerns, and strategic weight would be given to political rather than military or geographic positions. Nuclear weapons and clandestine nuclear stockpiles would be less relevant to the likely forms of conflict, and construction of nuclear weapons might be very difficult for those entities that might want such weapons. Thus, as international allegiance became relatively strong, national loyalties relatively weak, and the axes of probable conflict as likely to follow class or ethnic patterns as national patterns, the likelihood of large-scale war would be minimized.

There is a standard shopping list of issues—environment, resources, etc.—often said to be most effectively resolved through international decision making. Even though these technical issues may become more important over the next decades, they are unlikely to offer enough popular appeal to support a transfer of legitimacy to an international organization. In order to transfer legitimacy and political attention to any central institution, it is essential to create political and representative institutions and to develop services that the central organization can provide more effectively than local organizations. So far, the centralization in the above issue areas has consisted primarily of technical coordination of national political decisions, while the bulk of the political input has remained at the national level. And international technical organizations have proven unable, at least in the short run, to be a very strong force toward international integration.

One must therefore look to more far-reaching methods to create and maintain international legitimacy. Each of these methods would involve political choices that would appeal to some and not to others. The obvious, but politically difficult, example is international wealth transfer. The federal government's control of the income tax has clearly been a crucial lever behind its increase in power compared with state governments over the last half-century. If the concept of a subsidy-allocating welfare state survived in the developed world and were transferable to the international order, it could be a potent force for legitimizing international government, although it could also create a new basis for ideological conflict. Some hints of the emergence of possible transnational political action in this area are present in the growing developed-world concern about income distribution in the developing nations. The more and more frequent linking of questions of income distribution and global macroeconomic problems could also spur internationalization.

A second way in which international legitimacy could be fostered would be to give the international organization the power to intervene to right specific wrongs in what was traditionally the national order. In the United States, the enforceability of the Bill of Rights through federal decisions has been a potent source of federal power. International intervention in such critical areas as treatment of domestic minorities would probably not be effective for a long time—it has been hard enough in the United States for a federal government whose power is clear and has perhaps been possible only because of the prior legitimacy resulting from military victory in the Civil War. Neither would the support of human rights always be popular with majorities and dominant groups. Nevertheless, one might visualize an international Bill of Rights, to be phased in over time, which would slowly build constituencies and gain legitimacy through success in relatively limited forms of intervention. There are areas, such as ensuring higher education for minorities or arbitrating disputes between host countries and multinational corporations, that might be amenable to international intervention in an early phase.

The traditional source of legitimacy is the maintenance of order. Success at maintaining order is almost always popular and seems to bring legitimacy automatically. To generate support for internationalization, the order maintained need not be that of traditional criminal law. It could instead be concerned with specifically international crimes, such as terrorism or aspects of narcotics trafficking, as well as the prevention of war. These efforts could appear repressive to some while being considered beneficial by others. One also would face the problem that legitimacy and war prevention depend on each other. The central question at this point in the analysis, however, is whether an internationalized order, once achieved, could work effectively.

All these potential sources of legitimacy—income transfer, support of rights, and support of order—imply politics. There could never be a full consensus in any of the relevant areas: the positions of today's developed countries are far enough away from consensus among themselves, and there are even greater differences if one includes the positions of revolutionary cultures such as China, Tanzania, and Cambodia or those of the various traditional cultures in developing nations. Accommodation among these differing viewpoints would require political representation that, while a threat to existing national leadership, could be a source of strength to an international government by providing legitimacy. Direct popular election of representatives to the international organization would be highly desirable to increase this international legitimacy and to encourage the referral of problems to the international level. The internationalized world would thus become somewhat independent of national governments and would be able to deploy even limited resources in ways that would build constituencies and encourage transnational political alignments.

In addition to institutions to meet its security responsibilities, the international organization would have to have institutions to enforce its routine decisions—for example, to settle an investment dispute, to distribute food assistance, or to open a university for minorities. Even though many of these decisions would probably be viewed as benign by national governments, they would not necessarily be viewed as benign by all within the affected nations. Thus, some sort of centralized judicial system and a small marshal- or sheriff-type enforcement organization would be needed. The international government would not become the focus of political pressure and could not gain legitimacy unless its routine decisions were effective.

These characteristics—powers affecting some economic matters, some human rights matters, and some security matters; a directly responsible political authority; and a routine enforcement capability—would be the most essential if legitimacy were to be transferred. At some critical point, pressures for change would begin to operate in an amendment process at the international rather than the national level. The location of this critical point would be a matter of judgment. The process ought also to include a channel open to the people acting alone; the system could then evolve to meet new problems. The transfer of legitimacy would probably require greater international authority than that of the European Community, which lacks security functions or very significant direct representation, and less than that of the American federal government, which has great control over local economic and political institutions. Such a transfer of power would be substantial, but once it had occurred the system would be inherently stable against conversion of group-to-group conflicts into nation-to-nation conflicts in which nuclear weapons were relevant. "Normal" politics would replace military politics, and national incentives to maintain military forces would decrease of their own accord.

The security function—the way the system would deal with the unavoidable instabilities that remained—deserves special attention, particularly since it would contribute to the system's legitimacy. Terrorism would probably be a less serious problem in a liberal internationalized world than in today's or an incremental world: the increased opportunity for political representation would probably decrease the incentives toward terrorism. The response to the terrorism that might remain, however, would necessarily emphasize cooperation among police and security forces and thus would increase the risks of an illiberally centralized world. One would have to rely on the internationalized world's innate federalism and dependence on the citizen to provide safeguards against repressive action.

Ethnic and religious conflict would pose a very difficult problem for an internationalized system, as for any other system. Pressures that led to military conflict in a world where modification of national policies and boundaries was the key dimension of change would instead lead to political efforts in the international agency. When this process failed and armed conflict arose, international intervention would be necessary, but it would enjoy much greater legitimacy and a somewhat greater ability to deal with root causes of the conflict than in the incremental case. However, in the Ulster and Lebanese conflicts, even this higher level of intervention has proven able at most to contain the conflict; nevertheless, the linkages between international power politics and the internal conflicts that mark both of those examples would be weaker in an internationalized world, because outside powers would no longer vie for influence and the supply of arms could be controlled more effectively. Moreover, there would be more effective channels for dealing with the dispute after a cease-fire than there are now. A failure of the nation-state system to resolve such disputes might even provide the political context for transfers of authority to the international level. So while ethnic and ideological conflict would remain in an internationalized world, this world pattern would offer more promise of resolving such conflict than would alternative patterns.

The international model would have a special instability of its own: the possibility that the international organization could promote world polarization, leading to a global ideological conflict. Such conflict could take the form of a global revolution—classes or social groups working in parallel in different nations to modify the distribution of power at the international level. Or it could assume a more territorial form, such as capitalist against communist or North against South, that would present a greater risk of renuclearization. Such conflict might be more likely in the internationalized world than in the incremental world or the current world. For example, the possibility of a worldwide North-South conflict seems slight in today's world: individual nations of the South are likely to become co-opted and identify with the North as they gain in power, thus making creation of a powerful alliance within the challenging South more difficult. In the internationalized world, however, the international political institution itself might assist in this polarization by fostering regional identity and politically strengthening the otherwise weaker region, as its American federal analogue did before the Civil War. One cannot define security scenarios that would resolve this problem, and initial force levels would influence only some forms of global ideological conflict. It would be possible only to seek politically to avert the problem—for example, by ensuring that

187

the redistribution of economic and political power occurs at a reasonable pace or by promoting a balance within the international organization between those political alliances that are closely identified with geographic regions and those that are closely identified with social and economic groups. The stability of these political balances would be important in defining the international organization's initial powers, which in turn would shape its agenda and its politics.

Evaluation of the internationalized model requires acceptance of its rather sweeping basic assumptions. Nevertheless, leaving aside all consideration regarding the transition and assuming some wisdom in the design of the international organization, this model would offer by far the greatest promise of success in flexibly meeting the ideological conflicts that could tear apart the incremental world and today's nuclear world. The model would require national denuclearization, for the existence of large, known national stockpiles would make international legitimacy impossible to achieve. The model would probably also be the only one that could be really adaptive to the continued possibility of renuclearization.

SUMMARY OF THE TWO MODELS

A denuclearized world would require substantial international inspection and control of the nuclear industry. Conventional war would also have to be substantially restricted in order to weaken incentives toward renuclearization and to avoid a breakdown whose outcome could be catastrophic, given the chances of clandestine nuclear stockpiles and differential abilities to renuclearize. The two models offer radically different solutions to this problem of conventional war: the incremental model is built around minimum restraints, while the international model is designed to make conventional war as obsolete and irrelevant as possible.

The concept of the incremental world rests on the judgment that the nation-state could be preserved when nuclear weapons were essentially eliminated, and the concept's political support rests on the perception that the nation-state could be preserved *only if* nuclear weapons were essentially eliminated. Most political loyalty would continue to be entrusted to nation-states, and stability would depend on the nations' ability to resolve conflicts through careful diplomacy. Substantial new international authorities would nevertheless be necessary, for example, to assist the balancing of power and to deal cooperatively with economic and social problems. Diplomacy would have to forestall conflict at a very early stage, and some of the international organizations would almost certainly require powers far beyond those of current international bodies. The need to prevent conventional war would also require some international intervention arrangements to stabilize borders, to seize incipient national nuclear forces, and to conduct peacekeeping. This force would best have access to nuclear weapons. After the transition, conventional arms procurement would not necessarily have to be limited greatly, but the elimination of nuclear guarantees would probably dictate some control of conventional arms during the transition phase. Substantial control of conventional arms could be beneficial by reducing the size of the intervention force required to put down non-nuclear war and by reducing the risk of diplomatic war.

The dominant political motivation in the incremental world would be the prevention of conflict through elaborate military and political institutions and careful, traditional diplomacy. The international authorities would necessarily be heavily dependent on, and essentially in alliance with, national governments. International decision making to enforce denuclearization would be relatively easy, but that required to restrain conventional war would be so difficult as to leave one doubtful of long-term stability. As an alliance of national governments, such a world could become repressive in its efforts to contain revolution and ideological war. More likely, it would fail to resolve conflict successfully and collapse, as did the elaborate European structures in the 1930s. This would be quite similar to the non-nuclear world that produced World Wars I and II—it is doubtful that it could maintain the necessary level of responsibility or that its institutions would hold up in crises. And the rapid renuclearization that would be likely to mark the collapse of such a world would be exceedingly dangerous, for the nation with even a small head start at rearmament could practice nuclear blackmail with impunity.

The internationalized world would seek to prevent conflict by giving an international political body enough responsibility that it would attract the pressures for change that now operate upon national governments. National governments would thus become less and less important foci of the political pressures and aspirations of peoples. For the international body to be effective enough to achieve such a transfer of legitimacy, it would have to have relatively great powers over some traditionally domestic affairs and have a political organ directly responsible to citizens. Diplomatic conflict, it is to be hoped, would become obsolete as a result of this shift in legitimacy, and ideological conflict would take forms less likely to escalate to nuclear warfare. The international organization would still have to have some military intervention capability, but the need for international nuclear weapons would be less crucial than in an incremental world. Conventional arms could either be controlled at the outset or be left for ultimate limitation in response to political pressures working toward the weakening of national militaries.

The motivating philosophy would be the promotion of local political change through the establishment of an internationalized order. Rather than being in alliance with national governments, the international government would be in alliance with forces within nations, particularly the citizenry. Stability would depend in part on the character of these alliances; one would face a dilemma in choosing between alliances with the powerful forces, which would more likely be helpful in transferring power, and alliances with the weak elements, which would more likely be helpful in promoting international legitimacy and averting long-term conflict. The major dangers for this world would be "seizure" of the international order by special interest groups, its use for either repressive or revolutionary ends, and its breakup in a world-level civil war. In fact, the transition period, one of mixed national and international legitimacy, would probably be conducive to ideological war.

The fundamental advantage of an internationalized system over an incremental system would be that the institutions of the former would more likely be self-reinforcing and resilient than those of the latter. If diplomatic war were believed the more likely threat and were judged not difficult to avoid through partial measures, one might choose the incremental system. Likewise, if economic development were an adequate way to prevent ideological war, the incremental system might again be better, at least at first, because individual nations could probably operate more effectively in the economic area than could an inchoate international organization. However, ideological war is almost certainly the more serious threat in the coming decades, and it can be resolved only through power transfers, which would occur more easily in an internationalized system than in an incremental one. Moreover, combined resource, environmental, and population pressures might ultimately threaten the continued détente necessary to maintain the incremental system's stability. At this point, the internationalized system would be the only practical one. Nation-states might even be eager to cast off some of their responsibility!

The implicit alliance structure would also affect the future of individual freedom. A plausible risk in the incremental model is that national governments might become repressive in an effort to maintain the independence of their international policies and to control ideological war. On the other hand, the centralization imposed through the internationalized system would be one in which the world organization sought to look past the national governments. The foundation could be laid with individual freedom in mind, but one could not be certain that ideas of freedom and representation would grow along with internationalization.

THREE

The Transition to a Nuclear-Free World

The two worlds just discussed are both so utopian that it is hard to visualize any process of transition to them even by, say, the year 2000. At the very least, substantial cooperation from many nations would be required—the kind that might follow a major crisis and could subordinate secondary concerns such as the commercial benefits of the arms trade, the bargaining requirements of noncrucial bureaucratic and political actors, and the traditional but marginal disagreements on details of verification or strategic asymmetries. However, basic security problems, political goals, and philosophical positions can realistically be expected to evolve only slowly.

Ultimately, such a far-reaching transition would not be made simply because a pattern for transition existed which appeared to offer a reasonable compromise, or even benefits, to all participants. Only under the pressure of a great sense of urgency would political actors make the difficult political choices required in negotiating a transition. Hence, it is just as important to consider the character of the pressures and political choices that could lead to acceptance of a transition plan as it is to postulate a series of balanced transition phases.

Although the politics of the transition would differ in the case of each of the two world modes, there would be several major barriers in common. Three will be given special attention in this study. First, nuclear deterrence among the superpowers would have to be liquidated—and the liquidation of deterrence would require a broad range of associated changes. Second, both world models would require an elaborate and difficult alteration in the relations between North and South—between the traditional powers and the challenging newly nuclear, near-nuclear, and non-nuclear powers. Third, both models, the second more so than the first, would require changes in the relationship between a citizen and his or her government.

THE RELATIONSHIP AMONG SUPERPOWERS: NUCLEAR DETERRENCE AND SUBNUCLEAR CONFLICT

As pointed out at the beginning of this essay, nuclear deterrence cannot be absolutely liquidated. At best, the time from decision to destruction can be lengthened: from the half-hour characteristic of contemporary rocketry to the half-day that would be necessary for transporting clandestine weapons around the world, and perhaps eventually to the half-year required for reconstructing nuclear weapons technology. If the risk of abrogation of a denuclearization pact and unbalanced reconstruction of nuclear weapons is to be reduced, much would be gained by the increased time: decreased pressure on decision makers, greater chance for others to intervene in the decision-making process by political or military means, and less chance of effectively delivering a large-scale attack.

The usual response to calls for liquidation of superpower deterrence (although the above qualifications are not usually applied) is that liquidation would require passage through a series of progressively lower force levels that would be unstable in terms of deterring preemptive attacks. This problem could be avoided, however. Lawrence Weiler has suggested leaving the last nuclear weapons on submarines that would move out of range of their target nations at preset and observable times.[2] Leonard Beaton (for other reasons) has suggested inserting UN authority into the chain of command of nuclear weapons forces, so that the weapons would be available to national authorities only after a predeter-

[2]Verbal communication to author, 1976.

194

mined time delay or after an international decision had been made.[3] The time delay could subsequently be lengthened as weapons were destroyed at an appropriate rate. Exchange of observers among control rooms and careful phasing of the destruction of delivery systems of different speeds and vulnerabilities might also help resolve the problem. As discussed in Chapter 2, the problem of ultimate clandestine stockpiles would also not be so severe as it might first appear. If small open stockpiles were allowed for some time, or if the international organization retained nuclear weapons for a generation or so, the clandestine stockpile problem might be even less serious.

Thus, maintaining strategic stability in the process of liquidating deterrence would probably not be the hard problem; more difficult would be the military concomitants of, and political motivations for, liquidation. A number of military changes would clearly have to accompany the end of deterrence. From the viewpoint of the West, for example, renunciation of deterrence would be impossible without alternate provisions for the security of Europe and Japan. Barring an increase in local defense forces, a comprehensive European arms control agreement as well as general force reductions for the Soviet Union and perhaps the United States would be required. These would be difficult to achieve without corresponding Chinese reductions on the Soviets' eastern front and new security arrangements for Eastern Europe, and so on. Thus, pragmatic analysis shows that in the transition period, substantial conventional arms control would have to accompany the proscription of nuclear weapons, simply because nuclear weapons still have their defensive uses. Nevertheless, one could certainly devise a scheme of force reductions and a rate of growth of the international force and its powers that would leave each nation as safe as it is now at each point in the process and would lead to a denuclearized world with a balanced correlation of conventional arms.

The first steps would be for the United States and the Soviet Union to open up nuclear industries and nuclear production

[3]*The Reform of Power,* Viking, New York, 1972, pp. 201–211.

capabilities so that diversion to weapons programs could be detected and estimates of nuclear force levels refined and for the two countries to decrease their strategic forces to a point consistent with defense against any holdout nations and against nuclear threats to each nation's allies in Europe and Asia. Conventional force reductions, perhaps coupled with the creation of an international intervention force, or an international control structure for the use of strategic nuclear weapons could stabilize borders and permit further strategic reductions. The intervention forces and control structures would have to be created no later than the penultimate reductions of nuclear forces to some token level that would be maintained until the final reductions were made.

Negotiation of all arms control agreements has been extremely difficult, and no agreements to date have cut forces as deeply as suggested here. The practical political barriers are mind-boggling. Agreements so far, of political necessity, have had to be symmetrical. One can visualize the proliferation of Jackson Amendments that would follow upon the first phase of the liquidation effort! Nations have been unwilling to accept deep or asymmetrical reductions for the sake of the limited benefits following from arms control; they would accept such agreements only under strong political pressure or for the sake of a more profound goal. Only if such pressures and goals became active could the transition become conceivable; technical details could then be worked out as they were in the best days of the General Agreement on Tariffs and Trade, of the European Economic Community, or of the writing of the United States Constitution. It is in this sense that political will would be important.

Both the United States and the Soviet Union are heavily committed to incrementalism, both have respected the vetoes of several powerful domestic bureaucracies, and neither's recent policies have revealed much willingness to transfer power to international organizations. Of the two, the Soviet Union has been much less flexible. It is not only the captive of conservative institutions, it is also the captive of an ideology that is conservative in effect, albeit radical in form. The Soviet Union might assume that it could obtain superiority through conventional forces and clandestine stockpiles. In any case, the Soviets would be unlikely to risk destroying socialism in one nation even for the sake of a more flexible world political order that might further socialism in many nations. Nor would the Soviet Union likely give away its status as one of the world's two leading nuclear nations; this status is important in spreading communism elsewhere in the world. According to the conventional Kremlinological wisdom, the SALT agreements were possible only because they facilitated the purchase of technology from the West and codified Soviet-American parity and hegemony. The Soviet leadership's acquiescence may have been contingent on discouraging internal dissent and ensuring that the agreements not seriously affect their own military-industrial complex. If this conventional wisdom is correct, Soviet opposition to either type of denuclearized world would be quite strong. If denuclearization were acceptable at all, it would require a motivation substantially stronger than the mild mix of economics, strategy, and symbolism that produced today's arms control agreements. Although domestic upheaval might change Soviet policies, this study must assume a continued Leninist leadership unwilling to transcend the boundaries of its innate conservatism.

One motivation that might conceivably overcome this intrinsic conservatism of the nuclear powers would be the growth of general doubt about the continued stability of the nuclear world, doubt that would have to be coupled with a vision of a feasible alternative. The combination of doubt and vision could possibly move the American public and even the Soviet leadership. Some doubt about nuclear deterrence is perhaps present now; it would become more substantial following an accident or a near-war and might also develop as the number of nuclear powers increased. The vision of an alternative is still needed.

A second motivation would be a perception of the need for more decision-making time during nuclear crises, a need often emphasized by national leaders on both sides. This motivation would be especially significant because it would correspond so closely to the chief benefit that denuclearization clearly could provide—more time. Redefining nuclear arms control with the objective of providing increased decision time, rather than of reducing overall numbers or increasing formal strategic stability

197

might be useful. For example, during early phases nuclear submarines could be located beyond the range of their targets or control room observers could be exchanged. During later phases missiles could be eliminated or warheads stored separately from delivery systems. Although one would have to be very careful to avoid the dangers of deception and preemption, the increased decision time created by such steps could be extremely useful and lead logically to denuclearization.

A third motivation would be the need to forestall nuclear proliferation. The United States and the Soviet Union both have reason to fear proliferation and might have to accept significant limitations on their own forces in order to persuade potential proliferants to accept restrictions. This pressure could be the most effective one; its force would be the greatest if the threats of proliferation emanated from areas especially important to the two nations. Serious European consideration of an integrated nuclear force, for example, might create the needed pressure.

However, these pressures are unlikely to be strong enough to alter American and Soviet nuclear policies in the near future. And in any case, the agreements they might produce would more likely lead to an incremental denuclearized world than to an internationalized one.

Nevertheless, there is at least one transition pattern that would appear in principle to meet stability concerns and that might offer some potential for the public participation that would be characteristic of the international model. This is Leonard Beaton's proposal for inserting the UN into the chain of command for strategic nuclear weapons forces.[4] Under his proposal, the UN would hold an immediate veto over use of the weapons but would release them under specified conditions or after a vote. These release arrangements would presumably still permit immediate retaliation to a nuclear attack. To ensure the concept's political acceptability, the weapons would also be returnable to national authority upon request, but only after a delay of reasonable time (perhaps 24 or 48 hours). The concept would require substantial verification. Nevertheless, it would provide additional decision

[4]Ibid.

time, thus satisfying one of the objectives already discussed. Unlike most arms control concepts, it would be relatively expandable to include third nations, for the formal control provisions concerning the United States, the Soviet Union, and third nations would not have to be unequal. In fact, in an era of increasing missile accuracy, one could visualize Washington and Moscow seeking such an approach as a way to increase the stability of the Soviet-America deterrent balance. (It is not clear, however, whether one could have very great confidence in the control scheme if strategic cruise missiles were developed and proved unverifiable.) Assuming that Beaton's concept is technologically feasible, it could provide a basis for movement toward either the incremental or the internationalized world. The time delays could, over a period of many years, be progressively lengthened, international control over nuclear forces gradually increased, and conditions for release to national control gradually tightened. Elements of popular control could be inserted to help build international legitimacy: for example, the power of the UN to approve nuclear weapons use could include a requirement of approval by an elected international assembly, or a nation's domestic decision to request force release could be made subject to domestic legislative approval. As nuclear weapons would be somewhat detached from national executive authority and their value for diplomatic bargaining minimized, their prestige role, and ultimate governmental resistance to public participation in their control, would weaken.

Any form of denuclearized world would require the United States and the Soviet Union to accept substantial transfer of the national defense function to an international authority. Traditional national power interests would still be able to assert themselves through efforts to obtain dominant positions in the new international structure no matter what sort of structure were chosen. But it is particularly difficult to visualize how the ideological interests of the Soviet regime could be accommodated. Soviet participation would require a change in Soviet ideology and a judgment of Soviet leaders that their revised ideological interests could be met more effectively in the modified world structure. Considering the character of the possible motivations, successful

Soviet-American negotiation of a denuclearized world would be plausible only if the alternative world structures appeared extremely dangerous or if the Soviet regime changed substantially.

NORTH-SOUTH CONFLICT

Negotiation in the North-South conflict is dominated by the aspirations of Southern peoples seeking both economic and political advancement and by the concerns of Northern peoples seeking to retain their dominant economic and political position. Unless developing nations can obtain resources or power or both, proscription of nuclear weapons is an unattainable goal, for few developing nations would be willing to give away that bargaining chip which appears to bring power and resources. This link in the bargaining process between political-economic power and nuclear weapons may perhaps be implicit rather than explicit, but it is likely to shape any denuclearization effort. If bargaining does not occur, the North may seek to control the South in whatever ways it can. But the South would also have some sources of power; it could eventually build nuclear weapons and challenge the North on more equal terms. The bargaining approach therefore offers a safer transfer of power that *might* inevitably be transferred anyway (in less peaceful ways).

As in the Soviet-American case, a staged transition process could be negotiated which reasonably satisfied security, economic, and political goals. Being multilateral, seeking compromises among genuinely conflicting goals, and requiring communications among radically different cultures, the negotiations would be far more complex than those between the nuclear powers. They could, however, offer substantial potential for mutual benefit, and some aspects might receive relatively strong political support.

Arrangements in the nuclear security area would be the easiest to define but probably the hardest to negotiate. The developed world would seek immediate and effective controls on proliferation—meaning, in early phases, international control over the entire nuclear industry and, in later phases, international intervention rights to enforce that control. The developing world, however, would not wish to grant these controls and intervention rights without adequate assurance that its immediate and long-term economic and political concerns would be satisfied. Some of the potential great powers in the developing world currently appear likely to seek the regional benefits and prestige of nuclear weapons, suggesting that negotiations among the Southern nations would also be required. A shared fear of proliferation and a sense of long-term mutual benefit resulting from some Northern economic concessions might provide the necessary impetus toward the achievement of a transition agreement that would include enough international control of the nuclear industry to maintain the status quo in weapons production, coupled with arrangements to provide peaceful nuclear technology and economic and political concessions. Soviet-American arms limitations such as a Beaton-style international nuclear weapons control structure or perhaps some form of no-first-use agreement might be beneficial to the North and might also facilitate Southern agreement by reducing the symbolic value of nuclear weapons and the North's ability to make nuclear threats against the South. Voting power within the nuclear control structure could provide a substitute for the prestige derived from possession of nuclear weapons.

In the economic area there would be several tasks. One would be to negotiate a transfer of economic resources from North to South and perhaps from OPEC to non-OPEC nations, in return for a Southern commitment to renounce nuclear weapons. The required magnitude of this transfer would depend on the relative timing of the Northern denuclearization and the Southern commitment to refrain from nuclearization and on the extent to which such a transfer is needed to provide global stability. Another task would be to negotiate a centralization of global macroeconomic decision making. While such centralization seems far off today, the increasing integration of the world economy suggests a growing need for collective management for reasons quite apart from the goal of denuclearization. A further task, if the internationalized model is chosen, would be to design the new institutions to encourage citizen participation and foster international legitimacy. Of these tasks, so far only the centralization of economic decision making appears to have any momentum, and the associated institutions are still so fragmented as to have limited chance of gaining much legitimacy.

Several types of pressure could be used to promote the direct transfer of resources. The developed nations could find control of proliferation impossible unless they devised some formula for income redistribution, and the prevention of international political instability could require direct transfers of wealth. The currently discussed "global incomes policy," involving an effort to negotiate commodity prices and intervene directly in markets, could come to be seen as an economic and political morass and be replaced by a package of direct income transfers. But even elements of the global incomes policy of the proposed New International Economic Order, if carried out, might satisfy some of the requirements for controlling proliferation and decreasing political instability.

The growth of legitimacy and direct citizen responsibility in the economic area could be more difficult, but there would be pressures operating here as well. In several areas there could emerge an international structure that would build links with citizens and constituencies within nations. Arrangements to control multinational corporations would, for example, be a step in this direction. Likewise, as the inefficiency of contemporary foreign aid becomes more widely recognized and is attributed to the vested interests of recipient governments, foreign aid administrators may become more inclined to require that recipients make domestic reforms under international supervision. Another impulse could derive from the possibility that the existing international economic structure will be unable to deal with current problems. Integration—as it has in Europe—might give rise to demands for greater political control and encourage peoples to look increasingly to the international institution for economic change. These developments could be promoted by giving international agencies increased responsibility in areas such as settlement of disputes between host countries and foreign investors or allocation of trade adjustment assistance. In summary, in spite of, or perhaps because of, the difficulties of an increasingly integrated world economy, the economic institutional base needed for internationalization could emerge.

Institutional trends in a third important area of the North-South relationship—peacekeeping and intervention agreements—might also be relatively conducive to negotiation in the context of transition to the internationalized world, although the problems to be overcome are discouragingly great. The tasks are to develop the peacekeeping institutions that were shown above to be necessary for long-term stability in a denuclearized world (some of which are also needed in a nuclear world) and to negotiate some transfer of power over peacekeeping to the developing nations. Although progress in completing the first task slowed during the period from the Congo crisis to the recent Middle East arrangements, interest has since revived and could readily increase. Transfer of control over peacekeeping might be compelled by shifts in the world balance of power, by technological changes in weaponry that favor indigenous forces over intervention forces, and by the increased unwillingness of the West to participate in unilateral intervention efforts. Middle-range goals might include changes in the UN Charter and, although difficult to reconcile with Soviet ideology, formal restrictions on unilateral great-power intervention. Achievement of these goals, particularly if it were to equip the UN to deal with ethnic conflict, might create domestic constituencies. The pressures deriving from these constituencies might produce some instability; in the long term, however, they could make the transfer of power to the UN irreversible.

The Soviet Union has not been a strong participant in global North-South negotiations and would probably find it difficult to accept some of the aspects of the North-South transition described here. This transition could, however, probably proceed relatively stably for some time without the participation of the Soviet Union or some of the other nuclear powers, provided the structure included appropriate arrangements for nuclear deterrence against nonparticipants, conventional defense, and defense against subversion. Rules could perhaps even be designed for a Beaton-style nuclear control system to operate within the portion of the world outside the Soviet bloc; in some respects, NATO's arrangements (the "permissive action links") for restricting the use of nuclear weapons approximate such a system. The transition pattern would then resemble an alliance rather than a world order, but the difference would be relatively small if power and wealth were actually being transferred and the necessary institution were being created. If the system were to work to encourage political stability and progress, the holdout nations would not necessarily benefit by delaying to obtain better entry terms, and if the system were strong, the holdouts would not be able to attack it.

The North-South aspect of the transition is less implausible than the Soviet-American political transition. The North would gain stronger institutions to slow proliferation, and the South would gain a more favorable orientation of economic institutions and some control over peacekeeping; direct citizen participation and international legitimacy could be promoted. But the difficulty of negotiation should of course not be underestimated. The North would have underlying fears of economic ruin and the South of neocolonialism. The short-term balance of power in the negotiations would favor the North, which would hesitate to give up any of the dominance that it now possesses in the world. The problem would be that of a stronger power being asked to make concessions to a weaker power that is probably growing stronger; it is enormously difficult to negotiate power balances from an asymmetric starting point. At the time of the Baruch Plan, the United States, a status quo power, would not give up its nuclear advantage except under a structure that would protect the status quo. And the Soviet Union, a revisionist power, would not give up its opportunity to gain nuclear power except under a structure that would permit alteration of the status quo. The same problem would have to be faced today: to denuclearize the world would require a negotiated shift in the world's locus of power. Such a shift might be very desirable, but it would be difficult to negotiate and difficult to execute without systemic instability. And the time at which power balances favored negotiation might be too late for dealing effectively with proliferation. But the difference between the problem of the Baruch Plan and today's North-South problem is that today there seems to be greater recognition on both sides of the risks involved should the shift in the locus of power be allowed to occur through the spread of nuclear weapons rather than through the control of all nuclear weapons. In any event, without Soviet participation, and possibly with it, the global North-South negotiation—involving nuclear weapons, economics, and political power—might, at the outer limit of possibility, succeed.

CITIZEN-GOVERNMENT RELATIONS

The relationship between government and citizen would change only in degree in the incremental model. Such a world would require a sustained commitment by national governments to develop cooperative solutions to international economic and social problems, i.e., an elaboration of contemporary economic and social diplomacy. This diplomacy would involve cooperative formation of a series of specific programs, each of which would still have its own relatively narrow domestic constituencies. The "horse-trading" of the European Economic Community provides the classic example. International technocrats and leaders in each nation would constantly have to avoid or overcome conflicts and bargain among important domestic pressure groups and bureaucracies. Success would be feasible only through a prolonged era of cooperation among leaders of national governments and domestic pressure groups. The system would not be self-stabilizing, so national governments might be forced to shape or reject the demands of their constituencies much more than they do now.

In contrast, under the liberal form of internationalized model considered in this essay, direct citizen interest in the international authority would provide the crucial motivation for transnational politics and would substantially influence national politics. National governments would have to respond to only a limited range of pressures and would retain legitimacy in only limited areas. At least during the transition period and possibly later, the citizens' loyalties would be divided among several institutions, as they were in the early years of the United States or, in a different way, in today's European Economic Community. There would be transnational pressure groups, initially reflecting the interests of national governments but ultimately becoming political parties tied less closely to the government of each nation than to popular political forces within each nation. Undoubtedly, special interest groups such as multinational corporations, international labor movements, and international scientific societies would also seek influence at the international level. Alliances between political parties and these organizations would determine the ultimate locus of international political power.

There would be two mechanisms at work in this aspect of the transition, one depending on the agreement of governments and another deriving from independent change in citizen attitudes. National governments would not welcome any loss of power and would not directly negotiate for the creation of the centralized model—except perhaps on issues for which an international organization might offer national governments a scapegoat to justify their failure to come to grips with problems they cannot solve. Some aspects of the incremental model, however, could be negotiated during a period conducive to international cooperation, and some of the incremental institutions might evolve into fully centralized, internationalized ones. Other institutions could encourage political forces to seek further centralization. In the European Community, national negotiations led to a European Parliament that has been something of a force for centralization, although in retrospect it might have been useful and perhaps feasible to have given the European Parliament somewhat more power at the beginning. After central organizations were created, they would gain additional political power depending upon their relative effectiveness upon national political change and upon changes in the relevance of the issues in which the different levels have specialized. Ultimately, these forces would be reflected in constitutional change at the international level.

Loyalties also would evolve independently of national governments. The incremental approach would rely upon an attitude of openness to global solutions. This attitude is already quite widespread in the world, at least among younger people, although it may be weakening again in the United States. But this attitude is far different from that needed to transfer loyalty to an internationalized government, an attitude that would take time to develop and would probably rest on political and psychological bases that could evolve only after a period of cooperation. For example, attitudes in the United States toward the federal government in 1789 probably corresponded to the incremental model: the prevailing sentiment was to support a central organization that would help the states get along but at the same time to protect each state's negotiating position quite carefully. The primary loyalty was to the states and the secondary loyalty to the federal government. It was not until passage of the post–Civil War constitutional amendments that there developed great popular interest in using the federal government to achieve local political ends; this use of the federal government corresponded to the internationalized model but was achieved only in the wake of a drastic breakdown in the first model. After the Civil War primary loyalties went to the federal government; the states had to be kept in line in order to achieve collective goals.

This example and many of the European nation-building examples suggest that war has historically been necessary to legitimize the transition to the second phase. Clearly, some challenge is needed in order to place the question of integration high on the political agenda. Perhaps this could be a challenge short of war, permitting a formal transition after underlying political forces have produced a change in citizen loyalties. Increased international travel, communication, trade, and citizen identification with global concerns might support such an underlying change in loyalties on a world scale. Also possible, if less likely, would be a process of peaceful evolution of attitudes leading to a formal transition to an international structure in the wake of a peaceful challenge to the old order; the Meiji restoration, although not completely peaceful, is an example of this form of centralization.

Even allowing for the current wave of doubts about the utility of international organizations, the long-term trend of developed world public attitudes outside the Soviet Union may prove favorable to such an evolution, especially as the effectiveness of national governments declines in the face of growing interdependence. Attitudes in developing nations during the first generation of independence may be less favorable to international legitimacy—except in a few specific contexts. During the second generation of independence, these attitudes could turn toward internationalism or they could revert toward traditional cultures. Moreover, an attitude of simple globalism or internationalism would not be enough; there would also have to be a recognition of the ways that international interdependence affects individual rights and goals and enough understanding of this interdependence to influence the design of international organizations and to channel political pressures toward their creation. The strongest theories of interdependence so far available—the traditional free trade theory and the Leninist theory of imperialism—are much too weak to support profound change in the international system. Even if a new theory were created and the developing and developed world attitudes began to change in a direction favorable to internationalization, the ultimate transition to an international structure with substantial legitimacy could hardly take place before the turn of the century.

The character and timing of the challenges that could provoke a transition would be important. If the challenges came too soon, there would be a risk of global war. With national legitimacies still strong, conflict would more likely be between groups of nations than between the national and the supranational levels of authority. And if it should be true, as suggested at the beginning of this essay, that nuclear weapons ultimately give national governments power independent of their citizens, and if the transition should be delayed too long, citizen attitudes could eventually become powerless to produce change. Unification by conquest could be the only transition possible in a world of nuclear warlords.

FOUR

Conclusion

Only the incremental model of a denuclearized world would be at all conceivable by the 1990s. Although basically an extension of the nation-state structure, this model would include far-reaching international control of nuclear arms and some control of conventional arms. It would require an international authority for the enforcement of restrictions on nuclear weapons and perhaps for the non-nuclear protection of those nations that had disarmed or were disarming. This authority would need a nuclear capability, although not necessarily a large one.

Stability in such a world would require major changes in the political and economic areas and a major cooperative effort to build and utilize new institutions designed to alleviate those problems that would likely lead to war. These institutions would of necessity have substantial peacekeeping capabilities under broadened international control. Over the long run, such a world would probably be less stable than the predictable nuclear world. Its institutions would be brittle, and denuclearization could add more uncertainties than it removed. The incremental denuclearized world is therefore neither a desirable goal nor a necessary transition phase to an internationalized world.

A denuclearized world would much more likely be stable if the nation-state system were modified through the transfer of citizen loyalties from national governments to an international government. The international government would have to play a significant role in many political and economic areas in order to

209

acquire citizen loyalties. Through the growth of international legitimacy and the corresponding decline of national legitimacy, traditional patterns of warfare would become relatively unlikely, as what are now international politics came to resemble domestic politics. Such a regime is conceivable, but its creation would require significant time—extending at least into the twenty-first century. Although there would be a serious risk of instability during the creation of this regime, the internationalized world would be the only regime fully adaptive to an era in which nuclear weapons were proscribed, but renuclearization is always a possibility.

Nuclear weapons seem likely to produce fundamental changes in the nation-state system, and the stability of the current nuclear regime may well be illusory in the long run. But denuclearization without change in the nation-state system would probably produce a world worse than the current one. What is more important than denuclearization is the evolution of citizen loyalties and the establishment of international arrangements to resolve specific problems; the control of nuclear weapons is only one aspect of this crucial process.

During the late twentieth century, the goals that should be sought are those that would make the existing world safer and help support a later transition to an internationalized and possibly denuclearized world. These include the following:

1. In the arms control area, measures to control the nuclear industry, to slow proliferation, and to place international authorities into the chain of command for national nuclear weapons. Although reduction of force levels and stability of force deployments are important, a new goal should be given greater consideration: lengthening the decision-making time in a nuclear crisis.

2. In the area of international organization, measures to increase international effectiveness and legitimacy in economic and security-oriented agencies and to create direct representation and participation of citizens in international organizations.

3. In the North-South area, measures and concessions to en-

courage Southern participation in the control of proliferation and in the growth of international legitimacy.

Many of these goals could be successfully pursued even without the cooperation of the Soviet Union that, barring internal change, seems unlikely to be initially sympathetic. Achievement of these goals during the remainder of the twentieth century would be essential to entry into a fully internationalized world by the early twenty-first century and would be desirable in any event. If these goals were achieved, decisions on the formal transfer of greater power from the national to the international level and on full denuclearization could then be made at a time when both the understanding of and the opportunity for change would be greater.

Strategic Deterioration: Prospects, Dimensions, and Responses in a Fourth Nuclear Regime

David C. Gompert

ONE

The Limits of Stability

The essence of the world's strategic situation, as we have known it for the last decade and as we expect it to persist, is the availability to both the United States and the Soviet Union of sufficient deliverable nuclear power to render nuclear war between them improbable in the extreme. Moreover, the magnitude and basic symmetry of these two arsenals are such that this central balance—and the political power relationship it implies—cannot be fundamentally altered by any plausible, near-term quantitative, technological, or doctrinal developments. The present nuclear regime is extraordinarily stable.

Like any state of equilibrium, the current configuration of strategic power has a certain seductive quality. The imbalances of the 1950s and 1960s have been transformed by a seemingly inexorable process of production and restraint into the mutual checkmate conditions that prevail today. Just as this system of mutual deterrence seems capable of withstanding those pressures that would alter strategic conditions for the worse, it has also proven resistant to pressures substantially to reduce nuclear armaments or to codify international constraints on their use.

Most American military planners, while perhaps dissatisfied with this or that feature of the existing arrangement, are intuitively content that their national physical security and the protection of other vital national interests are ultimately assured by the sheer awesomeness of their enormous arsenal. Most Soviet planners no doubt feel a similar contentment. There is room for marginal deviation from equilibrium, for example, in one side acquiring an edge on the adversary in a particular weapon system. But such asymmetries as may result eventually prove either transitory or incapable of imparting significant advantages in the heat of a crisis. Preservation of a stable nuclear relationship has to a large degree displaced the quest for national advantage as the central precept of "responsible" strategic planning. Even when new weapons programs are initiated, their proponents are careful to pay homage to "the system" by contending that such capabilities would enhance stability.[1]

To leaders and strategists there is a comforting simplicity to the logic of the present regime. It provides security from nuclear violence not only by deterring each side from launching a premeditated strategic attack but also by inhibiting the use of even a single nuclear weapon under almost any conceivable circumstance. It discourages disorderly conduct in world politics. Each of the two global powers abstains from actions that might excite the adversary into contemplating the resort to nuclear weapons. Crisis avoidance has become a beacon for policy behavior by American and Soviet leaders. Neither side seeks to exploit the other's fear of becoming embroiled in a crisis, since such conduct might evoke an attempt at counterexploitation of one's own undeniable fears by the opponent. No prize of geopolitical competition is alluring enough to justify taking such risks. Both sides seem comfortable with the dependable, if imprecise, understanding of mutual prudence imposed by the imperative of avoiding a nuclear exchange.

That those in Washington and Moscow responsible for making national strategic decisions are content with—if hardly enraptured by—the constraints and the durability of the existing framework can be seen in the nature of important arms control agreements of recent years. These measures—the Non-Proliferation Treaty (NPT), the Strategic Arms Limitation Talks

---

[1]For example, proponents of greater emphasis on counterforce and damage-limitation plans and capabilities, policies traditionally considered "destabilizing," maintain that these preferred policies would in fact enhance rather than weaken deterrence.

(SALT) I accords, the Vladivostok understandings—were designed to consolidate the equilibrium, to formalize the acceptance of its conceptual logic, to shore up its weaknesses, to ratify its upper numerical boundaries, and to endow it with a large measure of irreversibility. At the same time, prescriptions for reducing or otherwise controlling nuclear weapons through sharp departures from the numerical and doctrinal bases of the present regime are met by official explanations that substantial reductions and other restrictions must await further consolidation and elaboration of current measures aimed at arresting the arms race. Still, undeterred by the proven resilience of the existing configuration of power, armchair negotiators press on, thinking and writing about less costly, less excessive, but, they argue, no less stable strategic arrangements.

Thus, most attention given to strategic nuclear matters is concentrated on ways to perfect the present regime or to progress toward a more "rational" nuclear world. Only those who must justify new weapons programs give much thought to the prospect of conditions getting worse. For all the wailing about various "potentially destabilizing" weapons, technologies, or doctrines, there is little inquiry into what destabilization would actually mean in terms of the behavior of various actors under international conditions ranging from crisis to calm. Most observers tend intuitively to believe that a serious degradation of strategic conditions is no more likely than a dramatic turn toward complete nuclear disarmament. But this writer believes—the above observations about the system's durability notwithstanding—that over the next 10 to 15 years deterioration is, in fact, more likely than major progress and, in any event, no less crucial a topic for analysis and prescription.

Even those who express a qualified faith in the durability of the current regime appreciate that the course of technology does not always respect our visions of a desirable future. As Harvey Brooks put it:

We ought . . . to remind ourselves that the rapid advances from 1950 to 1960 were not anticipated until they were almost upon us. . . . Scientists and technologists, in trying to foresee the state of the art more than five years into the future, have been notoriously myopic—conservative as to the actual possibilities and inaccurate in their anticipation of the direction of development. Thus, it would be injudicious to hope that the posture of mutual assured destruction is proof against technological change for more than five, or at most ten, years.[2]

The currents of world politics are as unpredictable as the course of technology. The moderation in ideological crusading and geostrategic competition between the two global powers, which has both contributed to and benefitted from the achievement of "technical" nuclear stability, is not an immutable fact of international life. The fabric of détente may prove no stronger than its weakest thread, be it the Middle East, Korea, Southern Africa, a restive Eastern Europe, or Western "meddling" in Soviet internal politics. Perhaps nuclear stability can be kept insulated from political vicissitudes. And maybe political prudence can mitigate the strategic effects of destabilizing technological developments. But the stakes of nuclear war and peace are too high—higher than they were when we worried more about them—for us to take shelter under such reassuring hypotheses.

This essay accepts Brooks's reminder and seeks to carry it one judicious step further. It attempts to analyze how strategic deterioration might come about, what it would mean for world order, and how it might be "managed" both to avert further disequilibrium and perhaps to guide the international system back toward more stable strategic conditions.

THE AXES OF DETERIORATION

Strategic deterioration can be defined as a sustained increase in the probability of general nuclear war resulting from changes in the numbers, distribution, or qualities of nuclear weapons; the doctrines that govern when, where, and how they might be used; the perceptions and rhetoric about their relevance to war, peace, and diplomacy; the procedures by which they are maintained; or

[2]Harvey Brooks, "The Military Innovation System," *Daedalus,* Summer 1975, *Arms, Defense Policy, and Arms Control,* p. 78.

the international norms and agreements that constrain them. To this definition we might attach two assumptions. First, as the probability of general nuclear war increases, the threat—stated or tacit—to resort to nuclear weapons, having become more credible, can exact a higher price in terms of other values, such as territory and resources, sovereignty over domestic affairs, freedom in the conduct of foreign policy, and individuals' perceptions of personal safety. Second, since any incidence of lesser forms of nuclear conflict will stand a good chance of leading to general intercontinental exchange, as the former becomes more likely the latter can be regarded as more likely also. Accordingly, deterioration may be thought of as a sustained increase in the probability of *any* form of nuclear combat.

Despite its exceptionally stable properties, the nuclear peace could deteriorate over the next 10 to 15 years along any or all three principal axes. First, the forces of nuclear proliferation, seemingly beyond the direct control of the two central powers, might produce so wide a distribution of nuclear weapons that one or both sides in most serious international conflicts would possess some sort of nuclear capability. Second, in the course of a reinvigorated arms race, both Washington and Moscow might pursue certain destabilizing policies—in research, development, deployment, and war-planning—creating conditions in which the presumption that neither would dare initiate strategic nuclear war might be called into question under circumstances of severe political stress. Finally, one of the two superpowers could so outpace the other in certain critical areas of technology and force deployment that the specter of nuclear war might become significantly less terrifying to the one than to the other. These conditions are examined below: first proliferation, then improved first-strike capabilities on both sides, and last, significantly superior capabilities in the hands of one of the two superpowers.

A disintegration of the institutions, norms, formal accords, conventions, and common doctrinal bases that have taken root over the past decade or so and currently govern strategic behavior might be deemed a fourth path of deterioration. Such a development might accompany, result from, or stimulate any of the three types of deterioration just identified. It might reflect a perception

219

by the parties to these institutions that long-held assumptions about strategic stability had been invalidated by new weapon systems. It might arise from the sheer unmanageability of a strategic environment in which nuclear weapons were rapidly spreading or in which the technological options open to force planners were multiplying. Or it might result from the intrusion of political conflicts into the management of nuclear stability, conflicts originating in other areas of intersuperpower relations less amenable to the pursuit of common interests than is the nuclear area. Whatever the case, the institutional atrophy (such as, a growing sterility of SALT, a divergence of American and Soviet strategic thinking, or a paralyzing politicization of the International Atomic Energy Agency) can be viewed as a fourth avenue of deterioration that could intersect with any of the three direct routes specified above.

TWO

Proliferation

While the development of certain technologies has helped to stabilize the Soviet-American strategic balance, the horizontal spread of nuclear technologies—civilian and military—is inherently unstable and destabilizing. There is no need to recite here the full litany of dangers attending the spread of inexpensive isotope-separation processes, the accumulation of reprocessed plutonium, and the diffusion of technology for effective delivery systems, to name but three of the most serious trends. These and other technological and industrial trends will persist in the years to come; the susceptibility of these technologies to effective international control is likely to decrease as their spread proceeds. We face a dilemma: measures to restrict the world market in nuclear technologies invite the production of homegrown facilities and materials, beyond the reach of international safeguards, but trying to preempt the growth of indigenous capabilities by maintaining an active, open market accelerates the diffusion of nuclear technologies under international safeguards that can be revoked or violated without risk of punitive sanction.

Whatever stability exists in the current international distribution of nuclear weapons stems from the fact that certain key states (most notably, West Germany, Japan, and Italy) have recently ratified or are poised to ratify their accession to the NPT. Each important state that ratifies the NPT helps refute the curious, though tenacious, notion that the detonation of a·fission device heralds a nation's arrival as a great power. Looking just at the politics of proliferation, the fulcrum of the problem is the continued refusal of a number of critical states to accede to the NPT. The confirmed or rumored acquisition of nuclear weapons by any of these states would eclipse the positive effects of ratification by, say, an equal number of other non-nuclear states. Unquestionably, much depends on the nature of world reaction to further proliferation, but if the two most recent cases (China and India) are thought to be prototypical, the international standing of the next few proliferants will improve in the years following their initial tests. Thus, proliferation to only one or two more countries might well revitalize the belief that possession of nuclear weapons, irrespective of military risk or gain, constitutes an almost unrivaled source of raw political capital.

While the technological aspects of proliferation are inherently unstable, the political aspects are not—yet. But a revived interest in nuclear "prestige" superimposed upon the already unstable technological conditions could create a groundswell of momentum. In fact, the less stable the technological conditions, the harder it will be to keep the politics in order, since the general spread of nuclear resources and skills could lead many governments to conclude that it would be foolhardy to foreclose their own options.

Should a few more critical states acquire nuclear weapons, even if only for vague motives of power and prestige, resultant perceptions of military insecurity at local and regional levels could compound instability. This progression—availability of technology feeding political motivation to acquire nuclear weapons, consequently destabilizing regional security conditions— can be brought into focus by considering how the Brazilian and Iranian cases might evolve should these two states go nuclear. As the regional balance of power tilted toward the nuclear state, rival powers (Argentina and Saudi Arabia) would feel increasingly compelled to try to restore some semblance of the political and military *status quo ante*.

A process of accelerating nuclear proliferation is more than a remote possibility. Not having nuclear weapons in 1990 might prove analogous to not having military aircraft in 1935. But the path toward that world might not be punctuated—as we tend to expect would be the case—with initial nuclear test explosions by new entrants to the nuclear club. While capabilities may spread and inducements mount, many states may elect to stop just short of actually assembling or testing weapons. Because of the ambiguities and anxieties it would generate, this sort of latent proliferation[3] might be as unstable as overt proliferation: as conducting a first test loses fashion, governments' suspicions as to their rivals' possible capabilities and intentions might motivate them to hedge by accumulating nuclear resources and formulating weapons plans that might otherwise have been eschewed, thereby aggravating the problem of latent proliferation over time.

As proliferation proceeded, once sturdy international nonproliferation institutions [NPT, International Atomic Energy Agency (IAEA)] would probably begin to disintegrate, and the real commitment of states to the norms upon which those institutions are built would correspondingly decline. Circumvention of the treaty by signatories could result, although withdrawal from treaty obligations pursuant to Article X (jeopardization of "supreme [national] interests") would constitute a more dignified means of escape. In any event, there would be little doubt that the nuclear age had entered a fundamentally new phase.

If the impediments to proliferation are indeed this weak—a debatable but not frivolous supposition—two tasks present themselves: first, to forecast and analyze conditions that might result if proliferation gains speed, and second, to identify possible measures for reinforcing existing nonproliferation institutions and systems, for bringing new inhibitive pressures to bear, and if these fail, for suppressing the risks of nuclear hostilities.

A PROLIFERATING WORLD: SUPERPOWER MODERATION AND REGIONAL NUCLEARIZATION

Destabilization of the existing six-nation nuclear regime would be tantamount to strategic *deterioration* if and only if, to be faithful to our definition, it increased the probability of any form of nuclear hostilities. There are two principal ways—distinct but

---

[3]For a full discussion of this phenomenon see Harold A. Feiveson and Theodore B. Taylor, "Alternative Strategies for International Control of Nuclear Power," in *Nuclear Proliferation: Motivations, Capabilities, and Strategies for Control,* 1980s Project, McGraw-Hill, New York, 1977.

related—in which nuclear proliferation might raise nuclear dangers: first, by compounding the difficulties faced by Soviet and American leaders in maintaining a stable central balance, and second, by increasing the chances of nuclear weapons being used in regional contexts, either by aggravating regional security problems themselves or simply by introducing the possibility of nuclear violence into what would otherwise be non-nuclear conflict.

The dynamics of a proliferating world need not and probably would not alter fundamentally and irretrievably the strategic relationship between the United States and the Soviet Union. This central balance has survived, among other disturbances, a massive unilateral deployment by the United States of multiple independently targeted reentry vehicles (MIRVs) and Chinese deployment of a substantial network of medium-range ballistic missiles (MRBMs) and intermediate-range ballistic missiles (IRBMs) that threaten Soviet but not American cities. Were the flames of proliferation to ignite worldwide, the central strategic relationship would undoubtedly be scorched. But because the superpowers possess so much more nuclear strength than does any other conceivable power or combination of powers, the basic conceptual logic and predictable behavior patterns of their bilateral relationship would probably survive intact.

Pressures that could upset the bilateral balance might arise if Soviet or American leaders resisted the possibility of their societies becoming increasingly vulnerable to the arsenals of a growing number of other states—some of which might be regarded as untrustworthy, others of which might be seen as potential adversaries that one or the other superpower might want to be able to coerce from a position of nuclear invulnerability. Ironically, each superpower might be more anxious about new nuclear states that are not closely aligned with its superrival than about those (Britain and France being the living examples) whose nuclear postures and policies are, for most practical purposes, integral to and constrained by the central deterrence system. The Soviet Union has not sought to deprive Britain and France of their second-strike capabilities in part out of knowledge that the political advantages of doing so would be limited by the persistence, if

224

not the expansion, of the American nuclear umbrella over its allies and also out of faith that neither British nor French weapons would be launched except as part of a Soviet-American exchange. Insofar as the superpowers will keep future proliferants at arms length, we may expect that they will feel a greater need to respond to the emergence of new nuclear powers than Moscow felt vis-à-vis America's nuclear allies.

The desire in Washington or Moscow to thwart the development of a survivable and deliverable nuclear force by certain lesser nuclear powers, along with the fear of accidental or anonymous nuclear attack, could stimulate or accelerate superpower research, development, and deployment of technologies that could begin to threaten the credibility of the rival superpower's deterrent—missile defense, bomber defense, antisubmarine warfare (ASW) systems, civil defense networks, and improved counterforce weaponry.[4] Even if no "strategically significant" destabilization resulted from such deployments on one side, the rival might begin to doubt that side's commitment to the tacit understanding (and in the case of antiballistic missiles [ABMs], formal agreement) that each superpower should remain exposed to devastating retaliation from the other. It might ultimately become clear that some lesser power, and not the other superpower, was the intended target of such damage-limitation measures. But amid the rush of events—and in the absence of deep mutual trust—the other superpower's strategists would be instinctively cautious. They could respond by reinforcing their own retaliatory capabilities or by following the adversary's lead in stepping up strategic counterforce and defense programs. In either case, of course, the physical and psychological conditions of the central balance could suffer: unnecessary and possibly destabilizing technological advances and weapons deployments could ensue, and bilateral arms control would be hamstrung by increased ambiguity and suspicion.

[4]It is reasonable to assume that the Soviet leaders will be more likely than American leaders to react with programs devised to neutralize new nuclear dangers, since most potential proliferants (e.g., Israel, Iran, Pakistan, South Africa, South Korea, Brazil, Turkey, and Spain, not to mention Germany and Japan) enjoy better relations with the United States than with the Soviet Union.

This is not to say that the Soviet-American strategic balance and dialogue are too fragile to absorb the sorts of shocks that proliferation would generate. The one important empirical datum we have—the SALT I and II negotiations conducted against a backdrop of a steadily improving and an increasingly anti-Soviet Chinese nuclear capability—suggests that the United States and the Soviet Union can sort out the primary strategic issues from the secondary issues. But future success in insulating the central balance could prove ephemeral: witness the hackles now being raised in the United States by the growth of Soviet strategic forces and civil defense programs that may, to a large degree, represent Moscow's anticipation of further improvements in the survivability and deliverability of Chinese strategic forces. Before assuming that the dictates of central stability will inevitably prevail, one should ponder the stresses that would be placed on Soviet-American strategic relations—particularly in the critical area of antiballistic missile restraint—if the Kremlin found itself trying to contend with *both* Chinese and Iranian efforts to attain a credible independent retaliatory capability against cities in Siberia and Turkistan, respectively.

These sorts of disruptions in the central balance could, of course, be averted altogether if the United States and the Soviet Union each or jointly were to decide not to respond at all to new sources of putative nuclear danger. If each accepts vulnerability to the forces of its archrival, would vulnerability to other, far less competitive nuclear states be such an intolerable fate? In principle, if both Washington and Moscow were willing to forfeit the option of using nuclear intimidation against smaller powers, neither would need security from the retaliatory forces of those states, for neither would ever threaten any action that would merit retaliation.

Yet it is doubtful that American and Soviet leaders—not to mention military interest groups—would subscribe to such an acquiescent policy. While the "mutual hostage relationship" of bipolar deterrence can be justified as essential to global survival, survival plainly does not depend upon the ability of, say, Turkey to maintain a balance of terror with the Soviet Union. The strategic sages who foresaw and prescribed the emergence of mutual deterrence in the late 1950s failed to extend their formulas for stability to then hypothetical conditions of nuclear crowding. What theory of strategic interaction or slogan of global imperative would save an American or Soviet defense minister trying to convince a domestic audience—or chief of state—that, say, Brazil or Turkey should be granted a second-strike capability against the American or the Soviet homeland, respectively? Indeed, for the superpowers to foreswear interest in a first-strike capability against smaller nuclear states would be to sweeten the reward to other small states for acquiring nuclear weapons.

Most important would be for the superpowers to minimize the confusion arising from the response of each to proliferation through consulting candidly on the purposes of new programs—a healthy habit in any case—and by limiting themselves to defense and counterforce systems that were effective against smaller, unsophisticated forces but virtually impotent against each other's forces. The day of reckoning would arrive when secondary nuclear states, perhaps driven by the defense programs of the superpowers, began to deploy forces sufficiently advanced and plentiful so that defending against them became essentially indistinguishable from defending against American and Soviet deterrent forces. Once lesser nuclear states had ballistic missiles that could be intercepted only by, say, space-based lasers or when they had long-range submarine-launched missiles that could be countered only by extensive "strategic antisubmarine warfare" systems, then even the most candid superpower consultations would not be able to dispel the ambiguities. The choice then would be either to relax duopolistic management of global strategic issues by admitting those states that had "arrived" as independent, potent nuclear powers or to retreat significantly from the principles and practices of mutual superpower deterrence. Of the two alternatives, the former would less impair the prudent management of nuclear weapons.

The foregoing analysis takes on a troubling new dimension with the recognition that quite apart from the issue of their direct mutual security concerns, American and Soviet leaders may be faced with the serious question of how to respond politically to the nuclearization of any of a number of chronically tense regions: the

227

Middle East, Southern Africa, South Asia, or the Far East. Simply stated, the choice would be either to try to stabilize regional nuclear situations by supplementing the embryonic deterrents of local powers with nuclear commitments by the superpowers or to attempt to insulate the central balance from the chaotic forces of regional nuclear instability and insecurity set loose by proliferation.

An interconnecting of nuclear relationships, the former course, would permit the superpowers to offset imbalances in regional nuclear matchups, including cases in which non-nuclear states were confronted by nuclear neighbors with crude but undeterred weapons. To instill caution in the stronger and confidence in the weaker nations, the United States and the Soviet Union could transform existing security ties or create new ties through which local nuclear powers were, in effect, drawn into the central deterrence system. An integrated world nuclear system of this sort might keep regional nuclearization from upsetting regional stability. But the great danger of concocting an intricate and expandable network of deterrence relationships to accommodate the appearance of new nuclear states would be that nuclear hostilities, if ever ignited, might travel along the very lines of commitment put in place to suppress nuclear conflict in the first place, turning a regional conflict into a global cataclysm. For example, Soviet and American nuclear guarantees to stabilize an otherwise shaky nuclear standoff in South Asia would make the prevention of global nuclear conflict dependent not only upon the avoidance of direct crises between the superpowers but also upon moderation in the potentially more volatile relations among India, Pakistan, and China.

The alternative approach, that of a compartmentalization of nuclear relationships, would seem both more likely and more desirable. True, the superpowers would continue to have substantive interests in the politics of nearly every region of the world, interests that would not be jettisoned simply because of the new regional dangers created by proliferation. But the incentives to remain or become directly involved in regional security issues would probably not increase with proliferation, whereas the disincentives would. New proliferants would probably not be embraced as suddenly important allies. China was not. India was not. There are definite signals from Washington that Israel, South Korea, and Iran would suffer at least partial estrangement from the United States if they deployed nuclear weapons. Diminutive nuclear capabilities (likened by some analysts to lightning rods) would be viewed by the superpowers more as liabilities than as assets. Regional nuclearization in the 1980s would be watched apprehensively by Moscow and Washington but would probably stimulate the interventionary nerve of neither.

The prediction and prescription of a compartmentalization of nuclear relationships raises two important questions: How would proliferation affect the basic structure of East-West security relations? And how could nuclear dangers be controlled in the absence of efforts by the superpowers to foster security in newly nuclearized regions?

Generally speaking, with the spread of nuclear weapons, superpower geostrategic maneuvering would become more restrained, not only out of a reluctance to get directly embroiled with lesser nuclear powers possessing crude and vulnerable forces but, more generally, because only exceedingly high stakes would justify involvement in local disputes in which the outbreak of some form of nuclear conflict was a real possibility. Long accustomed to avoiding confrontation within the central security theaters (Central Europe and the Far East), the superpowers would increasingly show a similar respect for the dangers of local crises in "outlying" areas where moderate behavior has historically been less exigent. Moreover, as allies acquired their own nuclear weapons, the diminished protective responsibilities of the superpowers would tend to shrink their spheres of influence and security ties. Vital American and Soviet interests would compete less frequently. Relations would mature and might even improve.

A wave of proliferation in the next 15 years would almost certainly have harmful effects on international security conditions below the strategic level of the superpowers.[5] These adverse effects would derive mainly from three special features of a

---

[5]Of course, a given case of nuclear weapons acquisition might actually be stabilizing insofar as it contributed to the restoration of a local power balance that had been upset by the introduction of nuclear weapons in the arsenal of one side and not the other.

proliferating world: the perceived coercive and military value of nuclear weapons to states facing local conflict or confrontation; the inflamed suspicions, cautious force posturing, reduced predictability of behavior, and increased risk of miscalculation that would result from the existence or suspected existence of undisclosed nuclear capabilities or of capabilities of undisclosed quality and quantity; and the unevenness with which nuclear weapons are likely to spread into various regions. These three factors—utility, uncertainty, and unevenness—no longer characterize the Soviet-American strategic relationship, their diminution having been a precondition for stability and success in enacting measures of joint control of the central balance.[6] All three factors would flourish below the superpower level in a proliferating world.

Those states that face local confrontations and disputes are among the most likely to seek nuclear status in the 1980s. Such states could become increasingly inclined to conceal the fact—but promote the fear—that they had assembled deliverable nuclear weapons. This element of uncertainty will become increasingly prominent as more and more nations, perhaps only for the purpose of developing civilian nuclear industries, attain the high level of technological sophistication and accumulate enough fissionable material to reduce the step to nuclear weapons status to a simple assembly problem. In addition, the spread of advanced conventional weaponry (particularly surface-to-surface missile systems) could eliminate the construction of delivery systems as a formidable hurdle. Proliferation might lose its drama; the *coup de théâtre* of the first nuclear test could be increasingly replaced by the quiet, almost casual substitution for conventional missile warheads of fission devices secretly manufactured with relatively insignificant quantities of plutonium from growing

---

[6]The *utility* of nuclear weapons to each superpower (especially to the United States) declined precipitously as its adversary acquired means of intercontinental retaliation. Now, only the tactical nuclear weapons—mostly in Europe and the Far East—have a specified role in military plans. *Uncertainty* largely vanished with rapid development of satellite reconnaissance photography and telemetry, which inform each superpower about the quantity and quality of its rival's forces. *Unevenness* ended with the Soviet build-up of the late 1960s to match American strategic offensive force levels.

stockpiles. By 1990, the nuclear community could consist of, say 10 "certain" nuclear states, 5 more "probables," and 10 more that apparently had no nuclear weapons but could within a matter of weeks. The new nuclear states would probably be clustered around areas of traditionally or potentially high tension—the Middle East, Northeast Asia, the Persian Gulf, Southern Africa, and perhaps Southeast Asia—and would vary markedly in the size and quality of their arsenals and in their willingness to use them.

A PROLIFERATED WORLD: WOULD THE FLASHPOINT BE LOWERED?

It is conceivable that the wave of proliferation could spend its energies in the creation of, say, a dozen new nuclear weapons states. Well over a hundred countries would probably resist the tide, because of technological retardation, national poverty, the absence of serious security problems, or sheer political and/or popular pacific will.[7] A dissipation of the pressures for proliferation would begin to relieve the acute security problems generated by the very process of proliferation. Uncertainties regarding the intentions of adversaries would, over time, probably be resolved one way or another. International norms and institutions for controlling nuclear weapons could be resuscitated and reformed to suit the new conditions. Nuclear industries could perhaps expand, unfettered by nonproliferation restraints (though still haunted by the danger of nuclear theft by terrorist groups). All these expectations are of course based to some extent on the assumption that the point of exhaustion of a proliferation trend

[7]It is sometimes suggested that as more states acquire nuclear weapons their importance as an international status symbol will diminish, thus contributing to the easing of pressures for proliferation. While there is a certain logic to this expectation, it is important to bear in mind that a similar decline in status seeking has not been evident with respect to other symbols of modernity, comparably dubious in utilitarian importance, such as the skyscraper, the national airline, the national steel industry, and the national civilian nuclear power program. Thus, while we normally think in terms of 10 or 20 nuclear states, the more distant future might hold a world in which very few nations will *not* have any nuclear weapons capability.

would be recognizable when reached. It is more likely that after a surge in which most middle-power industrializing states went nuclear, new additions would come with decreasing frequency; perhaps by the turn of the century the achievement by another state of nuclear status would be as rare an event as it has been to date.

Whether in the throes of accelerating proliferation or in the relative calm of a postsurge phase, a world of many nuclear states would differ fundamentally from a world of five or six nuclear powers. Foremost among the differences, of course, is that nuclear hostilities—though hardly commonplace—would be more likely to occur from time to time. As observed above, local conflicts could prove to be breeding grounds for a new generation of nuclear states, just as conflicts (World War II and the cold war) bred the first generation. And in regions where conflicts were absent or quiescent, the appearance of nuclear weapons could excite new turbulence, especially when uncertainty, unevenness, and perceived military utility characterized the introduction of nuclear weapons. The increase in the number of local conflicts and crises in which one or both sides possessed nuclear weapons would imply a higher probability of their being used.

This statistically higher risk would be amplified by the fact that at least some new proliferants might be less self-controlled and less prudent than the older nuclear states, an unpopular but almost certainly logical expectation. The political systems of the five members of the first nuclear generation (through China) are less susceptible—though of course not immune—to succumbing to "irrational" leadership than those of many prospective members of the next nuclear generation. Consider the factor of leadership composure in a crisis situation. Some observers would contend that Kennedy behaved somewhat irresponsibly in 1962 (the Cuban missile crisis), that Mao was incautious in 1969 (the Soviet-Sino border confrontation), and that Kissinger acted recklessly in 1973 (the "October alert"). How much greater would the chances of nuclear hostilities be if the weapons were in the hands of messianic states with messianic leaders or states and regimes threatened with extinction or states lacking in the considerable non-nuclear military capabilities and options possessed by the old nuclear states? Yet these are the countries whose leaders will be most likely to perceive a need for nuclear weapons—indeed, a pressing need as proliferation proceeded around them. Nuclear weapons may spread to the very areas where the inherent restraints on their eventual use would be lowest. Many proliferants of the 1980s will probably assemble their nuclear weapons in the heat of conflict. It is sobering to recall that only one of the five original nuclear powers initially produced nuclear weapons during wartime—and that power promptly incinerated two enemy cities.

The potential for internal turmoil also distinguishes the prospective nuclear young from the old. For example, control over nuclear weapons by a particular military service branch or, in the case of a large proliferant, a regional command could precipitate or decide a coup d'état or civil conflict. Inexperience in technical safety measures, deployment, and use doctrine and a lack of reliable command-and-control systems and procedures would amount to what might be called "nuclear immaturity." Each of the existing powers has experienced it, the latest case being that of the Chinese, who only recently seem to have developed a deep understanding that there is and must be a quantum difference between full-scale conventional and nuclear war on the spectrum of violence. And if politicians seem slow to grasp the uniqueness of nuclear weapons, professional military officers have been even slower to abandon or modify traditional concepts of war when a nuclear dimension is added.

These probable traits of new proliferants—inexperience, imprudence, internal instability, and involvement in specific conflict situations—mean that a straight-line projection of proliferation could increase exponentially the probability that nuclear weapons would be used in warfare. If "irrationality" (broadly defined) were the only problem, one could tender modest hope that the learning experience of living with nuclear danger would bring new proliferants quickly up to the standards of prudence respected by the existing nuclear states. Unfortunately, nuclear weapons would objectively be of some practical utility to future proliferants in the context of regional security problems. Conventional military ineffectiveness—abundant worldwide—is rampant in most parts of the Third World; the threat to use nuclear weapons to defeat or coerce a neighbor might be credible and therefore useful in regions where neighbors openly challenged each other's right to exist in present form (e.g., Southern Africa, the Middle East, the Korean peninsula, and perhaps Indochina). And even in strictly military terms, nuclear weapons can in fact provide the capacity for destroying armies, airfields, dams, industries, and capitals to states whose conventional impotence once placed such tantalizing targets beyond reach. It is comforting, and therefore popular, to assume that nuclear weapons will be as unusable once widespread as they are today. But this is simply not so. Nuclear hostilities would become more likely with proliferation, if not in the 1980s then in the 1990s.

A high and pervasive expectation that limited nuclear violence might occur would not reduce the political and psychological impact of its actual occurrence. The outbreak of nuclear conflict—or even the isolated use in combat or the accidental detonation of a single nuclear weapon—would generate a political shock wave affecting nearly every facet of international order and security. It has been suggested above that the spread of nuclear weapons would shrink the geographic scope of the superpowers' interests and moderate their international behavior, but should those weapons actually be used in some corner of the earth, the United States and/or the Soviet Union could be expected to react, especially after the danger of being drawn in had begun to pass. In other words, while neither superpower would consider proliferation itself so insufferable that it need accept or share responsibility for maintaining nuclear *peace*, nuclear *war* would not be similarly tolerated. Indeed, in the event of a regional nuclear war—or a serious scare—international consensus might shift from support of superpower noninvolvement in regional security matters to a demand for superpower nuclear peacekeeping. Failure of the international community, under superpower leadership, to react more than rhetorically to nuclear violence might encourage further outbreaks.

In situations in which one superpower had more vital interests than the other, a major unilateral exercise of power could occur in the wake of regional nuclear combat. Intervention in a small nuclear war might have its own nuclear overtones, possibly in the form of a threat to disarm the local user of nuclear weapons. In regions where the United States and the Soviet Union were about equally engaged, local nuclear hostilities could well lead to a severe global crisis and resultant deterioration of mutual super-power trust and restraint. Alternatively, the two countries might collaborate to disarm by ultimatum and jointly dictate a "solu-tion" conducive to the restoration of nuclear order (and, one would hope, prejudicial to the party that initiated the nuclear exchange). The greater the degree to which nuclear relationships were compartmentalized, the more likely it would be that a direct Soviet-American collision could be avoided but the more difficult it would be for the superpowers jointly to establish their authority in the wake of nuclear hostilities. Ironically, the superpowers would probably engage in enforcing international nuclear security only after it was too late, for the dangers of involvement before it was too late would seem unacceptably high.

The question of how to repair international security following nuclear hostilities is a highly speculative inquiry that would re-quire an extensive preliminary discussion of assumptions and variables. Rather than wading farther into those inhospitable waters, I have chosen to limit the scope of this analysis to condi-tions this side of actual nuclear conflict. The following discussion, in other words, assumes a proliferated world in which nuclear conflict—while perhaps highly likely—has not yet occurred.

CONFIDENCE AND OPENNESS IN A PROLIFERATED WORLD

So the question remains, What would have to be done to ensure nuclear peace—especially regional peace—in a proliferated world? The international mechanisms that have been developed over the past decade to impede the spread of nuclear weapons would be severely weakened by the cancerous political effects of a period of rapid proliferation. Circumvention, abrogation, and abuse of the withdrawal clause would leave the Non-Proliferation Treaty in shreds. Just as aspiring proliferants would tend to ignore the NPT's proscriptions, so might the superpowers and other established exporters of nuclear technology come to regard observance of their obligations as increasingly costly and naïve. And if the architects and staunchest defenders of the NPT-IAEA system fail to abide by their treaty commitments, the next nuclear generation would likely behave even less cautiously in exporting nuclear material, fuel components, technical assistance, and even assembled explosive devices masquerading as peaceful nuclear explosives. In any case, today's rules and institutions devised to prevent proliferation would seem not to be suitable or adaptable for use in controlling the *effects* of proliferation. Trying to inhibit the use of nuclear weapons is a quite different problem from trying to prevent their acquisition, though of course the latter problem could not be dismissed as long as some potential for further proliferation persisted.

If we think of the problem of maintaining nuclear peace in a proliferated world as having three essential components— *uncertainty* as to who possessed what nuclear weapons capabilities and where, when, and how they might use them; *unevenness* of the weapons' distribution; and the perceived *utility* of nuclear weapons in regional disputes—it follows that our remedies should be designed to foster certainty, evenness, and decreased utility. Also, we must distinguish those measures pursuant to these goals which should be undertaken at the global level from those which should—or must—have a regional orientation.

High hopes for success at either level are unwarranted. Efforts at the global level would be hampered by the likely (and desirable) increased compartmentalization of nuclear relationships and of security patterns in general, which would diminish prospects for fostering a global common interest. And regional efforts would be retarded by the plain fact that it is at this level that the incentives and adverse effects of proliferation would be most salient. Thus, while the superpowers have managed over the years to identify and cultivate a common interest in avoiding nuclear war, we cannot assume that a similar phenomenon would accompany proliferation and serve as the basis for international action, global or regional, to suppress nuclear war outside the domain of the central balance.

Still, it is possible to imagine a rather mixed and messy "regime"—of international constraints, institutions, procedures, and, above all, rudimentary acceptance of collective responsibility for nuclear peace—to control nuclear weapons in a proliferated world. Any mechanisms that could decrease uncertainties and misinformation about nuclear production capabilities and weapons systems would help reduce reliance on worst-case assumptions that influence a state's acquisition, development, and deployment of nuclear weapons. Rarely does the truth accord with the assumed worst case. And the likelihood of disclosure could inhibit nuclear ambitions. Therefore, it would be desirable to create an international agency to ascertain, evaluate, and disseminate information about states' nuclear programs. Such an organization—more appropriately instituted at the global than the regional level—could be erected out of the debris of the IAEA, which has unique experience in dispatching international scientific teams to crawl around reactors and other sensitive national nuclear facilities.

An international information service would require sufficient authority to extract information that military planners could rely upon with confidence in assessing other states' nuclear production capacities, research and testing priorities, nuclear material and weapons stockpiles, and actual force deployments. Whatever the institutional home of such a service, the chief obstacle to its effective operation would of course be national resistance to international intrusion into extremely sensitive industrial-military activities. A formidable problem under the best of conditions, this resistance would be toughened by the fact that proliferation in general is hardly likely to encourage a relaxation of concerns for national security and, by extension, of concerns for secrecy. Moreover, those countries that might stand to gain from misapprehensions about or concealment of their nuclear weapons capabilities would hardly queue up for charter membership.

The ambience of uncertainty regarding nuclear capabilities would probably be sufficiently disconcerting to most governments that a requisite number of them—especially those with nothing to hide—could be motivated to organize a potentially viable international information agency. The problem, of course, would be to involve the key nuclear, non-nuclear, and quasi-nuclear countries that might perceive significant disadvantages to membership in a highly intrusive system offering nothing more than interesting information about others' nuclear capabilities which would, in practice, be readily available to nonmembers in any case. Therefore, inducement and coercion would be necessary for such an organization to emerge from incubation.

Restrictions on access to civilian nuclear material and technology might be used to encourage membership and compliance. But this belief presupposes that the international institution would dominate the world commercial market both as a custodian of nuclear material, capital, and scientific talent and as a conduit for bilateral nuclear transfers. This preeminence might be achieved and the likelihood of straight bilateral deals diminished if it were made more attractive economically to transact with or at least via the international agency than to bypass it. The agency might be equipped to corner the investment market for nuclear power programs by offering softer credit terms than elsewhere available and by getting other international finance and assistance institutions to deny credit for nuclear-related enterprises not sanctioned by the central agency. The subsidization necessary to assure the agency an advantageous market position might be created by involuntary contributions from the nuclear weapons states. Thus, ways might be found to provide an international nuclear information organization with enough leverage over the nuclear power market to ensure near-universal membership as well as strict adherence by the members to the organization's rules on disclosure and inspection. Moreover, the greater the share of the world nuclear market controlled by the international agency, the easier it would be for the agency to keep itself informed about national nuclear activities and capabilities.

One of the main purposes of such an agency would be to disclose—and therefore possibly deter—clandestine deployment of nuclear weapons, particularly by states with an admitted or suspected capability of constructing nuclear explosives. A prohibition against any weapons deployments not announced and publicly justified in advance would serve as a nuclear "confidence-building measure" and might discourage not only covert undertakings but provocative new deployments in general. In the face of effective international information gathering and sharing, governments bent on continued concealment of the existence or scope of a nuclear weapons capability would find it difficult to deploy their devices in any militarily useful way without revealing their nuclear secrets. And governments with a known weapons capability might be more self-conscious about actual deployments if they knew that their neighbors and the rest of the world would promptly learn of them.

Monitoring could be accomplished by making it obligatory to provide advance notice of (and perhaps also justification for) deployments, preferably verified by international means. Realistically, the international agency would need access to information acquired by American and Soviet "national technical means."[8] Technical monitoring should not be made contingent upon national willingness to be monitored. Countries would thereby be unable to elude scrutiny through nonaccession; indeed, states remaining outside the regime should attract the most thorough technical monitoring of all.

In concentrating on new deployments, such a system would give preferential treatment to established nuclear powers with their weaponry already essentially in place. "New" deployments by "new" nuclear powers are in general more destabilizing (an unpopular but inescapable fact), for there is no reason to believe that deterrence along the lines of the Soviet-American model would be immediately operative wherever nuclear weapons might appear in the next 15 years. To the extent that a system such as this one would discriminate, it would do so against states that would represent the primary danger.

"New" deployments by "old" nuclear states (particularly France, China, and India) would also be subject to international disclosure, though in these cases one must assume that only involuntary technical means of verification would be available to the international authority. The United States and the Soviet Union might also be made subject to monitoring, though it must

---

[8]Giving the international organization its own satellite reconnaissance equipment would be an intriguing and technically feasible idea. However, the superpowers would be extremely unlikely to agree to relinquish their "patent" on this technology when to do so would be to forfeit control over a most effective means of collecting data on other states and, more to the point, on each other.

be realized that it would be within their means to exempt themselves. The involvement of these two powers in an international scheme of this sort would be so vital that lenient terms for their participation might have to be accepted by the other charter members. International disclosure of the superpowers' new deployments might be important for the viability of such a scheme only for psychological reasons—that is, to reduce the discriminatory appearance of the system. It is vastly more important that each know what the other is up to—as they most certainly will—than that everyone else know.

THE PROBLEM OF REGIONAL NUCLEAR SECURITY

Neither international sharing of information concerning nuclear production capabilities nor monitoring of weapons deployments would really confront head on the dangers of the outbreak of nuclear war in a proliferated world. Nor would it be sensible to expect the array of factors that have inhibited nuclear war since August 1945 to prevail in each and every plausible conflict situation in which nuclear weapons might be available for use in the next decade or two. The crucial question, therefore, is how to keep nuclear war—especially at a local or regional level—highly improbable when the familiar restraints are absent or inapplicable.

Nuclear instability would appear in a proliferated world order both as a general condition and as a mosaic of specific problems. As a general condition nuclear instability would take the form of an increased worldwide sense of insecurity stemming from the horizontal spread of nuclear weapons, rooted in a revival of the belief and fear that nuclear weapons had become more rather than less usable tools of war and power politics. Peoples the world over would suffer, at least psychologically, from the fact that new forces of nuclear disorder had been released, and the absence of any immediate nuclear threat would not make them confident of escaping eventual danger.

Specific manifestations of instability generated by proliferation, on the other hand, would be of two basic sorts: situations or areas into which nuclear weapons were introduced asymmetrically and situations or areas already excited by such severe military, political, and psychological insecurity that even a balance of nuclear forces might fail to deter the use of nuclear weapons in a crisis. (Relative stability would prevail both in areas untouched by proliferation and in situations or areas of nuclear symmetry in the absence of existing acute insecurity.)

General insecurity, real or imagined, could be allayed through subscription by the nuclear states—new and old alike—to the principle of no-use of nuclear weapons against those non-nuclear states that permitted international verification of their status. Such a measure would of course promote non-nuclear membership in the international monitoring system discussed above. It would encourage and sharpen general recognition of the qualitative difference between nuclear and non-nuclear weapons. And it would help contain the spreading sense of insecurity that would have been propagated by proliferation.

New nuclear states that acquired their weapons more for the sake of enhancing their global and regional prestige than for improving their military power might be quick—or at least not the last—to subscribe to the principle of no-use against non-nuclear states so as to demonstrate that they were not only modern and powerful but also magnanimous. Broad international adoption of the principle of no-use against non-nuclear states could help sooth regional insecurity caused by the asymmetric introduction of nuclear weapons. India, for example, would not be depriving itself of the prestige value of its nuclear capabilities in regional and global politics by vowing never to employ its nuclear weapons against a non-nuclear Pakistan. In fact, Indian refusal to make such a pledge might be taken as evidence that nuclear security in South Asia would actually be served by Pakistani acquisition of a nuclear deterrent force.

While a public pledge not to use nuclear weapons against non-nuclear states would hardly guarantee abstinence during actual conflicts, its effect would not be entirely superficial. Declaratory policy affects the plans and expectations of national strategists and soldiers. If they were told that nuclear weapons would not be available for use except in countering a nuclear threat, their strategies would stress conventional military options as alternatives to nuclear weapons. In this regard, the perceived military utility of nuclear weapons could be diminished by the availability of effective conventional weapons. The existing nuclear powers have, apparently, rarely had to consider using nuclear weapons for lack of suitable conventional capabilities. Proposals for curbing international trade in conventional arms must be weighed against the dangers that could arise if new regional nuclear states found themselves in combat without adequate non-nuclear forces.[9]

International subscription to the doctrine of no-use of nuclear weapons against non-nuclear states would be of dubious effect in situations of acute politico-military strife. Assume, for example, that South Africa acquired nuclear weapons to deter conventional invasion from the north or even to frighten its northern neighbors into suspending their support for insurgents waging warfare in South Africa and Namibia. South Africa presumably would not then foreswear use of its nuclear weapons against non-nuclear states. And for the international community to insist that the black Southern African states make a pledge of nonaggression as the price of South African adherence to that doctrine would be tantamount to awarding South Africa the very outcome for which it acquired nuclear weapons in the first place. Or assume that both Israel and Egypt-Syria (under unified command) had nuclear weapons. The no-use doctrine described in the preceding paragraphs would of course be patently inapplicable since both sides would have nuclear arms. Even an internationally established general doctrine of no-first-use of nuclear weapons against any state—a policy far more difficult to achieve—would probably not be accepted by either side in the emotionally charged Middle East conflict. Finally, imagine that South Korea had a relatively

[9]In another 1980s Project study, Anne Cahn and Joseph Kruzel discuss the dangers and dilemmas faced in implementing conventional arms restraint while nuclear weapons are proliferating. See "Arms Trade in the 1980s," in a forthcoming project book on conventional arms trade, McGraw-Hill, New York, 1977.

advanced nuclear force (perhaps nuclear-tipped cruise missiles) and that North Korea, in response, had just begun to assemble a small, crude nuclear force (consisting of old soft-site, liquid-fueled Chinese medium-range ballistic missiles). Even in the absence of conflict, the South would have a certain incentive to launch a disabling strike against the North's nuclear capability before the latter's vulnerability was reduced by the improvement of its forces. How might nuclear stability be injected into these types of situations?

The chief prerequisite to any serious attempt at reducing regional nuclear perils would be a recognition by all regional actors that the distinctive dimensions of local nuclear warfare would grossly exceed the political stakes over which conflict might occur. Such recognition would not come easy, for often—as in the examples just mentioned—parties to regional disputes do not respect each other's right to exist and so could become extremely desperate and reckless in the course of seemingly mortal combat. But to defuse regional nuclear dangers, it would not be necessary to effect a total reconciliation or even to obtain mutual acknowledgment that problems should be settled peacefully. It would be necessary simply to gain acceptance, if only tacit, of two related principles: that no regional state need fear for its very survival and that, high as the stakes might be, the extreme contingencies in which using nuclear weapons might be contemplated should be kept beyond the bounds of regional struggle.

Acceptance of these principles would obviously be no guarantee against nuclear hostilities or threats, just as the Soviet-American common interest in avoiding nuclear war is not fail-safe. And while the superpowers agreed to cultivate their common interest only after a stable deterrence relationship had come into being through a vigorous arms race, in a proliferated world fostering a regional community of interest in avoiding nuclear war could not await the attainment of strategic stability. Still, one can at least hope that the nuclearization of conflict-prone regions would cause leaders to reassess the sources and importance of their differences and perhaps to conclude that nuclear weapons had created more problems and risks than they had dispelled.

There are a number of substantive measures and policies that could, depending on particular circumstances, contribute to local nuclear stability in a proliferated world. Most would require acceptance of constraints by both proliferants and their neighbors. Some would bear a price for nuclear stability in terms of other values. All are aimed at reducing the utility or increasing the penalty for using nuclear weapons, thereby making nuclear threats also less rewarding.

1. *Bilateral and regional no-first-use agreements.* Nuclear weapons might be acquired primarily to deter conventional aggression. South Africa, Israel, and South Korea are three examples in which this might prove to be the chief motive behind proliferation. Elsewhere, however, governments would generally be more interested in enhancing their international stature and their security from the nuclear weapons or threats of other states. In these cases (conceivably Brazil, Argentina, Saudi Arabia, Iran, Pakistan, Indonesia, Vietnam, and Taiwan among others) one can imagine pairings or regional groupings of nuclear states in which each would formally declare that it would not *initiate* nuclear hostilities under any circumstances; each state would, in principle, simply be renouncing a use of nuclear weapons—for defense against non-nuclear threats—that had been of only secondary or tertiary importance in the original decision to go nuclear. Such groupings might include Brazil-Argentina, Saudi Arabia-Iran, Pakistan-India, Indonesia-Vietnam—and perhaps a tacit agreement between Taiwan and China.

Global no-first-use proposals have always foundered on the refusal of the United States and its allies to foreclose the option—and remove the threat—of using tactical nuclear weapons in the face of massive Soviet conventional aggression in Europe. But if based on regional pairs or groupings, no-first-use agreements could be struck among many future proliferants. Not only might such measures further the goal of engendering a sense of common interest in avoiding local nuclear war, they would also help to keep the nuclear weapons of parties to such arrangements divorced—in declaratory policy, and perhaps also in war plans, force structure, command-and-control procedures, and coercive diplomacy—from the non-nuclear issues and confrontations that might exist in each region.

In areas of more severe nuclear danger (the Middle East and Korea, for example) such agreements would be more difficult to achieve and, being less credible if achieved, would probably leave nuclear weapons closely and dangerously integrated or coordinated with conventional force postures and plans, as well as with hostile rhetoric. But insofar as non-nuclear military balance could be maintained and as mutual nuclear deterrence relationships evolved through improvements in the invulnerability of retaliatory forces, even nuclear matchups between Tel Aviv and Cairo, or Seoul and Pyongyang might become ripe for, and also be made stable by, the conclusion of no-first-use accords.

2. *Negotiated qualitative restraints on deployments.* Regional nuclear security in a proliferated world could also be strengthened by restrictions on how nuclear explosive capabilities were deployed into national military forces. Perhaps inspired by the international authority mentioned above, restraints might be designed to prevent or reverse the following sorts of undesirable developments: location of nuclear weapons near "front lines" where future hostilities might escalate to the nuclear level through accident, miscalculation, faulty command and control, insubordination of local military command, or simply the general assumption on all sides that nuclear weapons, once available, were likely to be used in any major military engagement; the deployment of systems that could threaten the nuclear forces of nearby states, by virture of accuracy, warhead yield, ability to penetrate point defenses, and minimal warning time before impact ("heavy" missile systems—both ballistic and cruise—would, on balance, be more destabilizing than bombers and light missiles in a regional nuclear context); programs and systems that could reduce civil and industrial vulnerability to retaliation—missile defense, wide-area air defense, and fallout shelters.

The thrust of such restraints would in effect be to replicate in regional contexts the conditions of strategic stability that now characterize the central balance, but *before* rather than after

245

years of arms competition. The animosity that now festers in several potential nuclear regions—especially the Middle East and Korea—would probably preclude highly intricate arrangements aimed at establishing significant limitations on how, where, and what nuclear weapons could be deployed. But even in these areas, rudimentary arrangements could be designed, almost necessarily with external pressure, that might at least begin to confine nuclear weapons strictly to a deterrent role.

Deployment restraints could be every bit as important in areas with a lone nuclear state, though in such cases the non-nuclear states might have to make concessions in the form of easing the conventional military pressure that had pushed the nuclear state across the threshold. Or such concessions might take the form of meeting hegemonic political demands. In the hypothetical case of a nuclear South Africa confronted by a hostile, non-nuclear alignment of black African nations, Pretoria might be coaxed into keeping its nuclear weapons in a relaxed state of readiness (perhaps with warheads separated from delivery vehicles) and away from the frontiers, but the asking price would probably be a significant reduction of black African military and paramilitary pressure. Such a pact with the Devil—a reward for his nuclear status—may be repugnant. But the suppression of nuclear danger is often a costly pursuit.

3. *Quantitative arms control.* After a state acquired its first nuclear weapon, subsequent additions to the national arsenal would bring diminishing increments of prestige. And once a credible deterrent force had been assembled, the incentives for a state to amass still more nuclear weapons would become significantly less compelling. Thus, some hope might exist for reaching bilateral or regional agreements restricting numbers of delivery vehicles or warheads.

The relationship between force levels and the likelihood of war is extremely complex and dependent upon numerous situational variables. Generally speaking, keeping regional nuclear force levels low would not alone reduce the danger of nuclear conflict; in fact, forces might have to be allowed to rise to a level that left no state with an invitingly vulnerable nuclear arsenal. But negotiated force limits might spare the states of a nuclearized region the expense of an arms race and the political aggravation such a race would add to already troubled relationships.

4. *The provision of conventional arms*. In the case of states whose acquisition of nuclear weapons would appear to be motivated largely by fears of non-nuclear military aggression (again, South Africa, Israel, and South Korea would be the prime candidates, with Thailand, Indonesia, and perhaps Libya among the other possibilities), such fears could be assuaged, and nuclear risks thereby minimized, through conventional arms transfers. But this approach is fraught with dilemmas for arms suppliers. For instance, long-range surface-to-surface missile systems with high-explosive conventional warheads might be made available so that the recipient could deter or respond to conventional aggression without resorting to its nuclear weapons. But such a measure would also equip the new proliferant with better *nuclear* delivery systems than it might otherwise have, should it choose to refit the missiles with nuclear warheads. There would also be the problem of judging whether the conventional arms being provided as a substitute for nuclear deterrent forces would be used aggressively, maybe even encouraging aggressive behavior on the part of the recipient. Another serious drawback to the conventional-arms-substitute approach is that it might actually encourage states to acquire nuclear weapons and talk rather recklessly of using them as a strategem for acquiring advanced conventional weapons that producer states might otherwise resist providing. But if pursued on a case-by-case basis, efforts to improve regional conventional balance might help keep nuclear weapons out of war plans and front-line military commands and might also permit implementation of some of the local nuclear control measures (no-first-use, deployment restraint, quantitative restraint) suggested above.

5. *International security guarantees*. Closely related to efforts at improving conventional military stability could be the provision of security guarantees (by the UN, the superpowers acting jointly, or regional political institutions) that would permit

247

certain proliferants to relax their nuclear readiness and perhaps agree to some of the restraints suggested above. This could mean freezing a status quo (such as in Southern Africa, the Middle East, Kashmir, or Taiwan) that might be far from satisfactory in the view of particular local interests or in its broader implications for international order and justice. And it could require forms and levels of international or superpower involvement in regional disputes which would contradict the partitioning of nuclear security relationships advocated earlier. However, in situations of apparent extreme nuclear hazard, the exercise of extraregional power and authority might prove unavoidable.

Similarly, where a lone nuclear power (perhaps India, Iran, or Brazil), unconstrained by any of the restraints just outlined, exploited regional fears to further its plainly hegemonic ambitions, some ad hoc external action might be necessary. It would be a dangerous precedent if a regional nuclear power successfully capitalized on the contraction of superpower nuclear commitments to bully its neighbors. The superpowers should therefore be prepared to act *jointly* to induce any future rogue nuclear states, at a minimum, to observe restraints on deployments and to accede to a declaratory policy of non-use of nuclear weapons against non-nuclear states.

6. *Rectification of nuclear asymmetry.* One would not be able to rule out the option of the superpowers encouraging or assisting certain states in the acquisition of nuclear weapons for the purpose of restoring regional equilibrium in cases where the antagonists of these states had acquired and appeared willing to consider the use of nuclear weapons.[10] There might be certain advantages in making this approach general, automatic, and preannounced, in that potential proliferants might be dissuaded from going nuclear by the knowledge that their rivals would immediately follow suit. But in the interests of

[10]In "Reducing Dependence on Nuclear Weapons: A Second Nuclear Regime," Richard L. Garwin proposes adoption of a variant of this approach—guaranteeing non-nuclear states access to the nuclear forces of the superpowers for retaliation against a nuclear attack.

discouraging routine superpower meddling in regional nuclear situations and avoiding a general international commitment that in all likelihood would not be honored anyway, it would be best to leave positive action to establish regional nuclear symmetry as an option of last resort and, even then, one that should be exercised only on the basis of joint superpower agreement.

As already warned, almost all of these measures would entail painful tradeoffs, especially in the sense that many of them would, in effect, reward proliferation by satisfying the wants and needs of new nuclear states in order that they not contemplate using their weapons politically or militarily. Furthermore, while the focus of all these measures would be distinctly regional, in almost all cases some external impetus, commitment, verification, and final recourse would be important. While the proposed international institutional arrangements for dispelling uncertainties in a proliferated world might provide a suitable framework for such extraregional pressure and involvement, in the final analysis only the United States and the Soviet Union would have the requisite coercive tools significantly to affect the policies of lesser nuclear states. Yet those tools would still be of limited utility, and their use would imply a degree of interconnectedness of nuclear relationships that would be both unlikely and undesirable in a world in which nuclear instability could arise in many places.

Thus, it would be preferable that those states that had obtained nuclear weapons in expectation of political and military gain show voluntary restraint. But such self-abnegation, and the order and stability resulting from it, would not come naturally in a proliferated world. Sovereignty would have to be much less absolute than it is today. Most fundamentally, the vast majority of peoples and governments would have to learn that security in a troubled age required a greater capacity for self-restraint and collective action than they had yet been able to muster. The superpowers in particular, while trying to preserve a stable, insulated bilateral nuclear relationship, would have to be willing and able to act jointly on an ad hoc basis to defuse situations of maximum danger without turning a case of regional nuclear insecurity into a global crisis.

The reader might ask how international institutions more intrusive than any existing today could gain legitimacy and near-universal acceptance and how the behavior of states could be made more responsible in a deteriorated strategic environment. It is useful to recall that success in establishing a basis for dealing with the nuclear aspects of the Soviet-American relationship *preceded* the evolution of political comity between the two. Despite bitter mutual distrust, each country was stirred by the recognition that its own security could not be adequately assured by weapons alone. The year this recognition really came into sharp focus, 1962—a year of confrontation—can be regarded as the gestation stage of the first serious bilateral efforts to construct a system of institutions and norms for the preservation of nuclear peace. Similarly, strategic deterioration of the sort we could expect in a world of widespread nuclear proliferation would not necessarily leave national leaders politically or psychologically incapable of trying new, bolder approaches to restore and preserve security. Often in history only cataclysm has given birth to new approaches. Sometimes, however, experiencing the danger of catastrophe but not catastrophe itself has sufficed. A proliferated world could be either a lawless world or a very sober one whose constituent societies were determined to find new sources of political will and to make unprecedented political sacrifices in order to survive.

NON-STATE ACQUISITION OF NUCLEAR OR OTHER DEVICES OF MASS DESTRUCTION

If the problem of maintaining security in a world of many nuclear states appears massive and complex, the question of how to deal with non-state acquisitors of nuclear weapons may, in some respects, be even less amenable to resolution on the basis of traditional concepts and policies. Non-state groups—terrorists, secessionist rebels, government factions vying for power—would likely be less responsive to the inducements and threats that could be brought to bear on national governments, the latter being heavily concerned with international respectability, inescapably accountable for their actions, and directly vulnerable to nuclear retaliation.

Over the next decade, small groups of political fanatics might attempt to obtain or manufacture primitive fission explosives. But this danger should not be overdrawn. It is and will continue to be difficult for small groups to assemble clandestinely the required expertise and material to construct fission devices. Nor is it clear that the typical purposes of terrorists would be served by detonation or threatened detonation of nuclear explosives. The effects of publicity generated by kidnapping, assassination, and other measured, if often indiscriminate, modes of terrorism have proven quite adequate for those willing to use terror to illuminate their grievances and to give their people an impression of positive action.

True, nuclear terrorism might also advance these objectives. But it is doubtful that it would appear sufficiently more effective to justify taking the risk of provoking an overwhelming and possibly fatal governmental or international response. And, even ignoring the risks, nuclear terror might be perceived as overkill even by terrorists or their supporters. The group that used or threatened to use nuclear terror might murder its own cause in the process. Of course, it is conceivable that pathologically suicidal groups with vague, nihilistic or anarchistic purposes might try to stage some sort of nuclear spectacular for reasons best understood by psychiatrists. If such action were threatened, common sense suggests that the best response would be to verify the threat's credibility, make the necessary tactical concessions, and subsequently proceed cautiously but ruthlessly to extinguish the source of the plot as a lesson to other deviants. Such considerations as the possible justice of the terrorists' cause would have to be suspended, but this action would not create the ethical dilemmas some observers foresee: one would neither hope nor expect that a national government—no matter how benevolent—making a similar nuclear ultimatum would escape subsequent international reaction; and the price for lenient treatment of a "just" nuclear threat would be the encouragement of nuclear blackmail by others perhaps less deserving of sympathy.

More likely than nuclear terrorism, and more serious, is the possible acquisition and use or threatened use of fission weapons by sizable subnational military or paramilitary forces within industrial or semi-industrial states—for example, serious insurgent groups with designs on state power, such as a possible unified leftist front in a fascist Argentina or rebel military-rightist units in a social democratic Turkey. Significant armed movements could accumulate the necessary human and material resources to construct such weapons more easily than terrorists could—through foreign support, indigenous development, forcible seizure of areas containing nuclear fuel-cycle facilities, or some combination of these routes. And nuclear explosives could provide such groups with the means to deter military action by the central government or even to achieve military or political triumph, rather than extinction as would be the fate of a future Japan Red Army or Baader-Meinhof gang with a nuclear device.

Attainment of a crude nuclear capability by one or more such subnational military groups would indeed constitute deterioration of the nuclear-strategic environment (more so than a freakish, though horrible, incident in which a small band of psychopathic terrorists blew up part of a city with a primitive nuclear device). A target government would probably feel it had little choice but to try to offset the new capabilities of its challengers: the equalizer would probably be fission weapons placed in the ill-prepared hands of the state's military forces. Or the government might instead arm itself with other weapons of mass horror, perhaps biological or chemical weapons. Whatever the form of governmental response, the likely immediate result would be the possession of primitive but highly destructive weapons by political authorities and military forces who were totally inexperienced in the safekeeping and use of such weapons. Of course, both the government and rebel factions might prove reluctant to visit massive destruction on territory that each regarded as homeland. But the fact that the competing forces would be locked in a life-or-death struggle for power might, on balance, make the use of nuclear weapons more probable than in the case of a confrontation between two nations over issues crucial to the survival of neither. This would be especially true in cases of civil wars that have a regional (as opposed to class) base, since geographic concentrations of opposing groups would reduce inhibitions against nuclear violence (though in such cases mutual deterrence might also be more likely to obtain).

Whether or not the embattled central government also acquired nuclear weapons, other states interested or involved in the nuclearized subnational conflict would probably quickly lose their stomach for intervention or active support for either side. The situation would have become too explosive for unilateral action by outside powers. But since the international community as a whole, and regional groupings in particular, would probably regard such a situation as an acute threat to the fabric of international security, *collective* action might be possible—perhaps in the form of a total quarantine of transfers of war materials into the inflamed nation. A quarantine might contribute to a cooling off of the conflict. But it would probably not be effective enough to cause the nuclear-armed forces to relinquish their weapons or turn readily to political negotiations. Indeed, deprived of the non-nuclear means for waging war, the antagonists might be pushed closer to the point of resorting to atomic weapons. Moreover, the various schemes suggested above for managing a proliferated world—monitoring of nuclear capabilities and deployments, international pledge of no-use against non-nuclear states, bilateral no-first-use accords, qualitative restrictions on deployment—would be virtually inapplicable to an intrastate nuclear situation.

To rescue such a situation from nuclear violence, the international community might have to initiate positive political intervention. The intervention could take the form of a cease-fire imposed by the Security Council and monitored by multilateral peacekeeping forces. Such a step would have to be taken automatically, with debate permissible only if necessary to confirm the presence of nuclear weapons in a given internal conflict. No attempt would be made to disarm the parties, but both would be required to submit to some form of international mediation of the conflict.

Such a plan would raise several questions: Would it be proper for the UN to intervene in an internal matter of this sort? If UN intervention were feasible and desirable under circumstances in which highly destructive weapons had been introduced into an internal conflict, would not such intervention be feasible and desirable in response to more normal internal conflicts? Would the necessary unanimity among Security Council permanent members be forthcoming?

The extraordinary threat to international peace that would be created by the introduction of nuclear weapons in an internal conflict would justify extraordinary international action. And the three leading permanent members of the Security Council (the United States, the Soviet Union, and China) would probably be able at least to agree that imposition of a cease-fire would be preferable to nuclear violence, especially if none of the three were deeply involved in the local situation. Whatever their parochial stakes in the conflict in question, the three would all have to recognize that, unchecked, escalation of the conflict to the level of nuclear hostilities not only would result in an intolerably high loss of life but also would have an unpredictable effect on the outcome of the conflict.

If a government besieged by nuclear-armed insurgent forces refrained from acquiring its own fission weapons and instead appealed for international help, the response of the international community would affect how frequently similar situations were likely to recur. Should the outcome of international intervention in such a situation be a settlement favorable to the nuclear-armed subnational forces, the utility of acquiring nuclear weapons would have been confirmed. To avoid setting such a bad precedent, the Security Council might have to come to the aid of a very unpopular, repressive regime.

The impracticality and dubious desirability of such international actions illustrates how difficult it would be to respond to the acquisition of nuclear weapons by non-state actors.

THREE

Mutual Improved First-Strike Capabilities

The grave and complex problems of a proliferated world discourage confidence in humanity's ability to adapt its politics and its institutions. By contrast, the task of perpetuating a stable nuclear relationship between the United States and the Soviet Union would seem to require only minimal restraint on the part of the leaders of those countries, restraint that should quite naturally flow from their declared common cause of averting nuclear catastrophe. As observed earlier, the existing central strategic relationship is based on an equipoise of two massive arsenals, each being, for now, safely beyond meaningful vulnerability by virtue of size, diversity of delivery systems, and the comparative backwardness of strategic defense and damage-limitation technologies. Soviet and American leaders of the present generation have, by their actions if not always by their words, exhibited a basic satisfaction—enlightened, pragmatic, or both—with the essential invulnerability of their rival's offensive forces and the vulnerability of their own societies to those forces. The leaders and their arsenals have been and probably will continue to be subject to competing pressures for change: on the one hand, to build more and better weapons (including some designed to provide national advantage should deterrence fail and war occur); on the other hand, to reduce their arsenals' size. Neither pressure would seem sufficiently strong to alter the basic equilibrium in the near future. And however strong the pressures may become, they will probably continue to be largely offsetting in terms of their political effects and their capacity to bring about significant changes in actual capabilities.

The strength of these pressures for change and their consequences for strategic stability will be determined by the interaction of future technological and political developments. Innovation in weapons design is only partially driven by political preferences, though the incorporation of innovations into actual forces can be tempered by political prudence. Conversely, a technologically stable relationship of nuclear forces will not guarantee moderation in Soviet-American politics, though it may provide some insurance that political deterioration will stop well short of open confrontation and frequent crises.

The danger is that *both* technology and politics will evolve in undesirable ways, that neither will be stable enough to arrest erosion of the other—in fact, that degradation of each will accentuate degradation of the other. The appearance of weapons systems designed to reduce retaliatory damage, for example, would be more likely in an atmosphere of political distrust; and the political atmosphere would, in turn, most likely become increasingly poisonous as such technical capabilities were introduced. There is nothing *inherently* unstable about present strategic conditions that would preclude the possibility that each leadership might begin seriously to question the other's commitment to mutual deterrence and alter its military posture accordingly. Neither numerical equality nor rough symmetry in the kinds of weapons on each side ensures stability.

There is, admittedly, little danger that the next five or even 10 years will bring so serious an unraveling of the political and technological threads of stability that Soviet-American nuclear conflict will become significantly less "unthinkable." But present conditions and orientations provide no assurance that by, say, 1990 stability as we know it will not have yielded to fragility.

It may be useful to consider briefly the characteristics of the forces comprising the central balance and the potential for technological instability. A critical index of stability, very simply put, is the ratio of invulnerable strategic delivery vehicles (bombers, sea-based and land-based missiles) to accurate hard-target warheads. The higher the ratio, the more stable the system—that is, the less inclined, even under circumstances of great stress, either side would be to initiate a nuclear war by launching a first strike aimed at disabling the enemy's retaliatory force.[11] As accuracy increases, the value of the denominator increases, and the system becomes less stable. As yields increase (either through higher quality or larger explosive payloads), warheads become more capable of destroying hard targets, the value of the denominator increases, and stability is again reduced. As the number of invulnerable delivery vehicles decreases, or as each delivery vehicle is rendered more vulnerable, the system also becomes less stable since the scale of likely retaliation is thereby diminished.

Of all the trends in weapons design that might threaten stability, among the most serious threat is the multiplying of the number of warheads on each missile. The effect of this technology—which both superpowers have mastered—is not unambiguously destabilizing, for while it is true that an increase in the number of warheads usable in a first strike would worsen the odds that a given retaliatory weapon could survive the attack, each missile that did survive would, with its own multiple warheads, be that much more potent as an instrument of retaliation. Thus, it might be argued that despite increases in warhead numbers, yield, and accuracy, the greater lethality of each surviving retaliatory weapon will ensure that the price for launching a nuclear attack can be kept unacceptably high. Such confidence, however, must be qualified by the recognition that an attacker with multiple-warhead weapons could destroy the enemy's retaliatory vehicles at a faster rate than that at which its own weapons were expended. This could lead to a situation in which the side that had been attacked, though still capable of delivering a devastating response, would be faced with an extremely unfavorable balance of forces after the enemy's first strike and might therefore, if rationality prevailed, surrender. Thus, on balance, the multiplication

---

[11]The larger the number of delivery systems, the greater the likelihood enough of them would survive a surprise attack to inflict "unacceptable" retaliatory damage; the lower the number of hard-target warheads, the lower the risks that the other side would fear its enemy was contemplating a first strike.

of warheads is destabilizing in that it puts the side that initiates nuclear war at a distinct advantage.

Along with further warhead multiplication, we can also expect that strategic delivery systems will become increasingly accurate and that warheads will come to have greater explosive yields. These improvements, which can occur independent of increases in the size (or throw-weight) of missiles, will further reduce the survivability of land-based retaliatory weapons. The destabilizing effect of all these developments (warhead multiplication, accuracy, higher yield-weight ratio) will be further aggravated if the present momentum toward production of increasingly large delivery vehicles—which would in turn permit still more warheads and higher yields—continues.

The cruise missiles now being developed for introduction into the American strategic arsenal in the near future may provide some relief from the sinking credibility of retaliatory forces. Because of their low velocity compared with that of ballistic weapons, cruise missiles are not well suited for use in a first strike, despite their high accuracy and ability to penetrate air defenses. Because they can be deployed in great numbers on aircraft, submarines, and surface ships, they could confront a potential nuclear aggressor with an untargetable proliferation of retaliatory weapons. But as cruise missiles become faster, their value as a first-strike weapon will increase, and so widespread deployments of them could ultimately prove destabilizing, especially if they turn out to be effective against not only land-based deterrent forces but also missile-bearing submarines.

These trends point toward a time, perhaps between 1985 and 1990, when fixed land-based missiles on both sides are likely to be highly vulnerable to destruction in a first strike. In addition, possible improvements in the capability of each side to locate, track, and disable strategic missile-bearing submarines (SSBNs)—now the least vulnerable strategic launch platforms—could dramatically reduce the numbers of submarine-launched ballistic missiles (SLBMs) available for retaliation after a first strike.

Continued pressures substantially to reduce launch-vehicle numbers through arms control measures could compound the problem. While reductions undertaken systematically and with due care for overall stability and force vulnerability would not necessarily be unhealthy, reductions might be undertaken incautiously in response to public pressures and budgetary constraints. Even in the absence of negotiated arms control, it is conceivable that existing strategic systems will be replaced at a less than one-for-one rate. Interservice rivalry and the natural instinct to maintain force diversity could lead to less than optimal reductions, such as an "across the board" paring of systems without regard to their relative invulnerability and second-strike value. Worse yet, reductions might be concentrated on older missile systems—relatively inaccurate, with single warheads— that are suitable only for retaliatory use against an attacker's cities and other "soft" targets, i.e., the sort of missiles that are most stabilizing. Such a trend would reduce the overall ratio of launchers to warheads, leaving the two strategic arsenals outwardly smaller but in fact more capable of knocking out the other side's retaliatory forces in a first strike.

The cumulative effects of all these probable developments would not, even by 1990, jeopardize the system of mutual assured destruction unless accompanied by two somewhat less likely developments: renewed emphasis on civil defense and the deployment of missile defense systems capable of protecting all or most of the homelands of the superpowers.

There is little reason to fear that the existing Soviet civil defense program (broadly construed to include shelter networks, urban evacuation plans, and dispersion of urban-industrial centers) even begins to permit Soviet leaders to think that American retaliation for a nuclear attack would not take a staggering, indeed unacceptable, toll. What does warrant concern, however, is the very fact that at least some powerful interest groups within the Soviet political-military-bureaucratic elite are advocating civil defense activities—apparently with some success. The program may appear perfunctory, but it hardly makes sense that they would intentionally develop an ineffective civil defense system. A more plausible explanation for the Soviet program is that there is at least a modicum of interest (probably a strong interest among a few and a modest interest among many) in a no-holds-barred civil defense system. This interest could become increasingly prevalent if the balance of internal political power shifts in favor of those elements that are proponents of or sympathetic toward civil defense. While it is highly unlikely that the United States would attempt to match Soviet civil defense developments shelter for shelter, domestic American political pressures in that direction would certainly grow if the Soviet programs were to gain new momentum.

Perhaps no development in strategic technology would more seriously threaten stability than the deployment of Soviet and American antimissile defense systems, particularly the sort capable of destroying or disabling missiles in "midcourse." Such capabilities—perhaps exploiting some combination of future advances in satellite, laser, and electromagnetic interference technologies—would be of greatest potential utility to the side initiating a first strike, for an attacker thoroughly prepared to deplete a fully anticipated retaliatory strike would have an edge over its unprepared victim with only a few minutes warning to defend against the initial attack. Of course, if the antimissile defense system were incapable of intercepting incoming retaliatory missiles before their multiple warheads had separated, it could be overwhelmed by sheer numbers. Moreover, once a missile had entered the ballistic phase of its trajectory, electromagnetic interference would not disrupt its guidance performance (though such interference might still be able to "defuse" the warhead). But effective midcourse defense systems could so drastically reduce the retaliatory damage from those land- or sea-based missiles that managed to survive a first strike that undertaking such a first strike would become a less extreme option in an escalating crisis than it is today.

A capability of this sort might strike many readers as being barely this side of science fiction even for 1990. But it should be recognized that the art of antimissile defense—compared, for example, with that of accurate intercontinental ballistic missile delivery—is grossly underdeveloped. Strict adherence by both sides to the SALT I ABM Treaty, which forbids research and development as well as deployments of missile defenses, would preclude the two countries' making the time-consuming effort needed to begin to close the gap between offense and defense. But neglect, abrogation, or a tacit mutual understanding to relax ABM restraints (perhaps in the face of a growing threat from one or more lesser nuclear powers) could give the military services and the laboratories enough room to develop highly sophisticated systems. For instance, unrestrained development of land-based and space-based antisatellite weapons systems could provide a technological base for effective ABM systems, the latter requiring little more than a multiplication of the former (since a missile attack would present many more targets than there are satellites) once the science of intercepting fast high-flying objects is perfected. In addition, progress in antiaircraft defense through the application of precision-guidance technology could jeopardize the ability of strategic bombers to penetrate enemy territory in performance of their retaliatory role, especially if they are not equipped with "standoff" weapons. And if, as is likely, the stand-off weapons are cruise missiles, they too may become more vulnerable to advanced antiair defenses.

Whether or not these plausible technological developments in fact occur will depend importantly—but not exclusively—on the political context of the strategic relationship between the United States and the Soviet Union. Greater political vigilance and a stronger commitment by both sides to the preservation of invulnerable retaliatory forces would obviously help to arrest destabilizing trends.

Strategic arms negotiations could produce restraints on deployments of heavy missiles, on antisubmarine warfare, on antisatellite programs, and on the multiplication of warheads not to mention an indefinite continuation of the ban on antimissile defense. Even some of the "softer" areas of strategic competition—civil defense, warhead and guidance improvement, and research and development efforts in general—might be susceptible to a degree of restraint through imaginative arms control approaches, improved means of technical surveillance, test restrictions, and an increased willingness (especially in the Soviet Union) to expose one's own arms development activities to the scrutiny of one's adversary. These measures would not freeze the physical character of the central balance, but they could, without endangering the national security of either side, help keep the Soviet-American nuclear relationship from threatening world stability and peace.

But such a future is not inevitable—perhaps not even probable. Equally plausible is a Soviet-American strategic relationship in which each side carries out the maximum permissible technological innovation, testing, procurement, and deployment within a negotiatory framework little improved from its present state. Or the SALT process might even come undone—and not necessarily through a traumatic fit of violation and counterviolation, abrogation, and ultimate disintegration, but rather through a slow withering and erosion of existing understandings in which key accords lapse and desultory efforts to reestablish limits are negated or undermined by an accelerated build-up of "bargaining chips" that cannot be bargained off.

Such a bleak future for SALT might result from political forces generated far outside the area of strategic interaction—domestic political shifts, a chain of geopolitical collisions, renewed ideological fervor and distrust, or a disintegration of the web of East-West economic ties. The management of the central balance is not easily protected from these political whirlpools. The declared mutual commitment to avoid nuclear war will not likely be renounced, but it might be heard less frequently and less emphatically in the context of a deteriorating political relationship. And the ability of Soviet and American political leaders to resist the programs advocated by those who do not share the commitment to stability built on self-denial could become increasingly constrained if the bilateral relationship became more vituperative.

Destabilizing political impulses might also emerge from within the area of strategic interaction. There will always be those who question the very fundamentals of mutual deterrence, parity, and stability, believing instead that national security can be assured only by a military posture that assumes the adversary is committed to predominance. Such sentiments are unlikely to attain political preeminence, but pressures along this line will persist and could easily mount.

Perhaps a more serious and less manageable danger will arise from a questioning of the basic elements of nuclear doctrine, motivated less by nationalistic or ideological temperament than by a careful, rational re-evaluation of strategic needs. Such a reconsideration—already in progress in the United States as of the last few years[12] and evidently a continuous process in the Soviet Union—is likely to revolve around the question of how nuclear hostilities should and probably would be conducted once initiated.

To elaborate, it is now being argued that plans for retaliatory strikes against cities, aside from being morally repugnant, in fact have little relevance to the way a nuclear war ought to and would probably be fought. Though the threat of destruction of population centers is useful in maintaining peace, the argument goes, actual launch against cities would be foolish. Rather, after suffering a first strike, retaliating against the attacker's unexpended strategic forces would be eminently more sensible in that a strike against its population would simply encourage similar subsequent targeting by the original attacker and leave intact its ability to do so. Thus, we may be witnessing an evolution toward a more "rationalized" doctrine, one that eliminates the anomaly of threatening population centers. The Soviets, in their stated doctrine, have always displayed to a significant degree this consistency between what they say their targeting policy will be and what they expect it will be. American doctrine has recently shown signs of moving in this direction.

But a doctrinal rejection of mutual assured destruction could produce an effect that is quite the opposite of what is intended. The forces needed to implement a "rationalized" doctrine—counterforce weapons—would, by and large, be the very forces that enhanced first-strike capabilities. The more doctrines were rationalized to correspond to anticipated or preferred nuclear war scenarios (such as that of limited exchange) and the more

[12]Former Secretary of Defense James Schlesinger of course earned the limelight in 1974–1975 with various public remarks about United States doctrine which contained some measure of counterforce strategy. The case was made originally and somewhat more conceptually by Fred Ikle in an article published on the eve of his nomination to be Director of the Arms Control and Disarmament Agency. See "Can Nuclear Deterrence Last Out the Century?" *Foreign Affairs*, vol. 51, no. 2, January 1973.

capabilities were shaped to correspond to the evolving doctrines, the more vulnerable would retaliatory forces become. To complete the paradox, as counterforce capabilities improved, the plausibility of "controlled" nuclear exchange between the adversaries would decrease. Since retaliatory restraint would invite further depletion of forces, both sides would increase their preparedness to launch as many weapons as possible as early as possible should war occur. Presumably, those who argue for a rationalized doctrine as a means of improving the chances of limiting or controlling nuclear war intend the opposite effect. But, indeed, the consequences could be worse than self-defeating. Not only would nuclear war be made no more controllable, but it would also be made at least marginally more likely by the fact that in a predominantly counterforce world the penalty for initiating nuclear hostilities would be reduced, and in a severe crisis the incentives for striking first and striking massively would be higher.

We are accustomed by intuition and education to associating stability with equality and mutuality. Strategic deterioration normally connotes imbalance in forces and asymmetry in constraints and prerogatives. In fact, pursuit of symmetry could aggravate strategic deterioration both by stimulating arms competition ("arms race instability") and by shaping conditions in which each side perceives a clear advantage in surprise and knows that the other side also sees that advantage ("crisis stability").

A crucial question is whether superpower X *compensates* for improved war-fighting capabilities of superpower Y by strengthening the invulnerability of its own retaliatory force or *imitates* the counterforce and defense emphasis of Y. Empirical evidence is ambiguous in this respect. Both powers have displayed a predilection for imitation, but both have also at times found compensation a preferable practice. Still, should either or both powers move to improve war-fighting capabilities over the next decade or so, the imitation phenomenon—as a means of establishing bargaining leverage, as a hedge against further deterioration, and as a policy to preserve symbolic "equality"—could well develop frightening momentum.

A willingness to confront counterforce build-up with counterforce build-up was unequivocally affirmed by a recent American Secretary of Defense, who is both representative of an important circle of strategic thinkers and influential well beyond that circle. Speaking of the possibility of improved Soviet war-fighting capabilities, he indicated: "They would then possess a major one-sided counterforce capability against the U.S. ICBM force. Such a majority asymmetry . . . is impermissible from our point of view."[13] The recent shift toward counterforce targeting and weapons—of which the proposed "MX" land-based missile is the prime example—in response to improved Soviet counterforce capabilities confirms the American inclination toward imitation. The Soviets, too, have shown an imitative streak. Had they been interested solely in the invulnerability of their retaliatory force, they might have responded to American MIRV deployment by concentrating more on development of their SLBM forces than on deploying their own land-based MIRVs.

In crude terms, the United States, having relied in the past on technological sophistication—greater reliability, higher accuracy, and more numerous and better warheads, thanks to miniaturization—now appears inclined to imitate the Soviet emphasis on missile "heaviness," or yield. The Soviets, having stressed yield—in part because of their lack of sophistication—are now directing their efforts toward warhead multiplication and enhanced accuracy. By, say, 1985, both arsenals will probably exhibit the full panoply of destabilizing qualities: a high ratio of warheads to launchers, ultrahigh accuracy, high yield-weight ratio, greater throw-weight. (This is not to overlook the possible defense-related programs touched upon earlier—strategic ASW, civil defense, antiair and antimissile defense—the strategic significance of which would not likely be felt until after 1985.)

It is true that a strong compensatory impulse exists too and could become stronger in the years ahead. Both sides, for example, are taking steps to preserve the invulnerability of the sea-based deterrents, principally by deploying longer-range SLBMs in response to ASW advances. Both have evinced an interest in

[13]James Schlesinger, *Testimony before U.S. Congress, Senate Subcommittee on Arms Control, International Law and Organization,* 93rd Cong., 2d Sess., Sept. 11, 1974.

maintaining strategic bomber forces. Both continue to work on ICBM silo hardening and mobile launchers. In certain respects, the cruise missile program can be seen as an effort to maintain retaliatory credibility in the face of a growing threat to "central" systems.

Still, on balance, neither the technological nor political trends are reassuring. Even the most favorable political atmosphere will not arrest certain technologies likely to progress by the force and logical sequence of scientific advance. If the politics of détente have not averted a destabilizing strategic arms trend—and it appears that they have not—what sort of politics could? However, the real danger is not that politics will fail to contain technology, but that politics, too, will go sour—in large measure as a result of developments in technology—sour enough to exacerbate technological competition and too sour to permit adequate management through negotiation and tacit understanding.

THE IMPLICATIONS OF MUTUAL
"FIRST-STRIKE INSTABILITY"

Even if one concedes that these various destabilizing tributaries might converge a decade or so from now, is it really sensible to talk of mutual first-strike conditions? After all, if just two SSBNs were expected to escape a coordinated first strike, the destructive capacity of just a fraction of their warheads should be enough to deter the initial attack. That is, even in a technological and strategic environment utterly inimical to retaliatory weaponry, a sufficient residuum of second-strike capabilities would persist to preclude either side's carrying out a thoroughly disarming first strike. This is the view of those who would be content with—and indeed advocate—"minimal deterrence."

In the abstract, the minimal deterrence view is quite respectable. But it is neither particularly helpful as a guide to policy nor useful in trying to comprehend the implications—the dangers and the induced behavioral changes—of reduced deterrent credibility.

Deterrence is not an "enough/not-enough" proposition but a

matter of "more or less." It so happens that the strategic situation of the last decade or so has been so far on the "more" end of the continuum of perceptions regarding the adequacy of retaliatory forces that it has been taken as an unequivocal "enough." But as the following simple examination of crisis decision making suggests, the persistence of what most people would regard as "enough" second-strike capabilities on the part of the United States and the Soviet Union does not assure nuclear security, much less a tranquil international order.

Under today's strategic conditions it is unimaginable that Soviet or American leaders would regard any competing interests as so vital that they would contemplate launching a first strike.[14] Indeed, no conceivable stakes are high enough to warrant behavior that might cause a crisis to escalate to the point that a nuclear attack would be thinkable. A decade or so from now, however, American and Soviet estimates of each other's retaliatory capabilities might be lower than today—perhaps considerably lower if some or all of the developments mentioned above were to occur. The minimum stakes—or costs of inaction or of backing down—required to cause serious contemplation of resorting to nuclear weapons in the midst of crisis would then be correspondingly lower. And the inclination of American and Soviet leaders to take the sorts of risks that would lead to confrontation might be greater. In other words, not only might crises be more intense—involving higher stakes for each side and therefore a greater willingness to suffer retaliatory destruction—but the expected severity of retaliation would itself be diminished. The inability virtually to disarm the adversary would not preclude at least consideration of resorting to nuclear weapons if the stakes of some future crisis dwarfed such issues as the placement of missiles in Cuba or the survival of the Egyptian Third Army.

---

[14]A distinction should be made between "first strike," which connotes a massive, surprise strategic attack, and "first use," which encompasses the possibility of the United States using tactical nuclear weapons in the face of Soviet conventional aggression, presumably in Central Europe but perhaps also in the Far East or even on the high seas. Judging from both existing doctrine and deployments, the United States would presently regard massive Soviet conventional aggression as sufficient grounds for first use.

The point is not that nuclear war might be likely in a deteriorated strategic environment, but that it might be significantly less unlikely. And the danger is not so much that either Soviet or American leaders would launch an attack to bring a confrontation to a favorable outcome; rather it is that if war were to begin to appear a strong possibility, both sides would, quite rationally, be sufficiently impressed by the advantages of striking first rather than second that one or the other would decide to preempt lest it be preempted. In such a situation the level of retaliatory destruction might be close to what some observers would consider enough to support minimum deterrence.

Moreover, confidence in deterrence must be qualified by the awareness of a potential nuclear aggressor that, irrespective of capabilities, retaliation may in fact not occur because political will is lost or a calculated decision is made that, once struck, retaliation is irrational. If a large fraction of one's own force were destroyed by a small fraction of the enemy's force—a real danger by 1990—retaliation for a first strike would only ensure that most or all of the enemy's unexpended forces, being vulnerable themselves, would be launched before being struck. In other words, the attacker's remaining forces would deter the victim's deterrent. This consideration might not increase the incentive to launch a nuclear attack, but it could lower the disincentives.

Perhaps most importantly, arguments about the adequacy of minimum deterrence in a deteriorated strategic environment tell us less about the nature of nuclear peace than about the avoidance of nuclear war. Obviously, the leaders of both superpowers will continue to be averse to nuclear devastation. But nuclear weapons might come to play a more prominent role in geopolitical competition in the 1980s and beyond than they do now. Either power might, from time to time, come to believe that it could convince the other that given the nature of the stakes and the temporary attainment of a high state of nuclear readiness, it was less fearful of a confrontation than the other was. A political or military initiative taken as a result of such a belief would produce either successful nuclear coercion or a dangerous crisis. More generally, greater emphasis on first-strike forces, doctrines, and rhetoric would—apart from its effect on the actual probability of a first strike—leave the two governments and the two societies far more suspicious and politically antagonistic than they are today.

Mutually improved American and Soviet counterforce and defense capabilities, as noted above, would lower the nuclear threshold in the event that vital interests collided. But might not the resultant awareness that international crises could more readily escalate to the nuclear level lead to more cautious superpower behavior—making nuclear war, though less potentially destructive and unthinkable, still not more likely than it is today? Probably not, for several reasons. First, in a world of degraded retaliatory capabilities, the threat to employ nuclear weapons would likely be far more decisive in influencing the outcome of a crisis than is the case today. Under today's strategic conditions, crises have an inherent potential for stalemate. There is no great psychological premium on nuclear readiness; each side can be fairly relaxed in the event the other places it forces on "alert," which simply means increased readiness of retaliatory forces. While local conditions (especially the balance of available conventional forces) can provide a critical edge (as they did when the United States mined Haiphong's harbor), both sides are likely to seek a mutually acceptable exit because of their equally felt fear of escalation (as was the case in the Soviet-American crisis during the 1973 Yom Kippur War).

But in an environment of improved nuclear war-fighting capabilities, the ability of one side to convince the other not only of the readiness of its retaliatory forces but also that its counterforce and defense postures were temporarily superior could heavily influence the outcome of a crisis. A nuclear alert under such conditions would mean mobilization of ABM and air-defense systems, ASW forces, civil defense, and hard-target offensive weapons. Thus, the side that took the initiative in a particular situation would have higher hopes of success. Each of the superpowers might therefore see and seize more opportunities favorably to alter the status quo by acting swiftly and without warning to effect a political or military fait accompli in an area of competing interests. Such action might be accompanied by increased first-strike readiness, which if properly signaled could persuade the other side not to react boldly to the initiative. Differences—

temporary but significant—in the level of fear of nuclear war would mean that crises or potential crises would increasingly have winners and losers. Imprudence would pay.

A conceivable consequence of a strategic environment that favored the side with superior first-strike readiness would be that both the Soviet Union and the United States would routinely maintain nuclear forces at a generally high state of readiness. The nuclear "trigger" would become more sensitive; the possibility of miscalculation or accidental initiation of nuclear hostilities would increase as "launch-on-warning" doctrines evolved into "launch-on-suspicion" policies.[15] "The fate of both the Soviet Union and the United States would then be dependent on the performance of electronic devices—radars and computers—and the technicians and junior officers who program, operate, and monitor them."[16]

Political moderation would also suffer insofar as strategic deterioration would debilitate efforts to maintain an accommodative political relationship between the superpowers. Arms control machinery would sputter and stall. At the very least, new accords devised to arrest the dangerous technological and doctrinal trends would be considerably more difficult to reach than today. At worst, extant SALT and test ban agreements would lapse or be

[15]While it is certainly true that in a world of counterforce capabilities, a measure of strategic stability could be preserved by a launch-on-warning policy (in that it would reduce the vulnerability of retaliatory forces), it must also be recognized that instituting such a procedure might itself contribute to strategic deterioration. It would make more sense to launch on warning those forces designed to limit damage by destroying enemy forces rather than enemy cities. Launch-on-warning, therefore, would probably increase the likelihood that the nuclear aggressor's first salvo would be: (1) massive; (2) primarily made up of more vulnerable weapons, leaving less vulnerable weapons to bear the brunt of retaliation; (3) targeted primarily against those weapons least likely to be launched on warning, i.e., systems reserved for retaliation against cities. Aside from these possible counterproductive effects of launch-on-warning, the utility of such a policy would be limited in the event that effective ABM systems were deployed by 1990.

[16]G. W. Rathjens, "Technology and the Arms Race—Where We Stand," in B. T. Feld et al. (eds.), *Impact of New Technologies on the Arms Race*, Proceedings of the 10th Pugwash Symposium, June 1970, MIT Press, Cambridge, Mass., and London, p. 11.

abrogated, the effect of course being that the two powers would no longer have to circumvent them but instead could proceed unimpeded with whatever research, development, and deployments they might choose. An unrestrained arms race might ensue, one that would differ from that of the 1960s in that stability would be progressively diminished rather than gradually strengthened. Attempts to preserve retaliatory credibility by deploying mobile and/or hidden forces would all but preclude arms control due to resultant verification problems. Should the superpowers come to appreciate that their strategic affairs ought to be steered back toward a more stable state, they would find the consultative procedures, habits, and institutions they developed through the 1960s and 1970s in serious disrepair. And one need only ponder how poorly détente would have fared without the arms control successes of recent years to appreciate how gravely the Soviet-American political relationship would suffer should those successes disintegrate.

Increased emphasis by Moscow and Washington on first-strike capabilities and doctrines would pose particularly acute security problems for other nuclear adversaries of each superpower. The Chinese, for example, would probably be incapable of matching a Soviet first-strike build-up by accelerating their ICBM and IRBM/MRBM programs. And a primitive Chinese SLBM capability—not likely for the next decade anyway—would be neutralized by significant American and Soviet progress in antisubmarine warfare. Similarly, French and British nuclear forces or even a unified European nuclear force would be less than convincing as a retaliatory threat to significantly improved Soviet counterforce and defense systems. If unable to strengthen their retaliatory forces commensurately, the Europeans, and perhaps the Chinese as well, would look more to the United States for nuclear security. Whether the Europeans and/or the Chinese would be willing to reciprocate by pooling their retaliatory power with the United States would depend primarily on the extent to which Moscow chose to play nuclear bully. The Soviets thus could well overplay their hand should they develop first-strike capabilities vis-à-vis Western Europe and China. In any event, with nuclear deterrence in general losing its value, "atomic diplomacy" might

271

be more frequently and effectively employed, and the two powers with preponderant nuclear might would have greater freedom of action in the game of nations.

RESTORING STABILITY

The most obvious means of restabilizing a strategic environment characterized by improved first-strike capabilities would be a mutual strengthening of retaliatory forces—reducing the vulnerability of launch platforms and vehicles and developing countermeasures to increase the probability of successful penetration of defenses. Barring active cooperative efforts by the two superpowers to dismantle ABMs, MIRVs, long-range sonar systems, and the like, alleviation of the deteriorated strategic conditions could well require extensive research, development, procurement, and deployment of new systems and countermeasures designed to bolster retaliatory capabilities. As already noted, some measures designed to preserve deterrence—mobile basing of ICBMs, concealment, multiplication of cruise missiles, deployment of submarine decoys—would make arms control agreements all but impossible to verify and therefore hard to negotiate. But since formal arms control would, in any case, be difficult to sustain in the sort of world projected here, the drawbacks of these unilateral restabilization measures should not be overdrawn. Silo-site and bomber-base defenses against missile attacks might be perfected, and the technology of midcourse antimissile defense might be improved to the point at which a defender, even without warning, could at least weaken the force of a first strike. Retaliatory weapons could be fitted with improved penetration aids and other equipment designed to blind radars and confuse air defenses, though the deployment of such advanced technologies could compound the problem of defending retaliatory forces on the ground. Perhaps the most promising area of development would be in underwater weaponry. The use of inland waters (e.g., the Great Lakes and the Aral Sea) as havens for submarine-based deterrent forces would defy advances in antisubmarine warfare, but would of course still not overcome the destabilizing effects of the deployment of effective antimissile systems.

These options would entail significant costs and might find little support within bureaucracies whose doctrinal and procurement priorities had been skewed by nuclear war-fighting concerns. Would there be more practical means of arresting the trend toward first-strike conditions? The answer is yes: given sufficient high-level political will on both sides, bilateral efforts would be preferable. A necessary precondition for any deliberate, mutual effort to restore stability would be a common recognition that the possible benefits of improved war-fighting capabilities were more than offset by the increased perils and tensions of a less stable nuclear environment. Leaders and strategists would have to see the illogic of the situation.

Such perspicacity might be rare. But if reason were to prevail, intermediate steps could be taken to recreate a measure of strategic security that would last long enough for the structure of a new stable relationship to be worked out between Moscow and Washington. Agreement on "readiness restraints" would seem to be a sensible course. National technical means could be used to monitor compliance with prohibitions on certain unannounced increases in first-strike readiness, such as stepped-up ASW activity, urban evacuation, ABM alert, and unusually high launch-readiness of ICBM systems with known counterforce features. Soviet-American communication links—in the areas of remote sensing, satellite communications, computer data sharing, etc.—to provide for shared warning and crisis management might have the same confidence-building effect as the "hot line" has today.[17] Deception would of course remain technologically feasible as well as sometimes advantageous. But it could be made technically more difficult and therefore more risky.

Bilateral consultative procedures could be instituted both to provide routine review of the status of forces under noncrisis

[17]Davis B. Bobrow, "Innovations in Shared Warning, Diagnosis, and Management of Conflict," discussion paper for 1975 American Political Science Association Meeting, September 1975.

conditions and to facilitate ad hoc consultation during periods of political stress. Such practices would be crucial in dispelling ambiguities and uncertainties of the sort that might cause either side to contemplate preemptive attack because of fears that the other side was preparing to initiate a nuclear exchange.

Admittedly, an arrangement to limit strategic readiness would likely be based on the assumption that the ultimate sanction against violation by one side would be a corresponding increase in readiness by the other. The value of readiness restraints in periods of tension or incipient crisis might therefore be limited. However, at least each superpower would be able to remain in a relaxed state of readiness under noncrisis conditions in the expectation that the other would observe the same degree of relaxation. Moreover, the danger of nuclear hostilities resulting from human miscalculation or technical accident would be diminished. Finally, improving the two-way flow of information concerning the readiness of forces would help assure that each side would have enough time to prepare retaliatory systems for sudden use (e.g., increasing the numbers of bombers airborne and strategic submarines at sea) and to communicate this enhanced readiness to the other side so as to deter attack.

For this and other arms control measures to be negotiated, American and Soviet political leaders would have to try in earnest to resurrect the substantive SALT dialogue that would be left for dead amidst the first-strike arms competition. No matter what stresses and strains weaken that dialogue in the coming decade, it is essential that the channel be kept open. Soviet-American negotiations have engendered a common theoretical base for arms control over the past decade, and each side has taught the other quite a bit about its own strategic fears and needs. The ability of the two countries to manage their nuclear affairs in less stable days than ours will depend heavily on the availability of bilateral consultative machinery.

But failing a mutually inspired, symmetrical approach to reduce nuclear dangers in an era of improved counterforce and defense capabilities, a unilateral effort by either the United States or the Soviet Union to redirect research, development, deployment, and doctrine back toward an assured destruction posture would be helpful. While only a sustained exercise of political determination could break the cycle of competitive improvements in first-strike capabilities, the side that chose to place top priority on restoring its retaliatory capability with an intensive technological effort could begin to overcome its rival's progress in counterforce and strategic defense, given the inherent advantages of offensive weapons over damage-limitation measures. The side that chose to exploit that advantage by concentrating on the development of survivable, deliverable weapons systems would not need to fear asymmetries in war-fighting capabilities. But as noted above, the impulse to imitate is always strong, owing to domestic politics and bureaucratic tendencies. Unilateral acceptance of the notion that assured destruction is enough, irrespective of the adversary's strategic priorities, would require greater self-confidence than either American or Soviet Union leaders have demonstrated since the dawn of the nuclear age.

In summary, it would seem that only a substantial technological and doctrinal reversal would restore MAD once lost. The process of such a reversal would be lengthy, costly, and extremely delicate, especially if it were punctuated by crises or quasi-crises between the superpowers that further injured mutual trust and disrupted their joint pursuit of a durable, stable strategic relationship. One would hope, however, that the logic of nuclear deterrence and a common recognition that no stakes are so high as to justify nuclear war would ultimately prevail and reverse the momentum toward instability that may gain strength over the next decade.

FOUR

Strategic Imbalance

Finally we come to the possibility of strategic imbalance. In order to examine the prospects and likely consequences of a significantly asymmetrical Soviet-American strategic relationship, we must consider two paths to such a situation, one in which the United States attained a significant edge and the other in which the Soviet Union surged ahead. Not only are both paths plausible, but their effects would likely be so different that tracing out a single abstract scenario of imbalance would not illuminate either case, and consideration of only one concrete case would not begin to explain the implications of the opposite possibility.

It is worth observing at the outset that barring the unforeseeable, all that would be required to avert strategic imbalance would be political determination in both the United States and the Soviet Union not to permit it to develop.[18] Each society is sufficiently well endowed with the human, financial, and material resources to preserve rough equality without gravely weakening its national well-being in other areas. If anything, on the strength of its resource endowments—scientific excellence, productive capacity, economic depth—the United States is technically in a better position to achieve superiority, while the Soviet Union, because of its authoritarian political system, probably has an advantage in its ability to concentrate its resources in military areas while endur-

[18]Of course, such a determination might lead to the symmetrical destabilization examined in the previous section.

ing the deprivation of other areas of national growth. Put somewhat differently, while American capabilities are greater, the United States might be more susceptible to a failing of political will should the Soviets press toward superiority.

The illustrative cases that follow are plausible but not nearly as likely as the possibility of a balanced, mutual improvement of nuclear war-fighting capabilities as discussed in the preceding section. And the reader is again reminded that the processes being examined would require more than a decade to unfold, rather than the five years or less that is the customary time frame for policy analysis.

CASE I: AMERICAN STRATEGIC SUPERIORITY

If so motivated, the United States could pursue certain development and deployment policies to produce an array of strategic offensive and defensive weaponry that would severely test the competitive capacity of the Soviet Union. The extent to which this could occur would of course ultimately depend on the degree to which this and future Soviet regimes were constrained from subordinating other national goals to the maintenance of strategic "equality." But equality can be an illusion, especially when capabilities are measured in visible, simplistic, quantitative terms; and it is conceivable that the Soviet leadership might satisfy itself with the illusion of equality, while real equality escaped its technological and economic reach. Indeed, a Soviet regime threatened with strategic inferiority might convince itself and others that the illusion was a reality.

The ability of the United States to pull away in strategic capabilities, of course, would also depend critically on the willingness of the American leadership and public to endure the costs of achieving superiority. In this respect, the illusive nature of "equality" could work in the other direction. Americans might be confident that they were maintaining equality—in visible, simplistic, quantitative terms—only when they had attained what might more objectively be judged as superiority.

278

Basically, the American potential for achieving a significant degree of strategic superiority—that is, enough to impart a psychological and political advantage in crises of very high stakes for both sides—has three fundamental roots. First, the country's scientific base is potentially more responsive than that of the Soviet Union to the qualitative demands of a future in which ultrasophisticated weapons technology will be increasingly crucial. The American scientific-technological position is particularly strong in such key strategic areas as miniaturization, acoustics, ballistic accuracy, navigation, and terminal guidance and could, with some effort, become superior in other areas, most notably laser technology. Second, the American economy is better suited than the Soviet economy to sustain a high level of defense expenditure without causing serious macroeconomic imbalance. While the Soviet consumer sector is more easily disciplined than its American counterpart, the sheer size of the American economy and the fact that major areas of the Soviet economy (e.g., agriculture and the production of consumer goods) are in sore need of investment suggest that Washington *could* significantly outspend Moscow in defense if it wished.

Finally, as will be explained below, trends in the structuring of American strategic forces are more conducive to the achievement of superiority than are those of the Soviet Union, especially when viewed in the light of the constraints and allowances of the principal arms control agreements now in force. The United States may be favorably positioned to exploit negotiated allowances, while negotiated constraints, in the long run, could operate to the disadvantage primarily of Moscow. Also, whereas the Soviets are now in the midst of introducing their most advanced generation of strategic systems, the United States is in a position to begin replacing an old generation of weapons—roughly comparable in sophistication to the latest Soviet models—with a new, more advanced order of weaponry. The Soviets are, very roughly, at least half a generation behind, and they would naturally be disinclined for some time to replace the generation just now being deployed.

American Incentives, Soviet Constraints

Public, academic, and bureaucratic support within the United States for maintaining unquestionable strategic equality relative to the Soviet Union is likely to gain strength from the currents of anti-Sovietism gaining momentum in American society today. Cynicism and disillusionment over the benefits of détente, revulsion to the nature of the Soviet political system, and a general return to a zero-sum-game mentality (though less ideologically charged than during the Cold War) appear to have coalesced into broad, bipartisan support for strategic equality (at a minimum) in all categories of weaponry. In allying with conservatives, liberal anti-Soviet forces may find it increasingly propitious to eschew the position that the United States is overprepared and to join their conservative stepbrothers in contending that the Soviets are exploiting détente while Washington is giving away the store. Further Soviet political gains in Africa, in Southeast Asia, in the Indian Ocean, and perhaps in European parliaments are fairly likely in the next few years. In response, Washington and the American people may look more and more to strategic arms (and less to an assertive foreign policy and conventional military strength) as the most effective equalizer in the global political balance of power. An American tendency to deprecate its own strategic capabilities would be amplified if political incumbents and challengers alike found it useful to do so in public debate—the former to justify higher expenditures, the latter to illuminate the shortcomings of the former. In general, then, in the coming decade we may find Americans less and less satisfied with the country's strategic strength, even in the absence of any rational basis for such dissatisfaction.

Should such pressures for unsurpassed American strategic power materialize, advocates of such a policy would not likely be sensitive to such esoteric indices of strategic capability as accuracy, superior forward-based systems, ASW kill probabilities, and warhead-multiplication potential. Equality, should it become a hot public issue, would be judged in terms of launcher numbers and megatonnage—two rather antiquated and illusory indicators, each of which now gives the impression of Soviet superiority. Thus, we would witness considerable pressure within the

United States to match the Soviets in numbers and to increase throw-weight. Such pressure, coinciding with rapid American progress in key technological areas, could produce a significant gap, depending of course on Soviet actions and reactions.

In contrast, the Soviets often overstate and rarely understate their strategic position. Their perceived ideological needs dictate immodesty. If Moscow found it difficult to maintain strategic retaliatory forces comparable to American retaliatory forces at a time when American counterforce capabilities were steadily improving, Soviet leaders would have little political incentive to publicize such a state of affairs. Instead, they would emphasize—to the international audience, to the Russian people, and perhaps to each other—the same simplistic, visible, and quantitative indices that some Western analysts use to inflate Soviet capabilities and deflate American capabilities.

Why would a Soviet regime be content to delude itself and others into overlooking a growing American strategic advantage rather than to mobilize the necessary resources to keep pace? Inability to sustain the requisite growth in defense spending would be a primary reason. It would be extremely difficult for the Kremlin to divert the resources from investment in agriculture, petroleum and mineral extraction, and consumer-goods production to support the massive outlays necessary to keep up with an intensive American strategic push. The shallowness and narrowness of the entire industrial sector is a deadly serious problem for the Soviet economy, a problem that will increasingly preoccupy the political leadership and compete with military needs.

Technology and Counterforce: The American Potential

Quite independent of strategic arms needs, the public and private sectors of the American economy will probably continue to apply massive doses of scientific-technological talent and funds to research and development in such fields as energy, oceanography, computer data processing, and space exploitation. Significant American advances can therefore be expected in information storage, pattern recognition, electronics miniaturization, acoustics, lasers, and satellites, to name a few of the more important areas of ultrasophisticated technology. To the degree that the

United States also intensifies research and development in these areas for *military* reasons, the speed and strategic significance of these advances will be commensurately increased. In particular, the United States has the potential to maintain a clear and increasingly crucial lead in three categories of strategic capability: antisubmarine warfare technology, weapon accuracy, and warhead multiplication.

The United States already has a significant lead in antisubmarine warfare capabilities, a lead that is unlikely to be shortened and that could in fact be lengthened either through broad, steady progress or as a result of a major breakthrough. American SSBNs are significantly quieter than their Soviet cousins and are likely to remain so, making them inherently harder to detect and track with acoustic ASW sensors. Moreover, the Soviet boats, in order to reach and operate in those areas of the high seas within range of their missiles' American targets, have to go through narrow sea passages, thus making their detection and tracking easier. (This requirement could be somewhat reduced by the late 1980s as the Soviets increase the range of their SLBMs). With passive sonar arrays and, more importantly, a formidable active continuous-tracking capability based on coordinated air, surface, and subsurface ASW units, the United States could make the ocean highly transparent by, say, 1990.

Not only is American sonar technology superior, but the tactical doctrine needed to translate this technology into a capacity for locating precisely, continuously tracking, and if need be disabling enemy submarines is much more fully developed and rehearsed than Soviet ASW doctrine. The Soviets do not have an impressive capability to keep the necessary surface combatants (i.e., those required for ASW operations) on station—fueled, armed, and prepared to track American nuclear submarines for protracted periods. American destroyers, on the other hand, specialize in antisubmarine warfare (at the expense of surface-to-surface and surface-to-air capabilities, some would argue) because of their traditional role in escorting aircraft carriers. Under-way replenishment and extended on-station time are the forte of the United States fleet and the sine qua non for extensive and sustained trailing of missile-bearing submarines. And while simple numerical comparisons of antisubmarine submarines favor the Soviets, American nuclear attack submarines (SSNs) are considerably—and perhaps increasingly—superior to their Soviet counterparts in their ability to track missile-bearing submarines.

Increased effectiveness of American ASW technology and forces would not in itself constitute a threat to the Soviet submarine deterrent force. But such developments could result in an American capability routinely to maintain a continual, active track on almost all *deployed* Soviet strategic missile-bearing subs and to keep ample antisubmarine forces on station to disable or disrupt the strategic mission of most of the subs being tracked. Such a capability could be expanded over short periods by shifting ASW vessels from tactical assignments (i.e., carrier protection) to strategic missions. The implications of an American potential to mount, on short notice, a coordinated, effective anti-SSBN effort would be even more serious if further increases in missile accuracy were achieved.

Accuracy is more important than yield in destroying hard targets, so the adage goes. Not only has ballistic missile accuracy traditionally been a specific American strength, but the United States has had more experience and a greater degree of sophistication in those technologies that rely on precision thrust control, inertial sensing, and terminal guidance—the keys to ultra-accuracy. Deployment by the United States of ultra-accurate missiles, by placing in doubt the survivability of the Soviets' fixed or even mobile land-based systems, would accentuate the importance of Soviet sea-based forces and thereby make American ASW superiority the crucial element in a strategic balance ultimately dependent on the comparative vulnerability of submarine-based deterrent forces.

American superiority in miniaturization permits greater sophistication of guidance systems; it provides for greater system redundancy in general and therefore greater reliability; it allows for higher missile yield-weight ratios; and it permits greater warhead multiplication. While all these advantages could contribute to an improved American counterforce capability, the prospect of greater warhead multiplication deserves special attention. The generation of MIRVed missiles that the Soviets are now deploying carries roughly the same numbers of warheads as do currently deployed American MIRVed weapons. But this symmetry in warhead numbers is not likely to last. Even though the Soviets are achieving MIRV capabilities well after the United States has achieved them, they still have to rely on their significant throw-weight advantage to achieve a level of warheads per missile comparable to the American level. With its proficiency at miniaturization, the United States has a substantially greater potential to increase its number of warheads per missile with throw-weight held constant, even on existing, deployed systems. And if the throw-weight gap were to shrink significantly in the next decade or so, the United States would be able to field several times as many warheads as the Soviet Union.

Consider the following illustration of how the convergence of several trends of American technological superiority could present a severe threat to the Soviet strategic posture. Further multiplication in the number of warheads deployed on American SLBMs combined with increased accuracy of those weapons (perhaps based on terminally guided, maneuverable reentry vehicle [MaRV] technology—again, an area of American superiority) could provide the United States with a single system capable of decimating all Soviet land-based retaliatory forces (ICBMs and bombers).[19] Soviet antisubmarine warfare technology, even by the late 1980s, will probably not be capable of eliminating or even significantly reducing such a threat. Moreover, the Soviets might find themselves heavily dependent on their own submarine-based retaliatory weapons, weapons in which they have so far not placed much megatonnage in contrast with their extensive MIRVing of ICBMs. And even should Soviet investment in its strategic submarine force increase over the next decade, that force could become more and more vulnerable in the face of steady or quantum American advances in ASW.

[19]In a recent article ("How to Avoid MONAD—and Disaster," *Foreign Policy,* no. 24, Fall 1976), Thomas J. Downey discusses the possibility of a Soviet MaRV/SLBM threat to American bombers and ICBMs toward the end of the next decade.

A possible fourth area in which, by the late 1990s, American technological superiority could yield an important strategic edge is that of missile defense technology. Intercepting large numbers of retaliatory vehicles before warhead separation may now seem infeasible because of technological retardation in this area, agreed ABM deployment restraints, and perhaps most importantly, restraints on ABM research and development. For the United States to develop and deploy superior missile defense systems, two conditions would have to be met: first, existing ABM limitations, which are indefinite in duration, would have to be formally abandoned or at least largely ignored by both sides; second, the United States would have to outperform the Soviet Union in an unrestrained or loosely restrained missile defense competition.

With respect to the lifting of ABM restrictions, several scenarios seem plausible. Fearing the threat of future increases in the ranges of Chinese missiles, the Soviets might seek to negotiate with the United States some degree of relaxation of current restraints, such as an increase in the number of permissible ABM-protected sites and allowance of greater flexibility in area defense. Or the Soviets—or the United States—might abrogate the ABM treaty if SALT foundered. Or, by tacit mutual consent, both powers might more vigorously pursue ABM research and development while still abiding by extant restrictions on actual deployments. Under any one of these scenarios, an ever-widening crack in the ABM-limit door could conceivably open in the course of the next decade. By the late 1980s, ABM competition could be in full swing, whether the door had been opened or knocked down. Should this situation occur, the American technological position would probably be stronger than the Soviet.

The strategic potential of laser technology is not yet understood. Nor is it at all evident that the United States now leads in this area. Potential use of lasers in energy generation, industry, tactical weaponry, and several other areas will continue to entice American researchers who are already pursuing mastery of this technology with at least as much intensity as the Soviets and who, with adequate resources, are capable of being second to none in

285

this area. Laser technology could, by 1990, provide the means to disable missiles in flight. Electromagnetic interference with guidance or other onboard functions of retaliatory vehicles is another real technological possibility. The United States probably has somewhat greater—though hardly decisively greater—sophistication than the Soviets in this field and presumably could acquire an advantage in its strategic applications as well. In sum, it is certainly reasonable to expect that if an ABM competition were to reignite, the United States would be at least as capable, and probably more capable, of deploying a system or systems—perhaps based on satellite-mounted lasers—that would cut deeply into retaliatory credibility.

Force Structure, Arms Control, and Expandability

> In the 1980s the greater flexibility of our force, and the greater vulnerability of their force, is very likely to bring about a situation in which the threat to their force is likely to be much greater than the threat to our total forces—regardless of what the weight of the individual warhead is.[20]
>
> Henry Kissinger
> December 3, 1974

At present, the Soviet Union has over three-fourths of its aggregate throw-weight in its ICBM force, while the United States has roughly one-fourth of its throw-weight in its ICBMs. The Soviets have chosen, at least for now, to concentrate their multiple warheads in ther ICBM force; the American MIRV program has been and will continue to be concentrated in SLBMs. Therefore, even if the ICBM forces of *both* sides should become highly vulnerable in the next decade, Soviet advantages in numbers of launchers, throw-weight, and gross equivalent megatonnage, even if maintained on paper, would in effect evaporate. What could the Soviets do to avoid a strategic trap—set as much by themselves as by their adversaries?

They could, within the bounds of SALT accords and under-

[20]Press backgrounder to Washington press corps following the November 24, 1974, "Vladivostok agreement."

standings, replace their ICBMs with SLBMs as the principal arm of the Soviet strategic arsenal. But doing this would involve enormous expense, especially as the Soviets are in the midst of a massive investment in land-based forces—in particular, the SS-17, SS-18, and SS-19 MIRVed ICBMs. They could try to make each ICBM count more. But here the constraints are even more severe: under the current SALT agreements, silo size can be expanded only slightly (15 percent); significant increases in numbers of warheads that can be deployed per missile above the SS-17 and SS-19 levels will be unlikely for some time given that the Soviet MIRV program is just leaving the infant stage; accuracy and yield-weight ratios might be improved, but both require the sort of qualitative sophistication that has characterized not Soviet, but American strategic programs. The imposition of new SALT restrictions on heavy missiles would further impede Soviet efforts to enhance the potency of their ICBMs.

Present arms limitation accords could work to the advantage of the United States in the long run. By building up to 2,400 delivery vehicles, Washington could further strengthen whichever component of the ICBM-SLBM-bomber triad it might choose—presumably SLBMs. The Vladivostok ceiling of 1,320 missiles that may be MIRVed provides room to deploy another generation of MIRVs with still greater numbers of warheads. Moreover, whatever throw-weight advantage the Soviets may have now could be erased should Washington wish to take advantage of the allowed silo expansion. Even existing American silos are, without significant modification, capable of taking larger missiles than those now in place.[21] The development of MaRVs and long-range cruise missiles would also enhance American force capabilities in a number of dimensions: flexibility, warhead multiplication, counterforce accuracy. Furthermore, the United States, by virtue of its MaRV and cruise missile potential, would be in a better position to defy improved and expanded Soviet missile and air defense capabilities. Thus, while American strategic forces are probably even now objectively more threatening to Soviet forces than vice versa, they are much more expand-

[21] Ibid.

able over time than are Soviet forces, given the constraints of cost, negotiated limits, and technological sophistication.

CASE II: SOVIET STRATEGIC SUPERIORITY

Soviet superiority in the late 1980s, should it come about, would be the result of a far different sort of process. It could be based on a massive civil defense program, on the creation of a vast antiair network capable of shielding the Soviet homeland from American bombers, on a continued build-up of increasingly accurate heavy missiles, and on intensive development of accurate, multiple-warhead submarine-launched ballistic missiles.[22] The attainment of Soviet strategic superiority might also be facilitated by a negotiated understanding to count French and British forces with American forces in designing arms control measures to "balance" Soviet and NATO strategic forces.

More importantly, Soviet attainment of superiority would require a willingness on the part of the Soviet leadership to make the necessary sacrifices—or, rather, to impose them on the Soviet people. It is not difficult to imagine a realignment of the Soviet internal political leadership that results in domination by less moderate groups. Understandably, given a history of recurrent foreign invasion and devastation under both tsars and commissars, there is a strong inclination within the Russian character to prepare for the worst. Regardless of any hypothetical expansionist intent, many (most?) Soviet planners believe that the Soviet Union ought to be prepared to win the next war, whatever its scope. The logical appeal of the Western concept of mutual deterrence has not and will not thoroughly overcome this war-fighting instinct.

At the same time, American leaders and society, faced with economic deceleration and constrained by competing domestic budgetary priorities, could become increasingly relaxed about the maintenance of strategic balance. The danger is not so much that the United States would fail to match Soviet counterforce and

[22]These are the aspects of current Soviet military policy to which some observers point in claiming Moscow is already seeking superiority.

defense advances, but that retaliatory capabilities would not be expanded and refined to compensate for Soviet programs. With the United States depending increasingly on the submarine-based deterrent, its land-based systems might be allowed to become highly vulnerable. And if Washington develops neither cruise missiles nor a new generation of strategic bombers, as ICBMs become less survivable the burden of deterrence on the SLBM force will be even greater.

While it is not likely that American strategic programs would lie dormant in the shadow of a continued Soviet build-up, it is possible. At worst, by 1990 the United States could find itself confronted with a Soviet capability to launch a crippling attack on American land-based systems, to disrupt—although perhaps not disable—submarine-launched retaliation, to protect at least some population and industrial centers with antiair and antimissile defense, and significantly to reduce casualties from retaliation with a civil defense program. The crucial question would be what fraction of its strategic force the Soviet Union would need to or choose to expend to make an effective first strike. Obviously, the smaller the fraction, the less likely it would be that the United States would in fact retaliate and the more tempted the Soviets might therefore be to launch an attack.

THE MEANING AND USES OF SUPERIORITY

Because the implication of cases I and II are so different, as will be discussed below, generalizing about strategic imbalance is neither easy nor especially enlightening. Still, three general observations should be made. First, looking strictly at the question of the likelihood of nuclear war, imbalance would probably be less dangerous than a mutual, balanced improvement of counterforce and defense capabilities. Given that nuclear war will remain a catastrophic contingency no matter what strategic environment prevails in the future, the most plausible impulse that might trigger a nuclear exchange will continue to be the desire to preempt should the perceived likelihood of the other side initiating a war rise sharply in time of crisis. The impulse to preempt would be stronger in the case of mutually improved first-strike capabilities than in either case of strategic imbalance. In the former situation, each side would have reason to fear that the other, also out of fear, might decide to strike before being struck. In the latter situation, the weaker side would suffer catastrophically whether it struck first or second, and the stronger side, aware of the constraints on the weaker, would sense no need for preemption.

Second, whatever the form of imbalance, Soviet-American arms control would likely become even more difficult than it is today. However dubious its importance in other respects, rough strategic equality provides a central organizing concept for arms control. We have seen in the negotiations on mutual force reductions (MFR) in Central Europe how badly handicapped an arms control effort can be when the participants do not start from a position that both sides recognize, openly or privately, as balanced. In essence, before there can be any hope for progress in actual negotiations there will have to be at least tacit agreement on one of the following guiding principles: (1) that the imbalance should be rectified; (2) that controls should affect each party in proportion to its power, thus leaving the imbalance essentially unaffected; or (3) that controls should apply equally in absolute terms, thus affecting the stronger proportionately less than the weaker. In contrast to the deadlocked MFR negotiations, the SALT experience illustrates the benefits of parity as a basis for arms control, for parity obviates the choice among these three approaches.

Finally, it is important to note that what most warrants analysis is not the nightmare of nuclear hostilities but the effects on the patterns of world politics, if any, of measurable differences in the deterrent and war-fighting potential of the United States and the Soviet Union. Such an inquiry must look not just at but also beyond the question of the symbolic relevance or irrelevance of strategic imbalance. It must examine the ways in which imbalance might affect the perceived opportunities and constraints, the plans and the rhetoric, of policy makers in Washington, Moscow, and elsewhere. It must examine possible changes in the political functions of nuclear weapons—the increasing extent to which they would define political power relationships and be used "diplomatically" to influence events—that might result from strategic imbalance.

The political consequences of imbalance would differ profoundly in the alternative specific cases of (I) American superiority and (II) Soviet superiority. This is because, for reasons of geography, history, and ideology, most politically important countries fear and will continue to fear the Soviet Union more than the United States.

Even in the case of American superiority, and under optimal conditions of peaked American readiness and Soviet negligence, the United States, should it ever launch a first strike, would suffer staggering losses from residual Soviet retaliatory forces. The extent of the probable devastation would certainly be considered "unacceptable" by American decision makers under *almost* any conceivable set of circumstances. Nevertheless, strategic superiority of the sort that the United States might achieve in a decade or so would translate into definite military and political advantages over the Soviet Union.

For example, the flexible-response strategy for deterring Soviet conventional aggression in Europe would be much more credible under conditions of unmistakable American superiority. Today, the Soviets must recognize the contradictions in NATO strategy—namely, that a flexible-response scenario is just as horrifying to the United States as it is to the Soviets. But if American strategic superiority were to make the prospect of escalation—controlled or uncontrolled—significantly more dangerous to Moscow than to Washington, then the American tactical nuclear deterrent would become much more credible. Put somewhat differently, given an asymmetric fear of nuclear war, the Americans would appear to be more prepared to cross the nuclear threshold before the Soviets in situations of escalating stakes. Moscow therefore would regard prospective crises, especially in Europe, with even greater circumspection than it does today. An American willingness to appear somewhat reckless would make the Soviets more cautious still. Moscow might be inclined to let off steam by talking tough, but the signals that count would reflect anxiety and conciliation. The predictability of the outcome of confrontations between the Soviet Union and a more powerful

United States might have the effect of reducing the incidence of such confrontations.

The United States would probably not be able—or willing to try—to exploit its superiority by engaging in initiatives in Eastern Europe, Indochina, or any other areas in which the Soviet Union has extensive, established interests, any more than the doctrine of massive retaliation enabled the United States to assume the political offensive or to abandon military restraint in the 1950s. Thus, it is unlikely that the possession of improved first-strike forces would stimulate aggressive behavior by the United States. Both superpowers would remain essentially status quo actors; mutual aversion to crises would continue. But in the event of a collision of the vital national interests of the two, the United States could be relatively confident of success. The Soviet Union would be less inclined to assert its claims and exercise its conventional military power in the ambiguous areas lying between the two spheres of influence. American power would probably seep into these areas—the Middle East, Africa, and the Indian Ocean being perhaps the most likely areas from which the Soviet interests and influence would recede.

The Soviets would probably be unable to redress the balance by restoring close relations with Peking. The bulk of China's strategic investment and deployment is now going into expanding and extending the range of its regional ballistic missiles deployed in Western and Northern China. And even a shift by Peking toward an increasingly anti-American nuclear posture (such as development of a submarine-based deterrent) would leave the Chinese extremely vulnerable to American first-strike capabilities. The strategic value to the Soviets of rapprochement with the Chinese would lie primarily in relief from pressing security concerns vis-à-vis China and in the resultant release of forces—strategic and otherwise—for possible use against the West. Though significant geopolitically, such a development would not relieve the imbalance of strategic forces between the United States and the Soviet Union. In any event, as long as the Chinese are given no cause to feel threatened by the United States, it is difficult to see what incentives they will have to gravitate away from Washington—which can offer a degree of security, a promising economic relationship, and perhaps eventual deliverance of Taiwan—toward Moscow, which can offer only to suspend a military threat that will probably become steadily less credible anyway.

Traditional American allies would certainly wish to maintain intimate political-military relationships with the United States. At the same time, somewhat ironically, as their fears of Soviet misbehavior abated they might begin to feel less politically constrained by their dependence on American security commitments. While they would want to ensure their continued association with the predominant superpower, they might also be less deferential to Washington in their diplomacy and in the conduct of their economic affairs.

Soviet allies might behave somewhat more obstreperously toward Moscow than they do now, not so much because of an interest in shifting toward the United States as from a recognition that increased Soviet strategic concerns might give them greater latitude to revise domestic and foreign policies pursuant to their own national interests. Of course, indiscipline in the Warsaw Pact is unlikely to get out of control no matter what the state of the nuclear balance so long as Russian troops occupy much of Eastern Europe. Indeed, a Soviet leadership less confident in its global capabilities might feel compelled to tighten control in the areas where its dominance persisted.

Since few states would have reason to suspect the United States of harboring expansionist designs on them, the extent to which American achievement of strategic superiority would stimulate nuclear proliferation would likely be negligible. In fact, a more robust American strategic capability and the resultant improvement in the credibility of American security commitments might reduce the incentives to go nuclear among those states— Turkey, Japan, South Korea, Iran, and West Germany—for whom the acquisition of nuclear weapons would be motivated largely by the need for assured nuclear protection from the Soviet Union.

To suggest that American strategic superiority would probably have these beneficial consequences for the West and for the international order in general is not to recommend that it be made the goal of the United States. In the first place, as was indicated earlier, the Soviet leaders would probably *not* allow it to happen, or they would at least do their best to keep pace no matter what the cost to the Soviet people in quality of political and economic life. Thus, case I is plausible but improbable. Pursuit of strategic superiority by the United States would most likely accelerate trends toward mutually, if not equally, improved first-strike capabilities. Second, there are more fruitful ways for the United States to direct its talents, resources, and energies than the quest for nuclear supremacy. Revitalization of American cities, upgrading of health care, improvement of education, and sustained development of alternative energy sources might not increase the influence of the United States in world politics, but the probable rewards of such efforts to the American people compare favorably with the uncertain dividends of strategic superiority. Finally, while one might not expect American leaders to resort increasingly to nuclear diplomacy in the event of imbalance favoring the United States, there might be a strong, if unintentional, tendency on their part to exercise America's power more and its leadership less. Power and leadership are obviously not strictly competitive tendencies: powerless leadership is a rarity, and even then quite shallow. But the United States, by virtue of its many strengths, enjoys an unrivaled potential for leadership in the 1980s—through creative diplomacy, an active commitment to the world's poor, self-confidence in its own institutions, and responsible management of its domestic and foreign economic affairs. To see the United States rely less on these sources of strength and more on political-military muscle would leave one less optimistic about general international conditions in the next decade.

If case II (Soviet superiority) is slightly less plausible, it is certainly more worrisome. The Soviet Union lacks the alternative, nonmilitary instruments of power and influence that the United States has in its economic base, its technological talents, and its diplomatic skills. As a result, in the event of nuclear imbalance heavily favoring the Soviet Union, there is reason to expect that Moscow would actively exploit such an advantage as opportunities arose.

True, the Soviets have been no less cautious than the Americans in their international behavior over the last decade or so, seemingly no more inclined to use their military power in general or to flaunt their nuclear strength in particular. The superpowers have both been relatively restrained, but American restraint has been largely self-imposed while the Soviets not only have lacked global conventional military reach but also have known that behaving immoderately practically anywhere outside their immediate sphere of influence entailed a risk of collision with the United States. One need not believe that the Soviets have vast expansionist aims to admit that their recent prudence does not in itself prove that with greater capabilities and greater confidence, Moscow will not be more opportunistic than it has been of late.

But how would nuclear superiority translate into operational political power? Again, the crux of the matter would be the asymmetric fear of confrontation, a function of the unequal fear of nuclear war resulting from the disparity in the damage each side would likely suffer in the event of nuclear war. Massive Soviet aggression in Europe would remain highly improbable. But Moscow might come to believe that more subtle and confined uses of military power (maneuvers on the eve of a Norwegian election, tightening the noose around West Berlin, a gradual stationing of Red Army units in Yugoslavia or increased Soviet use of Yugoslav airspace and harbor facilities) would be less likely to evoke a serious Western reaction. NATO's flexible-response strategy would be less credible since both sides would recognize that the Soviets could endure both the process and the outcome of escalation better than Western Europe and the United States. Sociopolitical conditions in Western Europe might deteriorate under the psychological burden of East-West strategic disparity. "Finlandization" of Western Europe would be possible, but perhaps no more so than a build-up of Western European nuclear strength with active German participation.

Elsewhere, the Soviets would probably become more adventurous, more successful in their adventures, and hence still more adventurous. Whether the Soviet Union is ultimately likely to do more harm than good in exercising its power internationally is a matter for each to judge on his or her ideological, philosophical persuasion. But it can be assumed that whatever interest the Soviets pursue, they would not be averse to emphasizing their nuclear prowess internationally if permitted to do so by a position of superiority. Lacking nonmilitary tools of diplomacy, a more assertive Soviet Union would in general mean an international order—or disorder—in which power would be more important than leadership, in which control would prevail over influence, and in which social and economic aspirations would defer to security concerns.

CONCLUSION

One must be wary of overdrawn—and of overdrawing—estimates of the significance of strategic disparity. Slight but acknowledged inequality would probably not noticeably affect international politics and security conditions—unless too many influential persons were convinced that it would. But significant disparities would matter at least at the margin. And marginal behavioral change by *both* the weaker and the stronger of the two states that dominate world politics would have important international repercussions.

It is all too easy to say that no rational leader would ever allow even, say, 10 percent of his or her people to perish, so why worry if it is 30 percent that is vulnerable one year and only 20 percent the next, or 20 percent for one country and 60 percent for the other. Indeed, our ability to estimate is so poor that we can at best say that national casualties would be, to pick an arbitrary range, certainly higher than 10 percent but probably no more than 60 percent—in other words, within a range of from 20 to over 100 million Americans (or Russians).

But we cannot ignore the danger that a gross difference in expected losses between the two superpowers would encourage the stronger to exploit the more acute fears of the side whose losses would be much greater. And if one side were to retreat from its tacit commitment to expose itself to the full fury of nuclear holocaust, a disturbing and exploitable asymmetry in the expected effects of such a contingency could develop. The problem lies in the question that haunts national leaders, strategists, and military planners in both the United States and the Soviet Union: Does it make more sense to arrange for maximal losses, in hopes that nuclear war can thus be permanently averted, or to prepare to minimize one's own losses—indeed to "win"—on the assumption that nuclear war may occur someday? Translated into forces and doctrine and expectable casualties, there is a massive difference between the two alternatives. If either American or Soviet leaders became obsessed with the need to prepare for nuclear war and designed their forces and revised their plans accordingly, would they face that contingency—or situations from which the contingency might arise—no differently than would the leaders of a rival that was prepared to deter but not to win?

The two hypothetical cases of strategic disparity outlined above entail what must be considered "significant" differences between the likely effects of nuclear war on the stronger and the likely effects on the weaker. Under such conditions, it would be foolish (if commendable) for the strong not to act more boldly and reckless (if admirable) for the weak not to act with greater circumspection.

Perhaps more important than static conditions of strategic inequality are perceptions of trends. For instance, when the Chinese express disappointment and concern over Soviet strength and American weakness, what they are really worried about is Soviet accretion and American decay. Static conditions reflect capabilities; trends reflect intentions, that is, they indicate complacency or strength of will. Static conditions are more easily analyzed and estimated, but perceptions of trends—however unrefined—are what drive behavior.

It is one thing to recommend against any effort by the United States to strive for a strategic advantage and quite another to prescribe a proper course of action for the United States in the face of such an effort by the Soviet Union. Since strategic imbalance would matter, and since Soviet superiority in particular would have undesirable international consequences, the question is not whether Soviet superiority should be resisted, but rather how. The choice would essentially be between compensation and imitation. And the dilemma would be that compensation alone (that is, programs designed to preserve a survivable, deliverable, retaliatory force sufficient to inflict roughly the same losses on the Soviet Union as the United States would suffer) might leave a strong impression of inferiority—disclaiming notwithstanding—with significant international political consequences. Yet imitation would likely lead in the more dangerous direction of mutual improved counterforce and defense capabilities. Both courses would involve considerable expense; neither would be desirable on the basis of budgetary considerations. So for Americans the choice would come down to one of the basic dilemmas of the nuclear age: to prepare for the worst or to do the best to ensure that the worst did not occur.

In facing this choice—as the United States in fact does today in numerous strategic policy issues—it is worth remembering that the Soviets are no less influenced by American actions than vice versa. What to Washington may seem justifiable imitation is likely to be seen as a provocation in Moscow. For example, today many Americans may deem it only prudent to develop a heavy missile in view of the greater yield of Soviet weapons. But in view of superior American accuracy, the Soviets may ask why the United States must also increase throw-weight. They in turn may be dissatisfied with their heavy but inaccurate weapons.

Thus, in acting to preclude a Soviet strategic advantage, the United States should develop forces that will both strengthen deterrence and, if copied by the Soviet Union, pose no threat to deterrence. With its technological superiority, the United States can and should ensure that nuclear war remains at least as terrifying to the Soviets as it is to American leaders and that any sustained Soviet effort to make nuclear war less terrible is offset. If the Soviets adhere to a similar policy, there is hope that the arms race will decelerate and that deterioration of the central strategic balance will be avoided—at least for the 1980s.

On the Choice
of a Nuclear Future

David C. Gompert

On the Choice of a Nuclear Future

IS THERE A CHOICE?

Human reason can influence but cannot determine the role and control of nuclear weapons in the future. The tricky course of technology and the occasional intrusion of irrationality will also have their say. But insofar as choice matters, the process of choosing might assume any of several forms. National leaders and the assorted experts who serve them might find it both expedient and proper to resolve nuclear policy questions (weapon development, force deployment, doctrine, arms control) essentially on the basis of the parochial needs of their individual societies. The aim of each nation would be to maximize its might and its options while minimizing risks and constraining adversaries to the fullest possible extent.

Instead, national leaders, aware that the availability of unspeakable destructive power requires "global leadership," might act as custodians of human survival as well as contestants engaged in a potentially deadly strategic competition. As particular nuclear issues arose, each would be dealt with in the light of its understood implications not only for national advantage but also for global security. Still another approach would concentrate energies and attention not simply on particular issues but on a general conception of a desired nuclear future, consistent with both national objectives and planetary safety. Judgments and actions on nuclear policy issues would then, in principle, promote the adopted conception.

This last method of nuclear policy making—like any effort to broaden and deepen the framework of policy—would allow for long-range planning, facilitate control over scientific-technological innovation, permit better public understanding of what the future holds and why certain policies are chosen over others, provide a basis for international consensus on how best to ensure the security of all, and improve predictability, continuity, and consistency in strategic policy. To choose a nuclear future is to infuse present-day decision making with a sense of direction.

And there is indeed a choice. The four nuclear regions delineated in the preceding essays differ vastly in their premises, their underlying values, their physical and doctrinal properties, and their implications. To borrow from this volume's introduction: the First Regime recognizes that nuclear weapons "have in fact fostered . . . moderation and stability in international politics;" the Second Regime sees nuclear weapons as "an inescapable burden" whose weight we should aim to lessen; the Third Regime views nuclear weapons as "an intolerable menace" which must eventually be eradicated; the Fourth Regime foresees deterioration and therefore seeks to "attenuate the perils of a forbidding nuclear future."

A critical and comparative review of the regimes might help sharpen the nature of the choice.[1]

THE FOUR REGIMES: CONSTRASTS AND CONSTRAINTS

The First Regime calls for retention of high American and Soviet nuclear force levels as a means of making the crucial central balance between the nuclear superpowers as insensitive as possible to vicissitudes in their political relationship, to future arms

---

[1] The comparative inquiry of this essay gives somewhat greater attention to the First and Second Regimes than to the Third and Fourth. This is because the Third Regime is not really a practical alternative for the 1980s and the Fourth Regime is not a prescription for desirable nuclear conditions but an analysis of how to get by if things get worse.

competition, to technical change, and to an expansion of the strategic power of other international actors, such as China or a more unified Western Europe. Implicit in this prescription is the question, Are the supposed benefits of arms reductions and a diminution of Soviet-American nuclear preponderance really worth the abandonment of a regime that, however grotesque it may seem, evidently works? It "works," suggests Michael Mandelbaum, in the sense that the supreme objective of avoiding nuclear conflict is and can continue to be realized not *despite* current nuclear arsenals and politics but *because* of them. The sheer size of American and Soviet arsenals and the fact that each society is virtually defenseless against the adversary's forces dictate prudence in geopolitical competition and extreme precautions in the command and control of nuclear weapons. Grave doubts that nuclear violence could be controlled discourage both powers from detonating even a single nuclear weapon anytime, anywhere. The regime stands on the record of an ever-fading danger of nuclear war and a claim that in the absence of evidence that other arrangements would provide better insurance, an uncertain future can most confidently be faced by the familiar system now in place.

The First Regime would preserve the various mechanisms that permit the fear of nuclear war—and indeed the fear of situations that might raise the risks of nuclear war—to contribute to the maintenance of conventional security, particularly at the apex of East-West confrontation, Europe. The paradox of the First Regime is that although nuclear war is indeed "unthinkable," a potential conventional aggressor is unwilling to run the risk that its adversary will accept a severe setback without escalating from conventional to "battlefield" nuclear to "theater" nuclear to "intercontinental" nuclear conflict. The possibilities for miscalculation, irrationality, and loss of control are too great and the consequences too disastrous to bet against the unthinkable, however favorable the apparent odds.

Thus, the First Regime would retain tactical nuclear weapons[2]

[2] In particular, those of the United States, which supplement NATO conventional forces in Europe and are deployed with land, sea, and air forces elsewhere around the world.

designed and deployed for possible use against non-nuclear aggression, thereby constituting a bridge between conventional conflict and the exchange of strategic weapons. In addition, the regime eschews formal pledges (unilateral, bilateral, or multilateral) to refrain from using nuclear weapons except in response to nuclear attack. The specter of total war can demand moderation even at levels of competition well below the nuclear threshold. But there must be plausible—if not necessarily entirely credible—paths from subnuclear aggression to the unthinkable, or much of the utility of nuclear weapons in promoting prudence and order will be lost.

The paradox that enables the First Regime to foster subnuclear security could be turned inside out, however, making it a blueprint for Armageddon. The more credible the links (tactical nuclear weapons and a strategy that embraces a willingness to use nuclear weapons first), the more likely it is that a low-level crisis will in fact have a nuclear denouement. The Second Nuclear Regime regards this condition as intolerable. The architect of the specific Second Regime in this volume, Richard Garwin, believes that the only rational, legitimate purpose of nuclear weapons is to deter the use of other nuclear weapons. While the First Regime involves continued dependence on the conditon of mutual assured destruction, nuclear weapons and doctrine would not be strictly confined to a strategic retaliatory role. The essence of the Second Regime is that nuclear weapons should be so confined. The Second Regime would sever the links between conventional security and nuclear weapons; it would abolish tactical nuclear weapons and discard doctrines and force deployments that imply the possibility of using nuclear weapons for any purpose other than to guarantee a convincing retaliatory threat. It would seek to push nuclear weapons as far as possible into the background of competitive international politics, seeing such weapons as simply too dangerous to serve as a source of general discipline in world affairs, as is their role in the First Regime.

While both these regimes entail continued dependence on mutual assured destruction, they differ markedly in their recommendations as to how and in precisely what form the Soviet-

American mutual deterrence relationship ought to be preserved. The First Regime stresses rough quantitative equality of Soviet and American nuclear forces, even though stability could survive considerable inequality. Given the complexity of nuclear strategy, differences in weapons quality, and the dissimilar security needs of the two superpowers (owing to geographical factors, vastly different national experiences with war, dissimilar alliance relationships, Soviet fears of China, and the like), numerical equality of forces is admittedly an arbitrary state. But the importance of equality as a symbol cannot be dismissed as being meaningful only to those who are ignorant of the nuances of "stability" or "equilibrium." Equality is a litmus (to the trained and untrained observer alike) for the crucial—and otherwise not easily discernible—fact that neither superpower is intent upon superiority, just as neither would settle for inferiority. Equality is important essentially because any significant departure from it would signal dissatisfaction with—and therefore the possibility of genuinely serious future departures from—the strategic status quo.

The Second Regime would tolerate—though certainly not require—significant nuclear inequality. As long as the United States (or the Soviet Union) retained an unchallengeable capacity to retaliate in the wake of a nuclear attack of any scale, considerable imbalances and asymmetries in forces would be of little moment. Our addiction to the symbol of equality may be understandable in a world where nuclear weapons have come to play so prominent a role in the perceptions and exercise of relative national strengths and wills. But in the Second Regime's world of "lesser dependence" we need not—indeed, should not—vest nuclear weapons with any significance beyond the narrow function of deterring nuclear war. The possession by either side of forces far in excess of those conceivably needed to fulfill the deterrent function would constitute not abundant strength but worthless surplus.

Lesser dependence on nuclear weapons implies fewer nuclear weapons. Thus, the Second Regime allows for significant though gradual reductions (preferably bilateral, otherwise unilateral) in strategic forces. To guard against adverse consequences of future developments in critical areas of strategic technology,[3] the Second Regime embodies alternatives to the high force levels retained as insurance against instability in the First Regime. Among these alternatives are a *launch-on-warning* option (in which at least some vulnerable retaliatory forces would be released before being decimated by an oncoming nuclear attack), *penetration aids* (to frustrate any attempt by an attacker to defend against retaliation), and defensive systems to protect retaliatory forces from nuclear attack. These fallback measures are not without cost and risk. For instance, launch-on-warning is a euphemism for making the nuclear trigger more sensitive, and the perfection of systems to defend retaliatory forces (and thereby strengthen the condition of mutual assured destruction) would mean the advancement of technologies that might be adapted eventually to defend *against* retaliatory forces and thereby weaken MAD.

Some observers might argue that hedging is unnecessary, that reductions can be safely undertaken without compensatory measures. Perhaps they are right in principle, as long as at least one important component of a retaliatory force remains patently "survivable." They might also be correct in arguing that the withdrawal of tactical nuclear weapons from Europe need not be offset by a significant Western conventional military build-up, as Garwin would have it. But in practice, movement toward a Second Nuclear Regime would require negotiations "at home" every bit as tough as those with the adversary.[4] An American President committed to making progress toward the Second Regime would have to convince not only domestic groups whose overwhelming interest is that of maximizing national defense capabilities (if need be, at the expense of strategic stability), but also allies, who might see in the Second Regime a serious danger of their being thrown upon the mercy of Soviet conventional military preponderance. The path to the Second Regime would not be without hazards. Domestic reaction against too rapid an attempt to move toward it

[3]In particular, the deployment of weapons that could destroy or provide protection from retaliatory forces, thereby weakening deterrence.

[4]Here I am thinking primarily of internal debate on the American side, but the observations would be generally valid for Moscow too.

could push the strategic relationship in the other direction. Failure to satisfy allies that a world less dependent on nuclear weapons would not be a world more perilous for their societies could result in their acquisition of nuclear weapons. Failure to insist on reciprocity and rough symmetry during transition to a Second Regime could invite an adversary to place *more* rather than less emphasis on nuclear weapons in world politics and to try to glean advantage from its larger, less constrained nuclear force. Impatience in instituting desired conditions may in fact make the path to such conditions longer and rockier.

Neither of the first two regimes presented in this volume accepts much deviation from the principle of MAD as the keystone of nuclear security in the 1980s. Each assumes that there can be no hope of adequately defending societies against nuclear attack and that seeking to do so would only call into question the continued willingness of Moscow and Washington to be deterred. But is there no hope that governments will eventually be able to resume their traditional first duty of defending their citizens, rather than offering them as hostages to the adversary's nuclear force in the interest of maintaining the balance of terror? Is there not a regime (absent from this volume) that stresses defense over deterrence, if not for the next decade then perhaps for some decade beyond? Is the supremacy of nuclear offensive might over any conceivable defense measure God-given, permanent? Or might there be a cyclical relationship between nuclear offensive advantage and defensive advantage, as there was in prenuclear warfare since the birth of human conflict due to the sinuous course of military technology?

It is not impossible—though today it seems science fictional—that effective defense will eventually be available, owing to progress or breakthroughs in such areas as missile intercept technology, antisubmarine warfare, civil defense, lasers, particle-beam techniques, and the altering of ambient electromagnetic conditions to impede delivery of offensive weapons.[5] In such a world,

[5]Those convinced that such a future is inconceivable should ask themselves if intercepting a ballistic missile appears any more hopeless now than delivering a missile within a target area no larger than a football field on another continent must have appeared 30 years ago.

reduced destructiveness, viewed with ambivalence today, would become an unambiguous goal. Arms control might be easier, since it would not have to allow for the retention of massive retaliatory forces. Reductions and the deployment of strategic defenses would go hand in hand. The sheer difficulty of successful execution would replace the fear of mutual annihilation as the principal disincentive to resorting to nuclear hostilities. Conceivably, the futility of trying to overwhelm or outsmart defenses could, over time, lead to a de-emphasis on weapons of mass destruction altogether, a general nuclear obsolescence. In any event, the central question is this: Would we prefer a world in which the inhibitions against the use of nuclear weapons (out of fear of retaliation) would have been relaxed and the severity of nuclear conflict drastically reduced over a world of high restraints whose failure might leave hundreds of millions dead?

In his essay on the Second Regime, Richard Garwin argues, in essence, that the supremacy of the offense—manifested in the capacity to incinerate cities—is an ineradicable property of the nuclear age. No matter how sophisticated defensive systems may become, there is, for the indefinite future, simply no conceivable way to assure protection of every large population center from every avenue of nuclear attack. And since even the most limited form of nuclear exchange would mean millions of casualties, reliance on defense instead of on deterrence based on MAD is unacceptable—indeed mad.

This question of defense versus deterrence is one of great immediate importance and controversy, relating not only to the design and targeting of American strategic weapons but also to Soviet attitudes toward the prevention and conduct of nuclear war. In both respects, this issue is certain to be with us in the 1980s, owing to the blossoming of several technologies (terminal guidance, multiple warheads, improved destructive yields) that when merged permit the construction of weapons potentially capable of decimating would-be retaliatory forces. Some analysts would argue that the ability to limit damage in the course of a nuclear war (namely, by attacking nuclear weapons instead of cities) is not only morally desirable but would also have the effect of enhancing rather than weakening deterrence. According to this view, deterrence based solely on mutual assured destruction is not itself adequately credible, since each side suspects that in the event of war the other side would lack the nerve or lose the incentive to initiate a process of mutual obliteration. If deterrence fails, would not rational leaders—their prewar declarations notwithstanding—use their weapons against military targets rather than cities, in the interest of depleting the adversary's capacity to do further harm? Therefore, the argument goes, the better one is prepared to conduct nuclear war as it is likely to be fought, with suitable weapons suitably targeted, the more likely it is that the other side will be deterred.

This is not the place to join the debate about whether or not the United States should evolve a strategy of defense and damage limitation and develop its forces accordingly. (Several of the authors in this volume discuss the question in some depth.) But it is worth pointing out that the same reasoning that supports a shift away from MAD today could, if extrapolated, support an argument in favor of a future nuclear regime based on effective defense and renewed governmental commitment to protect its citizens—that is, the "missing regime" of this volume.

The problem, of course, is how to get to such a defense-oriented regime from here. The abandonment of MAD in favor of defense would not take place overnight. It might require passage through some dangerous phases during which the fear of nuclear war would be eroded by the belief that it could be limited, before systems were developed that could provide a commensurate reduction in the destruction that such a war would bring.[6] Moreover, conditions could emerge in which a temporary asymmetry in the ability of each side to limit damage might disturb the mutuality of interest in avoiding nuclear hostilities or threats. (For example, missile defense would be a key element in a defense-oriented regime. But there is a danger that the forerunner

---

[6]If a *limited war* is one in which, say, only 1/7,000 of all nuclear destructive power is released, one would have the equivalent of World War II inside of a few days.

of an effective missile defense system would be one that works well only when mobilized in expectation of imminent attack.[7] In that case, the risk would increase that one side would prepare to defend itself against retaliation and then proceed to attack the unprepared adversary.) So even if the idea of a defense-oriented regime is appealing as an outcome, there are many troublesome questions about whether the path to that outcome might not be prohibitively treacherous.

Indeed, a number of developments that one might see as pointing toward a defense-oriented alternative to the First and Second Regimes are depicted as elements of strategic deterioration in the so-called Fourth Nuclear Regime. But the Fourth Regime cannot be viewed as a first step toward a rational alternative to a MAD world for one simple reason: It would be characterized not by the orderly, coordinated process that might permit the replacement of MAD but by distrust, political discord, and the competitive pursuit of technological advantage. The Fourth Regime anticipates a vicious circle, in which destabilizing technological developments aggravate political relationships, whose deterioration in turn hinders efforts to avoid further technological destabilization. It does not predict such a future; it simply cautions that such a future is far from impossible and therefore requires attention.

The Fourth Regime, as conceived by this writer, is essentially a First Regime gone bad: the ambiguities that permit the First Regime to foster prudent superpower behavior become dangerous irritants in their relationship; equilibrium at high force levels becomes disequilibrium at such levels, possibly inspiring even further swelling of nuclear arsenals; the proliferation of nuclear weapons reduces the capacity of Soviet-American mutual deterrence to impart stability and security throughout the international system. In illuminating the fragility of current arrangements that now seem so durable, the Fourth Regime brings home the dilemma of deciding whether our efforts should be directed toward further strengthening the existing (First) regime or rather toward

---

[7]In general, the more advanced a "system" is—be it missile defense or color television—the less time it takes to "warm up" and the easier it is to keep routinely at peak performance.

instituting a much different regime for the next decade and beyond.

The dilemma is compounded by the fact (or argument) that—as pointed out above—in trying to move toward a new regime, such as the Second Regime, we may in fact succeed only in making the existing regime more susceptible to deterioration. For instance, the lowered force levels that make the Second Regime intuitively attractive could instead aggravate a situation in which the invulnerability of retaliatory forces is eroded by technological developments. Moreover, a renewed arms race starting from the lower force levels of the Second Regime might be worse than one proceeding at a similar pace from a high-force-level base, since the same measure of *absolute* change in nuclear capabilities would be of greater *relative* consequence in the former case than in the latter. The relaxed attitude toward force inequality that is permitted by the Second Regime's lessened dependence on nuclear weapons could instead result in undesirable shifts and uncertainties in world political alignments, if strategic deterioration has the effect of making nuclear weapons *more* salient in international relations. The launch-on-warning options that provide the Second Regime with a hedge against the loss of retaliatory credibility could instead encourage American and Soviet leaders to be far more trigger-happy in a crisis.

This discussion of the First, Second, and Fourth Nuclear Regimes illuminates one conclusion above all: As long as nuclear weapons exist, there are serious drawbacks to any regime that purports to manage them:

- The stability of the tested First Regime (of high force levels, tactical nuclear weapons, and multipurpose deterrence) might not prove durable when faced with the tests of the 1980s—proliferation, advances in "destabilizing" technologies, and the erosion of superpower preponderance and authority.

- The Second Regime (of lower force levels, constrained deployments of nuclear weapons, no tactical nuclear weapons, and a new strategy for the maintenance of security in Europe based on conventional balance) might deprive the world of the value of nuclear weapons in promoting order without measurably improving security from nuclear holocaust.

- The Fourth Regime is a real possibility, if not in the 1980s then in the decade beyond, and neither the First nor the Second Regime would preclude the deterioration embodied in the Fourth.

- Finally, a defense-oriented alternative to these regimes is neither compelling as an end in itself nor very attractive at all if one considers the dangerous gulf that separates it from a world based on mutual assured destruction.

In short, although we may be satisfied that we have met the great challenge of living with nuclear weapons at a given moment in history, we need only contemplate the challenge of doing at least as well in the uncertain future to be reminded that the nuclear age is an endless minefield. So we are brought to the inevitable question of whether we can put the nuclear age behind us. This is the question of the Third Regime—the "denuclearized world."

Complete, certain, and lasting denuclearization would of course require far more than a missile bonfire. It would require the burial of all knowledge, material, and equipment that could assist a government in rebuilding nuclear weapons—in effect, the death of a technology, which is as patently impossible as the end of, say, manned flight. Thus, the Third Regime's chief concerns are those of making the penalties for violating nuclear disarmament high and keeping the incentives low. Perhaps the clearest message of John Barton's essay is that unless accompanied by fundamental changes in the global polity, denuclearization is neither practical nor especially desirable. The persistence of conflict among sovereign nation-states—many with the competence to "renuclearize"—implies a Third Regime plagued by suspicion, where the reappearance of nuclear weapons might result in force levels so low and so asymmetric that mutual deterrence would not operate. In other words, global "politics as usual" would not provide a context with sufficiently high penalties and low incentives to assure lasting nuclear disarmament. Only when and if the loyalties of people are transferred from the national to the global level and national governments are relieved by higher authority of the right and duty to resort to force on behalf of their citizens is the abolition of nuclear weapons likely to become practical and desirable.

So our study of nuclear alternatives does indeed distill down to the fundamentals of political choice. How we deal with nuclear weapons in the future ultimately depends on the kind of world order that awaits us—or the kind of world order we would seek to fashion. The replacement of the nation-state—at least in crucial security areas—by some form of global authority is, in my personal estimation, not an altogether compelling goal, even though it may be the only route to real denuclearization. Quite apart from the question of feasibility, one need only think of the ills of today's world attributable to the imposition of political superstructures on individuals, communities, tribes, and other groups of common culture to question the wisdom of forming the far greater concentrations of authority that effective world government implies.

PROLIFERATION AND THE NUCLEAR REGIMES

Still, we are arrested from casually dismissing denuclearization by the thought of the spread of nuclear weapons beyond the six nations that now own them. Although the essays in this volume were meant to examine alternatives for managing *existing* nuclear weapons and nuclear relationships, there is no escape from the fact that any nuclear regime will fundamentally affect and be affected by further proliferation. The continued existence of nuclear weapons implies a growing possibility of their spread, which in turn, would compound the problem of maintaining a regime to manage them.

The question of which nuclear regime is best, given the issues raised by proliferation, has three components:

- Which regime would most inhibit (or least encourage) proliferation?
- Which regime would best attenuate (or least exacerbate) the consequences of proliferation if, or as, it occurs?
- Which regime is least susceptible to being undermined by proliferation?

313

The answers are as complex and ambiguous as the maze of factors that explain why states want nuclear weapons. And they will vary markedly from one respondent to another. Nevertheless, given these caveats, some preliminary observations can be ventured.[8]

The First and Second Nuclear Regimes provide strikingly different antiproliferation platforms. The First Regime retains the means by which nuclear states (especially the United States) have extended believable protection to non-nuclear states: tactical nuclear weapons deployed abroad to supplement conventional deterrence and to link the full atomic might of the protector to the security of certain allies; a declared intent to use nuclear weapons in the event of attack—conventional or nuclear—on certain allies; and continued high force levels, second to none, to impress allies and others that the protector's umbrella is not being closed. The thought of abandoning these features of the First Regime should give pause to anyone who accepts the argument that proliferation would be stimulated by waning faith on the part of numerous non-nuclear states (for example, South Korea, Israel, Taiwan, Japan, West Germany, Turkey) in the willingness and ability of traditional protectors (in these examples, the United States) to strengthen their deterrence of conventional attacks by the threat of nuclear escalation. Furthermore, a number of possible measures to arrest proliferation—sanctions, nuclear guarantees, constricted diffusion of civilian nuclear technologies—might best be championed (if not imposed) if the duopolistic Soviet-American hierarchy of the First Regime were preserved.

But the weakness of these arguments lies in the fact that the more protective Moscow and Washington are of their nuclear supremacy, even in the presumed service of nonproliferation, the more other governments might be convinced that nuclear weapons are indeed useful instruments of security, status, and diplomacy. For this reason, the Second Regime, in advocating a

---

[8]The focus here is on the First and Second Regimes, since in the Third the issue of proliferation gives way to the larger problem of preventing renuclearization and in the Fourth extensive proliferation is assumed already to have taken place.

contraction in the deployment, quantity, and role of nuclear weapons, seeks to depreciate their value in the eyes of those who lack them. And since the Second Regime would aim to limit the use of nuclear weapons to the deterrence of nuclear attack, non-nuclear states would be free from the danger of such attack—provided, of course, the nuclear states acceded to such a norm—thus strengthening their incentive to refrain from acquiring nuclear weapons.

The flaw in this conception is that a good many potential proliferants are interested in nuclear weapons for reasons that have little to do with emulating the superpowers or deterring nuclear attack. Some states, such as Israel or South Africa, may be tempted to acquire nuclear weapons in order to deter non-nuclear aggression or coercion; these ranks might swell to include, perhaps, Korea, Japan, West Germany, or Turkey if, as the Second Regime would have it, American nuclear weapons were no longer available for this purpose. Others, such as Iran, Vietnam, or Brazil, may see nuclear weapons as a valuable addition to the portfolio of power with which they seek to fulfill regional hegemonic aspirations, irrespective of the purposes to which the superpowers put their weapons. And still others, such as Pakistan, Egypt, Taiwan, Saudi Arabia, Indonesia, or Argentina, might doubt that their nuclear or prospectively nuclear neighbors would abide by the Second Regime's proscription of the use of nuclear weapons against non-nuclear states and might therefore acquire nuclear weapons themselves. Thus, while a perfected Second Regime, accepted by all nuclear states, might be effective in curbing proliferation, an imperfect, nonuniversal Second Regime would not dispel all the motives for nuclear proliferation and might even aggravate the problem by eliminating some of the First Regime's antiproliferation features.

Recognizing this, Richard Garwin endorses the idea that the superpowers should dedicate some of their weapons to the protection of non-nuclear states whose rivals acquire nuclear weapons. In essence, he is suggesting not only that nuclear weapons be used only to deter other nuclear weapons, but also that no nuclear weapons be left undeterred. So deprived of their value in coercive statecraft, nuclear weapons would interest only those states that required them for deterrence, and the incentive to acquire nuclear weapons for deterrence would, in principle, also fade with nuclear states vowing not to use nuclear weapons except in response to nuclear attack. Moreover, in those instances in which this new nonproliferation order failed to dissuade a state from acquiring nuclear weapons, it would still be deterred from using them against non-nuclear states by the threat of retaliation by the superpowers.

I need not dwell on the massive practical problems that cling like barnacles to the hull of this smooth concept. But two observations are in order. First, collective security schemes (of which this is a derivative) require above all "that the premise of the 'indivisibility of peace' . . . be deeply established in the thinking of governments and peoples" and that the "geographical remoteness of aggression [be] irrelevant" to the guarantors.[9] Thus, not only must the superpowers resolve that nuclear conflict *anywhere* warrants nuclear punishment, but also—if the scheme is to win international acceptance—other states must share the belief that no breach of the nuclear peace should be deemed to fall outside the retaliatory "jurisdiction" of the superpowers. Can we begin to believe that the United States and the Soviet Union would (and should) detonate their nuclear weapons—otherwise tightly sheathed by the Second Nuclear Regime—over, say, Calcutta in response to Indian nuclear aggression against Pakistan? Or against a South Korea that uses nuclear weapons in the face of conventional aggression from the North?

But before declaring this proposal beyond redemption, it should also be noted that the idea of the nuclear states extending their deterrence to non-nuclear states is an idea whose time has hardly passed. Nuclear guarantees play a central and positive role in the current Western security system, and it is often suggested that such measures be extended to discourage certain other states from acquiring nuclear weapons. But one is bothered by the universality and automaticity of the proposal to leave *no* nuclear weapons undeterred, even though one knows that selectivity and

[9]Inis L. Claude, Jr., *Swords into Plowshares,* 4th ed., Random House, New York, 1974, pp. 250–251.

unreliability have long plagued collective efforts to achieve international security.

We have already begun to cross the fuzzy line separating the two questions, Which regime would most inhibit proliferation? and Which regime would best moderate its effects? The Fourth Regime elucidates what may be the next decade's central strategic dilemma if proliferation continues: How should new nuclear capabilities and dangers be treated? A world of, say, a dozen nuclear states (at least one in each major region) is hardly an unreasonable expectation for the late 1980s. Should existing security arrangements be adjusted to "domesticate" each new nuclear state—creating a global network of deterrence relationships—in order to impart the stability of the central nuclear balance onto regional nuclear situations? Or should the United States and the Soviet Union try to insulate themselves and the management of their deterrence system from the shock waves of proliferation? An interconnection of nuclear arrangements, as in the former approach, might make the use of nuclear weapons in regional conflicts less likely, but it would also heighten the risk that regional nuclear hostilities would bring into play the nuclear weapons of the superpowers, thereby igniting a much wider nuclear outburst over an issue of relatively minor importance to all but the states of a particular region. Under the alternative approach, the "compartmentalization" of nuclear relationships would reduce the danger that localized nuclear hostilities would spread, but it would also limit the degree to which the arsenals of the superpowers would restrain the contestants in a regional dispute.

Consider, for instance, the hypothetical question of how Washington and Moscow should deal with a nuclear confrontation between North and South Korea, given the conflictual history of Korea and the precariousness of any situation involving low levels of vulnerable retaliatory forces.[10] Each superpower

---

[10] A situation in which each of two hostile states possesses relatively few nuclear weapons but also the means effectively to attack the enemy's small arsenal is dangerous because there is a definite incentive to strike first in the course of a serious crisis.

could indicate that behind the deterrent forces of its respective Korean ally stood the threat of its own retaliatory forces. In so doing, Washington and Moscow would be shoring up an otherwise shaky nuclear standoff with timber "borrowed" from the central balance and also giving themselves substantial leverage with their respective clients.

The Fourth Regime warns against this sort of response to the spread of nuclear weapons. A global network of deterrence relationships, stable in theory, would be fraught with ambiguities and doubts in practice. The dangers of nuclear accident, miscalculation, or madness are such that regional nuclear violence sometime in the next decade (in Korea, Southern Africa, the Middle East, South Asia, or across the Formosa Straits) is hardly implausible, even with superpower engagement to foster nuclear stability. A compartmentalized nuclear world whose deterrence relationships are kept bilateral and insulated from other nuclear relationships may be as likely as it is desirable. The superpowers will have a powerful disincentive to identify closely with new nuclear states: the geostrategic gains, restraining influence, traditional interests, and improved local nuclear stability that could encourage the superpowers to fashion new, or retain old, security relationships with proliferants will, in most cases, be heavily outweighed by the perception that nuclear troubled waters are too dangerous to fish.

Just as neither the First nor the Second Regime offers an ideal platform from which to curb proliferation, both have shortcomings in dealing with its effects. The First Regime's aversion to rigid constraints on nuclear weapons and policies may be less tenable in a world of many nuclear states. Freedom to deploy, threaten, use, and maintain high levels of nuclear weapons would be available not just to the superpowers but to numerous other nuclear states. Even an advocate's brief for the First Regime, such as the one in this volume, conveys no assurance that nuclear weapons will dependably moderate outlying regional politics as they have East-West relations, at least not until regional nuclear situations are politically and technically stabilized in the way the central balance has been for a decade, that is, with high and symmetric levels of survivable forces.

Because it puts constraints on the quality, quantity, testing, placement, and use of the superpowers' nuclear weapons, the Second Regime seems better designed than the First to encourage or impose constraints on other nuclear states. In this respect, even if the United States were capable of implementing most of the Second Regime through unilateral action, the problem of how to manage a proliferated world points toward two good reasons why the United States should instead pursue the Second Regime through international action. First, while the United States, by making the force posture adjustments suggested by Garwin, may be able safely to accept the Second Regime no matter what the Soviet Union does, the same is not true for other nuclear states. If anything, a Second Regime accepted by the United States but not by the Soviet Union would make other nuclear states (China, France—and in the future possibly Israel, Iran, South Korea, Taiwan, Japan) quite unwilling to accept controls on the use, quality, quantity, testing, and deployment of their weapons. Second, by negotiating the Second Regime internationally—even if only bilaterally at first—the United States would be cultivating the institutional arrangements upon which the regime would ultimately have to depend in the face of long-term political and technological change and the further spread of nuclear weapons. The United States may not be imperiled by the inadequacy of international institutional means to control the nuclear prerogatives of other nuclear states, but the interests of international security, particularly the avoidance of regional nuclear conflict and coercion, would be served by the development and strengthening of institutions, rooted in the purposes of the Second Regime, whose activities and authority should eventually impinge upon all nuclear weapons programs.

The final question, Which regime is least susceptible to being undermined by proliferation? recognizes that the chief threat to strategic stability may arise not from the internal dynamics of Soviet-American technological-political competition but from the erosion of their nuclear duopoly. Efforts by the superpowers to prevent their societies from becoming hostage to every nuclear newcomer could endanger the sparse mutual trust that characterizes the Soviet-American nuclear relationship. Attempts to create defenses against lesser nuclear states could advance the very research, development, and deployments that would make management of a stable central balance more difficult than it is today. There may be strong public and interest group pressures— today largely suppressed by acceptance of the balance of terror— for civil defense, ballistic missile defense, improved bomber defense, antisubmarine warfare advances, and counterforce guidance and payload design. In a Soviet-American context such programs are recognized as being destabilizing; in a world of multiple nuclear threats against American and Soviet cities, they may be hard to resist politically and bureaucratically.

On top of this danger is the possibility that Moscow and Washington will each be so suspicious of its rival's ability to join forces with other nuclear states that the mutual commitment to Soviet-American parity will be hard to sustain. The Soviets in particular may find parity less reasonable once encircled by nuclear states. How, then, could the central balance be insulated from proliferation?

In the First Regime, the maintenance of extremely large Soviet and American offensive nuclear arsenals provides a double thickness of insulation. High force levels place the preservation of credible deterrence beyond reasonable doubt. If Moscow or Washington should choose to respond to the appearance of a new nuclear threat with programs for the defense of its citizenry, the other superpower could more confidently ignore such programs the more offensive power it had at its disposal. Destabilizing competition between the United States and the Soviet Union would not be aroused by actions taken in response to proliferation for the simple reason that even a strategic defense system capable of providing either with considerable protection against, say, China would be so pitifully inadequate vis-à-vis the rival superpower's force as not to appear threatening. Relatedly, the First Regime is insulated from proliferation by the preservation of nuclear duopoly. As long as the gap between the nuclear capabilities of the superpowers and the capabilities of other nuclear states is kept exceedingly wide and as long as the superpowers persevere in their mutual determination to maintain a special bilateral relationship in nuclear affairs, the stable international structure that is built upon duopoly will persist. The thought of continued duopoly will evoke little enthusiasm except at the East and West poles. But from the narrow perspective of maintaining a global structure conducive to nuclear stability, have we any reason to believe that the breaking down of nuclear hierarchy would make the world safer from nuclear war? And from the broader view of a moderate international order, should we be content (or eager) to see the weakening of a structure that, for all its inequalities, has at least not been plagued by the hyperbolic violence of the first half of the twentieth century?

There is, however, a danger that the superpowers, in trying to preserve nuclear hierarchy, would succeed only in encouraging others to build more and better weapons, in turn requiring the superpowers to accelerate to stay ahead of the pack. The logic of the Second Regime, wherein a nation's nuclear posture is predicated solely on the need to deter a nuclear attack, implies that the United States—and preferably all nuclear states—should refrain from trying to prevent any other nuclear state from fielding its own credible deterrent force. In theory, the Second Regime itself would be unaffected by proliferation for the simple reason that a precondition of the achievement of the Second Regime is the acceptance by governments of the vulnerability of their societies to nuclear destruction. As long as a state has a sufficient survivable offensive capability to deter its most powerful rival, it will be able to deter all other nuclear threats. And since, in theory, nuclear weapons would not be usable except to deter or retaliate, the fact that additional states have acquired the means to deter one's own forces should have no effect on one's force levels or doctrine. One need not compensate for the acquired ability of others to deter an action—that of using nuclear weapons except in retaliation—that one had no intention of taking in any event.

Of course, the Second Regime would be significantly messier in practice than in theory. Garwin concedes that the superpowers might agree to erect defenses that would be effective against the forces of lesser nuclear states without jeopardizing the stability of Soviet-American mutual deterrence, if it were technologically feasible to do so. But such a measure would violate the core principle of the Second Regime, since it would imply less than total willingness on the part of the superpowers to see their own nuclear weapons deterred. Thus, proliferation could bring a retreat from the Second Regime once American and Soviet leaders were faced with the prospect that their societies might become vulnerable not just to each other but also to the retaliatory forces of a growing circle of other nuclear states, some of whom might be trusted even less than Washington and Moscow trust one another.

At the mention of proliferation, the mind's eye sees nuclear accidents; the Middle East or other trouble spots consumed by nuclear combat; nuclear terrorism directed against London, Paris, or New York. Yet the most important consequences of the spread of nuclear weapons may have little to do with the never-never land of nuclear violence. Proliferation implies structural change in the international system: if not the death of bipolarity, at least the significant fragmentation of the security alignments and security issues that to this day powerfully influence world politics. This process would have several aspects: the loosening of security commitments, causing nuclear clients to build their own deterrents; the diffusion of technology and the rising out of poverty of a growing number of developing countries, providing the resources to build such forces; the reluctance of the superpowers to be drawn into a potentially nuclear fray, accentuating the regionalization of security matters; the erosion of the political-ideological consensus that once cemented each of the two great blocs, leading to wide acceptance of the notion that peace is not indivisible—indeed, that the prudent course in a pervasively nuclear world is to partition peace, lest war prove indivisible.

Neither the First nor the Second Regime guarantees that proliferation can be arrested, that its effects can be contained, or that the regime itself can endure the basic changes proliferation would bring. The First Regime is a holding action: the superpowers would insulate and preserve their nuclear relationship by clinging to the massive, stable mutual deterrence system that has kept the Cold War cold. The Second Regime would push nuclear weapons into the background of world politics: if the role of nuclear weapons were strictly limited to deterrence, the effects of proliferation on the structure and conduct of world politics would be less profound than might otherwise be expected (though, in that case, the retirement of nuclear weapons from politics would itself constitute a fundamental change).

To repeat, the importance of nuclear weapons transcends the questions of the likelihood and character of nuclear war. Significant changes in the way nuclear weapons are managed or mismanaged may intrude into seemingly unrelated issue areas and affect basic patterns of international relations that lie beyond what have traditionally been viewed as security affairs.

NUCLEAR PEACE IN THE 1980s

This volume's presentation of alternative regimes offers an opportunity to consider the ramifications of significant change in the management of nuclear weapons. We have already noted that the Third Regime would demand—as well as help instigate—profound political transformation, not all of it necessarily desirable. If the Third Regime is to be judged in part by the appeal of the sort of world it implies, the practical choices for the 1980s—the First and Second Regimes—should be similarly tested. How would the regimes differ in their effects on diplomacy, citizen-government relationships, and the course of relations between East and West and between North and South? How would each regime affect the nature and distribution of power in world politics?

While one cannot hope to deal satisfactorily with these issues in a short essay, one can at least scratch the surface and bring into focus some of the questions the reader might ponder in weighing distinguishable nuclear regimes. Three areas of inquiry might be helpful in this regard:

1. What sort of nuclear regime would best facilitate the proper handling of the "new" global issues of economic and functional interdependence that will require attention and action in the 1980s?

2. To what extent will each regime encourage continued amelioration of relations between the societies of East and West?

3. How will nuclear capabilities affect relative power and influence among nations in the conduct of bilateral and multilateral relations? How might the various nuclear regimes differ in this effect?

In the past three decades, the specter of nuclear war, magnified by the fears and fallacies of Cold War, skewed international priorities and obstructed our view of such other problems as population growth, world food supplies, the maldistribution of wealth, and the dissatisfaction of identifiable groups the world over with established political structures and divisions. That these issues are now commanding greater emphasis can be partially explained by the fact that the current nuclear regime—its assumptions, institutions, and magnitudes—has won wide official acceptance. Managing the details of the regime still requires constant attention, but the basic structure is no longer the subject of heated dispute that it was through the early 1960s. Replacing the regime, even with one intrinsically more satisfactory, would return nuclear weapons to center stage at least temporarily and could disturb relationships (between friends and between foes) that have come to take as given the basic elements of the current nuclear regime.

For instance, a more relaxed American view of the need to maintain rough numerical nuclear parity with the Soviet Union might be read in Western Europe as portending a contraction of American commitments. Probable European responses to such a perception—ranging from accelerated Anglo-French-German nuclear weapons cooperation to a more neutral European orientation in East-West matters (that is, "Finlandization")—mostly imply basic changes of the sort that would amplify security issues and impede cooperation among Western states on issues of trade, economic policy coordination, energy, and the like. Once the necessary adjustments were made, there would be no reason why cooperative action on such issues could not be put back on track. But the transition to a regime implying a diminished role for nuclear weapons could be a disruptive process. Many quite desirable relationships and institutions are strengthened by the fact that a mature existing nuclear regime, however imperfect, provides fairly predictable, unobtrusive management of nuclear issues. A significant change of regime, however justified, would require debate and renegotiation at a rather fundamental level, causing nuclear weapons to compete once again with other issues begging for priority attention.

But departures from a status quo always bear a price. One must ask if the benefits of the conditions toward which one is aiming more than offset the risks and costs of the transition. Would the Second Regime bring about international conditions that would permit governments to concentrate more fully on the "low politics" issues of adequate nutrition, human rights, pollution abatement, the use of the seas, and so on? And would the Second Regime, once instituted, be more durable and less contentious in the long run than the First Regime—requiring less reassessment, renegotiation, and adjustment?

The answers may depend on the extent to which the Soviet Union would subscribe to the regime. It may well be within Washington's capacity to move far toward the Second Regime without Soviet reciprocation. But unless Moscow evinced sympathy with the principles of the Second Regime and a practical inclination to accept symmetrical constraints on its nuclear forces and policies, it is doubtful that the regime's lesser dependence on nuclear weapons would translate into a reduced preoccupation with the issue of nuclear security. If, however, the Soviet Union could be brought into harmony with the goal of confining nuclear weapons exclusively to a mutual deterrence role, the prospects would brighten that the business of dealing with other interested problems could be relieved of the nuclear distraction.

But the choice among regimes and among paths toward their achievement could alter international politics more substantively than is revealed by the question of the competition among issues for the attention of policy makers. In the first place, relations within the community of advanced market-economy states would almost certainly differ from one nuclear regime to another. Under the First Regime, the United States intentionally jeopardizes the physical security of its society by confronting the Soviet Union with a threat to escalate as necessary to turn back Soviet aggression, however minor, in any corner of the Western world. With American nuclear weapons in forward deployments on land and at sea, Soviet aggression, whatever its local context (except for the area of the Warsaw Pact), can reasonably be interpreted as a strategic challenge to the United States. This is how the United States has chosen to define the stakes, by declaration and by the escalatory bridge it has constructed with its forces and doctrine. The American commitments to security in Europe and the Far East are, in principle, open-ended. Since it is never certain that an American President would in fact execute the threat to escalate as necessary, America's allies are highly dependent on American intentions and therefore generally adhere to a political course that keeps Washington predisposed to fulfill the ultimate commitment.

The Second Regime would qualitatively change this situation no matter what quantity of conventional forces the United States provided to offset the withdrawal of nuclear forces and the open-ended commitment they symbolize. Security in Europe and East Asia would not only be less dependent on nuclear weapons but would also, perforce, be less dependent on the readiness of the American Commander-in-Chief to place his nation, as opposed to his troops, in harm's way. The American security commitment would be effectively closed-ended—no longer an unexecuted promise but a finite, present contribution to collective defense. American allies could no longer depend on Washington's willingness to engage in nuclear escalation, but only on its willingness to expand and expend conventional forces. American intentions would become less critical to the defense of Europe and therefore less of a factor in Western relationships.

Furthermore, the Second Regime implies that American society could escape virtually all harm in the event of East-West conflict, since the full force of violence, being non-nuclear, would be more or less confined to Western Europe, the Mediterranean, Northeast Asia, or whatever the local theater. If anything, the United States would become *more* dependent on the willingness of its allies to allow their territory to be used as a battlefield in the common defense. In the First Regime, the allies can have some "hope" that hostilities, if not quickly extinguished, will move rapidly from the local theater to direct Soviet-American strategic exchange. Such hope would evaporate in the Second Regime. The allies might be less inclined to resist Soviet advances below the level of an all-out offensive, where the risks of resistance are high and the immediate costs of acquiescence seemingly low. In effect, the intentions and will of American allies in the face of lesser Soviet aggression (which is already more plausible than total aggression) would become more important.

But what does all this war-gaming have to do with peacetime political patterns? Simply stated, dependencies stem not from the distribution of burden already accepted but from expectations of future behavior. In the First Regime, American future behavior is the key; in the Second, the burden of choice shifts to the allies. Under the Second Nuclear Regime the United States would become less important and its allies more important in deterring unfriendly Soviet actions along the frontiers of the Western security area, largely irrespective of the relative magnitudes of American and European physical contributions to NATO. Before mourning—or cheering—the interment of that component of American hegemony that is built upon its nuclear commitments, one should realize that according to the politics implicit in the Second Regime, both the United States and its allies would be accepting a trade-off: the United States would bear less risk while enjoying less political deference, whereas its allies would bear greater risks while enjoying the greater freedom of action that reduced dependence yields. Still, this shift would subtly but importantly affect not only politics among the Western industrial states but also the behavior of those states with regard to issues not confined to the West.

The practical implications of this should not be overdrawn. The advanced market-economy states will continue to hold common values, perspectives, and interests on a host of important issues. They are, typically, democratic societies, troubled by inflation and irregular economic growth, dependent on OPEC oil, offended by tyranny, generous when they can afford to be, suspicious of the Soviets, and committed to the preservation of Western culture and the rule of liberal law and order. Moreover, American leadership derives from conditions and dependencies that will persist no matter what nuclear regime is in place: the central role of the dollar in the international monetary system, American technological-scientific excellence, American managerial skills, American conventional military power, and the relative (though decreasing) insensitivity of the United States economy to vicissitudes in external economic relations and conditions.

Obviously, such a community would not disintegrate over a modification in nuclear security arrangements. But it would change. Relations between the United States and Europe and between the United States and Japan could become more competitive. Less dependent on American intentions, Europe and Japan might be more inclined to seek "a separate peace" with other actors in the system in order to ensure satisfactory outcomes on a variety of issues—oil and other commodities, economic relations with the Communist states, accommodation with radical regimes in the Third World. But here again, it would be a mistake to expect the choice of nuclear regimes to determine the course of these politics. At most, the Second Regime might only accentuate trends that have already gathered momentum under the First Regime.

The relationship between the United States and the Soviet Union will be crucial to world politics and security under any imaginable nuclear regime for the 1980s and beyond. Since it is not clear whether nuclear stability begat political accommodation or vice versa in recent years, commenting on the future connection between the management of nuclear weapons and the course of Soviet-American relations is a highly speculative venture.

Much depends on *how* the nuclear regime of the future evolves and not just on what its mature features will be. A First Regime maintained by the invisible hand of strategic competition would, even if stable, hardly lead to further easing of the sense of ultimate insecurity and perpetual confrontation that is still strongly felt in both capitals and by both societies. Indeed, the present pause in Soviet-American relaxation may signal that unless fundamental changes are made, the tension in the relationship will ease only to the point at which nuclear stability, perhaps the superpowers' only true common interest, is assured.

A Second Regime achieved without significant American insistence on Soviet reciprocity might imply—accurately or inaccurately—a willingness on the part of the United States to accept asymmetry in other areas of interaction: assured supply of resources (grain, natural gas) upon which the other party depends, competition for influence in the Third World, involvement or disinvolvement in local conflict, covert operations, support for states or groups hostile to the other's interests, consultation on matters of mutual concern, and so forth. A Second Regime accompanied by a massive, compensatory build-up and forward deployment of conventional military forces might elevate tensions above the level prevailing in a continuation of the present nuclear engagement. And even if the United States and the Soviet Union were comfortable with greater reliance on conventional forces, would the societies of Eastern Europe, whose territory is the bivouac for a large part of the Red Army, feel the same way?

But before convincing ourselves that the risks of change are too great and the payoffs too dubious, we should reassess the present condition. It is widely assumed in the West that any departure from tested security policies—massive central nuclear forces, extensive deployment of other nuclear forces, a stated willingness to use nuclear weapons first if necessary, an insistence on what is considered symmetry—would invite Soviet aggression. This is not necessarily an unreasonable assumption. There are too many unfulfilled tsarist and Soviet expansionist aspirations, too many opportunities for gain in the more fluid world of the 1980s, to expect Soviet self-restraint. But, never questioned, the assumption of immutable Soviet imperialism may conceal the fact that Soviet leaders, too, have powerful apprehensions, that they see present threats where there are only ghosts of old aggressions. "Soviet security" is not a term frequently used outside the Kremlin. Inside that citadel of xenophobia and paranoia, security means relief, at last, from the forces of anti-Sovietism that would challenge the status quo in Eastern Europe and ultimately threaten the Soviet system. So the choice of a nuclear regime for the future must recognize that improved Soviet security (as perceived in Moscow) is not necessarily deleterious for world peace and order. In fact, a reduced American dependence on nuclear weapons, as embodied in the Second Nuclear Regime, could weaken politically those within the Soviet ruling elite who insist that Soviet security requires unsurpassed military strength.

In this regard, there may be an alternative to Garwin's prescription for a strengthening of NATO conventional forces to offset whatever weakening of deterrence in Europe might result from the withdrawal of tactical nuclear weapons: mutual force reductions. In moving toward the Second Regime, perhaps the United States should make its removal of nuclear weapons conditional upon the withdrawal of Soviet tank forces and Moscow's acceptance of restrictions on maneuvers and other unsettling military activities short of attack. Of course, such an approach need not, perhaps should not, preclude qualitative improvements in NATO's conventional military posture.

These considerations notwithstanding, it would be imprudent to assume that a Second Regime without reciprocal Soviet adherence would, over time, encourage moderate Soviet behavior nonetheless. We simply do not know if Moscow *needs* to be deterred. Ironically, accepting nuclear inferiority and terminating the threat of escalation might be the best way to find out, unless conventional security is assured through more capable defense, effective conventional arms control, or both.

Looking more generally at the implications of the Second Regime, those states that have derived political benefit from the possession of nuclear weapons would find themselves somewhat less advantaged. Not only would nuclear weapons be less useful in providing protection for other states, thereby earning reduced political dividends for the protector, but they would also have less coercive value. The nuclear threat is, in any case, a disappearing species. There is little reason to believe that the First Regime's eschewal of a formal no-first-use pledge would mean that the superpowers would practice nuclear intimidation against weaker states in the 1980s any more than they have in the 1970s. But by formally—if not convincingly—ruling out the possible use of nuclear weapons in the course of conflict with non-nuclear states and by eliminating the tactical nuclear weapons that might be thought most suitable for such use, nuclear states (especially the superpowers) might meet greater resistance in attempting to coerce other states.

At the same time, it is far from clear that the international system would be less conflict-prone under the Second Regime than under the First. The superpowers might be less bold in confronting other states but perhaps also less cautious in competing with one another. The mutual aversion to potentially uncontrollable collisions that the First Regime engenders could fade under a Second Regime whose very purpose is to eliminate the danger that collisions cannot be controlled. And the constrained ability of the superpowers to coerce other states by brandishing their nuclear forces might encourage the expansionist ambitions of such emerging regional powers as India and Brazil, whose relative restraint in the past may to some extent be attributable to their fear of nuclear threats.

Under the Second Regime, nuclear weapons would be deprived of much of their significance in the relative standing of states. Political power and influence would be increasingly measured in terms of economic strength and conventional military capabilities. Given the considerable non-nuclear resources of the United States and the Soviet Union, the order of hierarchy would not change. But the pyramid would flatten somewhat. And "non-nuclear great powers" (especially Japan and Germany) would enjoy greater standing. Multipolarity—prematurely proclaimed in recent years—would become more of a reality.

The choice of a nuclear future is more than a matter of deciding how best to suppress the threat of nuclear war. Indeed, were that the sole criterion, we might have little incentive to look beyond the current system. But as the essays in this volume show, the importance of nuclear weapons in shaping the future demands that our political vision not be limited by the blinders of immediacy, obstructed by presumptions of infeasibility, or diverted by promises of panaceas.

331

Appendix

Franklin C. Miller

Nuclear Weapons in Today's World: A Synopsis

The world of nuclear weapons is often regarded as arcane and highly technical, the exclusive preserve of military planners and physicists. While the specific details of weapon manufacture and employment are in fact cloaked by secrecy and remain behind the scientific and engineering walls which shield any high technology, the general issues raised by the presence of nuclear weapons in today's world are neither hidden from public view nor difficult to comprehend. They are, moreover, issues which affect all our lives, and as such merit attention by a much wider group of people than those who deal with them on a daily basis.

This appendix is designed to help the newcomer understand the basic issues of nuclear weapons policy. It does so by reviewing the central concepts that have shaped present-day nuclear doctrine, the size and composition of existing nuclear arsenals, and the nature of recent arms control measures and initiatives. To help the reader see behind the veil of jargon that surrounds most discussions of nuclear weapons, the appendix also contains a glossary.

STRATEGIC CONCEPTS

Perhaps the clearest way to convey a sense of contemporary nuclear strategy is to review nuclear weapons doctrine as it has evolved in the United States over the past three decades. The role of nuclear weapons in national policy has been the subject of an intense debate within the American scientific and military communities throughout this period. In the course of this debate, concepts and doctrines have been put forward with a clarity and a richness of detail matched nowhere else, and as a result the international impact of the American discussion has been profound. European strategists have largely echoed it. There is also some evidence that Soviet strategic thought has been importantly affected by American writings; in contrast to the voluminous Western strategic literature, however, the various positions in the Soviet nuclear debate have only rarely been permitted to ventilate in public.

In the immediate post-World War II years, even after the explosion of the Hiroshima and Nagasaki devices demonstrated the immense power of the new weapons, the atomic bomb was regarded simply as a somewhat bigger bomb to be used in the same way the largest high-explosive bombs had been used in World War II. If the United States were to be involved in a future war, the American strategy would be to fight a series of World-War-II-like campaigns, using atomic and conventional bombs against enemy cities. The United States had, in Henry Kissinger's words, "added the atomic bomb to [its] arsenal without integrating its implications into [military] thinking."[1]

The first Russian atomic test, and subsequent development of a nuclear weapons stockpile, the experience of limited war in Korea, and the rising cost of American peacetime defense gave rise in the early 1950s to the concept of *massive retaliation*, the first national strategy to consider nuclear weapons as other-than-ordinary bombs. In the often-quoted words of Secretary of State John Foster Dulles, the United States would respond to aggression anywhere "by means and in places of its own choosing." In essence the United States posed a threat to respond to any Soviet or Chinese breach of peace by attacking the aggressor's homeland with nuclear weapons.

By the late 1950s, inadequacies in the massive retaliation doc-

[1]Henry A. Kissinger, *Nuclear Weapons and Foreign Policy*, Harper, New York, 1957, p. 8.

trine had become apparent to American strategists. The fundamental weakness was that the threat of a nuclear response to minor provocations was inherently not credible, thus encouraging an adversary to conduct its "offensive" through a series of small acts, each safely below the level that would conceivably justify massive retaliation. Soviet development of an intercontinental nuclear capability further undermined the American strategy, for there now existed the danger that the act of massive retaliation in the face of aggression would itself evoke similarly catastrophic nuclear retaliation against the United States.

The 1960s saw the adoption, therefore, of a two-tracked strategy that sought to separate the problem of containing communist conventional military aggression from the problem of deterring a Soviet strategic nuclear attack. The concept of *flexible response* called for renewed emphasis on Western conventional military strength, a declared willingness to "escalate as necessary" to turn back aggression, and the forward placement of weapons that were both tactical and nuclear, weapons that were meant to show that the chasm between non-nuclear and nuclear warfare would be bridged if necessary as part of a flexible, escalatory response.

The choice of means to prevent a strategic nuclear attack on the United States proved to be more difficult. In the early 1960s a philosophy of *damage limitation*, which called for United States nuclear forces to be able to strike and disable Soviet strategic forces, was dominant. In the event that a number of Soviet weapons survived such a strike and were launched at the United States, a combination of so-called active and passive defense measures were to be relied upon to reduce the number of American casualties.[2] But as the size of those Soviet forces grew and their deployment became more diversified, the problems of conducting a damage-limiting (first) strike multiplied. By the late 1960s damage limitation had fallen into almost complete disre-

---

[2]Active defenses, composed of antiballistic missile and antibomber systems, detect, intercept, and destroy incoming enemy weapons systems. Passive defenses are civil defense programs—bomb and fallout shelters, evacuation plans, food stockpilings—designed to protect civilian populations.

pute, culminating (in 1972) with a Soviet-American agreement to limit severely the antiballistic missile systems (ABMs) of each. A retaliatory policy known as *assured destruction* became the guiding principle of American strategic deterrence.[3] Under assured destruction, the United States would maintain a strategic weapons establishment large and diverse enough to destroy so much of the U.S.S.R.'s population and industrial base, even after a Soviet first strike on United States nuclear forces, that Soviet leaders would be deterred from ever starting nuclear war. The requirements of the flexible response strategy caused the United States strategic arsenal to be maintained at a level that exceeded the minimum number of weapons necessary for assured destruction. The additional missiles and bombs were needed so that military targets in Eastern Europe and the Soviet Union could be attacked without drawing on those forces required to maintain a credible strategic retaliatory posture.[4]

As the Soviet Union's nuclear forces rose to a level in the early 1970s at which the U.S.S.R. had a similar capability, assured destruction was said to have become mutual (thus leading to the acronym MAD, for *mutual assured destruction*). The emergence of mutual assured destruction confirmed Robert Oppenheimer's prophetic comment that the nuclear-armed United States and Soviet Union were analogous to two scorpions in a bottle, neither one able to sting the other without being fatally stung itself.

The desirability of maintaining nuclear peace and stability

[3] In giving up the damage-limiting strategy, the United States eschewed a preemptive first strike policy. Preemptive use of strategic nuclear weapons to disable an adversary's threatening nuclear force is not the same, however, as "first use," which means that a nation will initiate the employment of nuclear weapons in war. First use was, and remains, an integral part of the flexible response strategy. Of the five nuclear powers, the People's Republic of China (PRC) is the only one to have formally pledged that it will never be the first to use nuclear weapons.

[4] In part because they were not facing the extended deterrence problems of the United States, and in consideration of the high cost associated with strategic nuclear weapons, Britain and France opted to build small nuclear forces which their governments considered adequate for the minimal deterrence posture. The PRC is presently in the process of building a minimal deterrence force; whether long-range PRC plans call for force levels above those needed for that role is unclear.

through MAD has been seriously challenged in recent years. The United States was predisposed by its basic strategies and its targeting plan to respond to even a limited nuclear attack with the initiation of full-scale nuclear war and to direct its retaliation against the enemy's cities and industry rather than its unexpended strategic forces. This posture was deemed by many important strategists to be irrational, inhumane, and noncredible in that it implied that the United States favored retaliation against the Soviet populace over the possibility of limiting the destructiveness of nuclear war. Accordingly, the implementation of a flexible strategic targeting policy was begun to give the United States the option to employ selectively one or a number of strategic weapons, aimed at military targets in the Soviet Union, in response either to a massive Soviet attack on U.S. allies which tactical nuclear weapons had failed to halt or a limited Soviet strategic nuclear attack. Recent U.S. Department of Defense reports have begun calling the combination of MAD and flexible strategic targeting *assured retaliation*.

As was noted earlier, the Soviets have revealed little about their strategic nuclear thinking and policy. It can be inferred both from the manner in which the Russians negotiate at arms control sessions and the few writings that have been reproduced in the West that there exists a wide range of views on nuclear strategy within the Soviet bureaucracy, running from arms control/ deterrence advocates to those who regard nuclear weapons merely as standard combat weapons. Some American analysts believe that the Soviets are content with the present MAD relationship; others posit that the Soviet Union is actually seeking a damage-limiting capability for the 1980s.

FORCES

The strategic nuclear forces of the United States and the Soviet Union are quite similar. Each nuclear force has three basic components: long-range bombers with nuclear bombs and air-to-surface missiles; intercontinental ballistic missiles (ICBMs); and submarine-launched ballistic missiles (SLBMs). These are the so-called *central systems*, as distinguished from numerous types of lesser nuclear weapons possessed by the superpowers but not commonly considered to be "strategic" or to contribute importantly to the maintenance of an assured destruction retaliatory capability. In the United States, the submarine-launched missiles, intercontinental missiles, and bombers are known collectively as the strategic "Triad." The Pentagon justifies the existence of the Triad on the grounds that three separate systems compound the difficulties faced by an opponent in trying to defend against retaliation, minimize the risk that the entire strategic deterrent force will become vulnerable as a result of a technological breakthrough, and ensure against major systems failure.

Of the three arms, the SLBM force is probably the least vulnerable to a preemptive attack because of the low state of the art of antisubmarine warfare (ASW). (Those submarines, not at sea, i.e., in port, are, of course, as vulnerable). On the other hand, there are two shortcomings associated with SLBMs: first, the difficulty of communicating with submerged submarines, and second, the fact that SLBMs are not as accurate as either ICBMs or bombers.[5] The United States has 656 SLBMs carried on 41 nuclear powered submarines (16 missiles per submarine). Of these 496 are Poseidon missiles which carry 10 to 14 multiple independently targeted re-entry vehicles (MIRVs) over a range of about 3,000 miles. The rest are older Polaris missiles that have the same range as Poseidon missiles but only carry three multiple re-entry vehicles (MRVs) each. Under current plans, the Poseidon-bearing submarines will receive the MIRVed, 4,000-mile range Trident I missile during the late 1970s and 1980s.

The Soviet SLBM force is numerically slightly larger than its United States counterpart. It consists of a small number of older submarines which carry three single-warhead, 750-mile range missiles each and 34 newer vessels which, with 16 1,750-mile

---

[5] Accuracy may be viewed in several ways. From the technological standpoint of weapons design and engineering, accuracy is a highly desirable commodity. It is also important and necessary when the limitation of collateral damage is a consideration. An arms control perspective sees highly accurate warheads as potential first strike weapons and hence as an undesirable destabilizing threat to the nuclear balance.

range missiles (the latest model of which has been tested with MRVs) are quite similar to the American Polaris submarines. The Soviets also have deployed two versions of a third-generation submarine which fires a single warhead, 4,200-mile missile. These vessels—13 so-called Delta Is, which carry 12 missiles, and four even bigger Delta IIs carrying 16 missiles—are the largest submarines in the world. As a rule, American submarines are quieter (i.e., produce less machinery noise) than the Soviet ones and are therefore less liable to detection, tracking, and destruction by antisubmarine forces.

The ICBM force is more vulnerable to attack than the SLBMs in that the location of the silos from which the missiles are launched is known to the other side and therefore can be targeted by their planners. However, the reinforced concrete silos provide considerable protection against incoming missiles that are not exceptionally accurate. Moreover, ICBMs can be launched instantaneously, a feature that further decreases their vulnerability to attack. The American ICBM force consists of 550 MIRVed Minuteman III missiles, 450 Minuteman II, and 54 older "heavy" Titan II missiles. The Minuteman has an 8,000-mile range while the Titan's is 7,250 miles, but the latter carries a much larger warhead than the former. A replacement for Minuteman, designated MX, is undergoing preliminary research and development. If deployed, the MX will be larger than the Minuteman and may be launched from mobile launchers instead of silos. The Soviet ICBM force, with over 1,300 missiles, is larger than the American force (which may be partially explained by the fact that the Strategic Rocket Force is the most bureaucratically powerful branch of the Soviet armed forces). Two types of Soviet ICBMs, the SS-9 and the SS-18, are capable of carrying a 25-megaton warhead, the largest in the world. The ranges of Soviet ICBMs vary between 5,000 and 7,500 miles. In general, the Russian missiles are larger and carry heavier warheads than those in the American inventory, but American weapons are more accurate and currently have more warheads per missile.

Of the three types of strategic delivery forces, the bombers are most easily destroyed on the ground. Some portion of the bomber force is routinely on "ground alert," ready to take off within a prescribed minimum period of time, and thus able to avoid being destroyed by an enemy surprise attack. In a crisis situation, a percentage of the force could be placed on airborne alert. Given the warning time available in all but the worst possible hypothetical surprise attack, most of the bomber force could be airborne in time to escape destruction on the ground. Although they, therefore, possess a degree of relative invulnerability, bombers must also face enemy air defenses which may shoot down a high percentage of the planes before they reach their targets. This can be compensated for by placing greater reliance on air-to-surface missiles so that the bombers need only close within missile range of their targets rather than having to penetrate all the way in to drop their bombs. There are 387 B-52 long-range bombers in the U.S. Strategic Air Command (SAC). These aircraft, which are capable of flying 10 to 12 thousand miles without refueling, can carry four 20-megaton bombs (the largest weapon in the United States arsenal). In addition, they can carry up to 20 nuclear-tipped short-range attack missiles (SRAMs) which have a range of 100 miles. All told, more than half of the total U.S. megatonnage is currently carried by bombers. A new, longer range, air-launched cruise missile (ALCM) is under development. A new manned bomber, the B-1, may soon begin to enter SAC ranks as a supplement to and eventual replacement for the B-52. The Soviet Union's long-range bomber fleet is significantly smaller than the American, consisting of 135 aircraft, all but 35 of which are propeller-driven. They, too, carry both bombs and surface-to-air missiles, but their percentage of total Soviet megatonnage is significantly smaller than the corresponding U.S. figures. The Soviet Air Force is also beginning to receive the first of some 200 aircraft of an advanced design. These "Backfire" bombers are said to have a potential range of 6,000 miles, which (assuming optimal, i.e., Arctic-basing policies) would make them theoretically capable of strategic attack upon the United States if they land in Cuba after carrying out their mission. The Backfire is also equipped for mid-air refueling, which extends its combat radius considerably. It should be noted that, as weapons incapable of inflicting a first strike blow, bombers are "benign" and pose no threat to strategic stability.

While their arsenals are dwarfed by those of the nuclear super-powers, the three smaller nuclear weapons states do deserve some mention here. France has developed a "mini-Triad," having a fleet of four ballistic missile submarines, a 120-aircraft bomber fleet, and land-launched ballistic missiles. Britain relies on a deterrent force consisting of four ballistic missile submarines (whose missiles are of United States design and manufacture) and a 160-plane manned bomber force (which is rapidly becoming obsolescent), but no land-based missiles. The Chinese have elected to concentrate on bombers and land-launched missiles. Of the latter, they have so far deployed missiles of less than intercontinental range, capable of striking most of the U.S.S.R. but not the United States. Their delivery vehicles—both bombers and missiles—are based on mid-1950s Soviet technology, and are fairly vulnerable. The bombers are slow; their land-based missiles use liquid fuel, requiring that they be fueled just before launch, a time-consuming process that could be fatal if an opponent had all the missile launch sites targeted. It has long been reported that the Chinese are interested in developing ICBMs and SLBMs; that they have not done so, to date, might indicate a policy of giving priority to improvement of their regional nuclear capability over the development of an intercontinental capability.

ARMS CONTROL

Strategic arms control efforts over the last decade or so have had four basic aims: limiting, and eventually reducing, existing strategic weapons systems; retarding the development and deployment of new, especially destabilizing, weapons; restricting both the numbers and types of nuclear explosive tests; and preventing the proliferation of nuclear weapons. Arms control initiatives have been pursued on both the bilateral (United States-Soviet) and multilateral levels (perhaps more properly defined as intersuperpower and nuclear/non-nuclear levels). In essence, these efforts have been based on a shared recognition of the fact that nuclear weapons do not guarantee security and are, above certain levels and of certain types, wasteful or even counter-productive. The two-track approach to arms control reflects a belief, held especially firmly in the United States and the Soviet Union, that while preventing the spread of nuclear weapons requires wide participation, controlling the Soviet-American strategic relationship can only be efficiently accomplished between the superpowers, with a minimum of intrusion by other states that lack a serious appreciation of the exigencies of maintaining a stable central balance.

Intersuperpower agreements include (1) the 1963 Limited Test Ban Treaty, also signed by Great Britain, which prohibited nuclear weapons tests in the atmosphere, outer space, or underwater; (2) the 1972 United States–Soviet agreement restricting antiballistic missile (ABM) deployment; (3) the 1972 United States–Soviet Interim Strategic Arms Limitation Agreement (SALT I), which placed a restriction on the number of strategic launchers each of the two superpowers was permitted; (4) the 1974 Vladivostok accord between the United States and the U.S.S.R., limiting each side to a total of 2,400 strategic delivery vehicles, of which no more than 1,320 could be MIRVed; and (5) the 1976 Threshold Test Ban, wherein the United States and the Soviet Union agreed not to test nuclear weapons with yields over 150 kilotons.

The 1968 Nuclear Non-Proliferation Treaty began life as a United States–British–Soviet attempt to halt the spread of nuclear weapons; it has since been signed and ratified by almost all the nations of the world. It seeks to prevent the further spread of nuclear weapons. It prohibits signatories which currently possess nuclear weapons from transferring either nuclear weapons or weapons production technology to non-nuclear weapons states. Additionally, non-nuclear weapons states signing the treaty pledge to abjure from acquiring or producing such weapons.

A genuine multinational approach to all questions of strategic arms control is practiced by the United Nations Conference of the Committee on Disarmament (CCD) which meets at Geneva.[6] Written agreements produced in part by this body include treaties banning nuclear weapons storage and use in outer space and on the seabed. Beyond these accomplishments, the CCD has been

[6]Formerly (1962–1969) the Eighteen Nation Disarmament Committee (ENDC).

modestly useful in providing the wider international community with a means of holding the superpowers accountable for their arms control policies.

One of the greatest stumbling blocks to strategic arms control agreements has been the fear of covert cheating by an opponent. The development of high resolution surveillance satellites (i.e., those able to take extremely detailed and accurate photographs from space orbit) appeared to solve this problem by providing a sure means of verifying that a treaty signatory was fulfilling its obligations. The development of MIRVs posed a severe difficulty in this regard, as the satellites could detect missile silos but were obviously unable to determine whether the missiles under their closed lids were loaded with a single or multiple warhead. An agreement was worked out in the 1974 Vladivostok accord whereby once a particular type of missile was tested in a MIRV mode, all missiles of that particular type were assumed to carry MIRV warheads. A more troublesome verification problem may now be arising as a result of the development of strategic cruise missiles, the number of which are in a given ship, plane, or stockpile being very hard to verify in the absence of on-site inspection.[7] The issue has yet to be resolved, and may or may not be included should the second round of the Strategic Arms Limitation Talks (SALT II) between the United States and the Soviet Union produce a treaty.

There are several methods of calculating the destructive potential of nuclear forces. One of the simplest of these, tabulation of the total number of warheads each side possesses, is shown below in Table 2, section A. Such an index may be misleading, however, as the quantitative comparison ignores qualitative differences among warheads: all nuclear weapons do not generate equal power. The actual explosive force (or "yield") of nuclear weapons is measured in thousands (KT) or millions (MT) of tons of TNT; while the yield gives some indication of potential destructiveness, the relationship between yield and destruction is not one to one. Accordingly, the concept of equivalent megatonnage (see Glossary), which seeks to define destructive power

[7]On-site inspection has long been a problem in arms control negotiations, as it represents an intrusion into national territory.

TABLE 1

Strategic Nuclear Delivery Vehicles[a]

Type and System	U.S.			U.S.S.R.			
	Number	Range (miles)	Warhead	System	Number	Range (miles)	Warhead
ICBM							
Titan II	54	7,250	5-10MT	SS-9	252	7,500	18MT; 25MT 3 x 4 or 5MT
Minuteman II	450	8,000	1-2MT	SS-11	900	6,500	1-2MT 3 x KT
Minuteman III	550	8,000	3 x 170KT	SS-13[b]	60	5,000	1MT
	1,054			SS-17	20	6,500	4 x KT
				SS-18	36	7,500	18MT; 25MT 8 x MT 6 x KT
				SS-19	100	6,500	
					1,368		
MRBM/IRBM[c]				SS-4	500	1,200	1MT
				SS-5	100	2,300	1MT
					600		
SLBM[d]							
Polaris A 3	160	2,800	3 x 200KT	SSN-5	21	750	1MT
Poseidon C 3	496	2,880	10 or 14 x 50KT	SSN-6	544	1,750	1MT
	656						

United States

			Maximum Weapons Load (pounds)
Air-launched missiles			
Hound Dog[e]	400	600	1KT
SRAM	1,500	100	1KT
Long-range bombers			
B-52D/F	387	11,500	60,000
B-52G/H		12,500	70,000
Medium-range bombers			
FB-111A	66	3,800	37,500
Carrier-based aircraft[f]			
F-4		1,997	16,000
A-6		3,225	18,000
A-7		3,400	15,000

Soviet Union

			Maximum Weapons Load (pounds)
SSN-8	220 / 785	4,220	1MT
AS-3	?	400	1KT
AS-4	800	450	1KT
TU-95	100	7,800	40,000
Mya-4	35 / 135	6,050	20,000
TU-16	450	4,000	20,000
Backfire B	30+	5,500	20,000
IL-28	260	2,500	4,850
TU-22	170	1,400	12,000

[a] When MT/KT is not preceded by a number, the exact yield is not available.

[b] A new missile, the SS-X-16, is under development to replace the SS-13. It will have twice the latter's throw-weight.

[c] The Soviets are developing a new mobile missile, the SS-X-20, capable of carrying a MIRVed warhead.

[d] A new short-range (600 miles) SLBM, the SS-X-13, is reportedly being deployed on some Soviet SSBNs. It is said to have a possible tactical antiship role.

[e] The Hound Dog missile is being phased out of the United States inventory.

[f] There are approximately 30 to 40 aircraft on each carrier.

SOURCE: International Institute of Strategic Studies, *The Military Balance 1976–1977*, London, 1976; Donald H. Rumsfeld, *Annual Defense Department FY 1978*, Washington, D.C., 1977; and General George S. Brown, *United States Military Posture for FY 1977*, Washington, D.C., 1976.

more precisely, was developed. Section B sets forth the gross equivalent megatonnage of the American and Soviet nuclear arsenal. Yet another way in which nuclear forces are compared is through the weapons-carrying capability of their delivery vehi-

TABLE 2
Aggregate Figures

	U.S.	U.S.S.R.
A . Nuclear warheads mid-1976*		
ICBM	2,154	2,195
SLBM	5,120	785
Bombers	1,256 (?)	270
	8,530	3,250
B . EMT (equivalent megatonnage)†		
ICBM	1,150	2,950
SLBM	780	785
	1,930	3,735
C . Missile throw-weight (in millions of pounds)		
ICBM	2.4	7.0
SLBM	0.9	1.2
	3.3	8.2
D . Bomber payload (in millions) of pounds)‡	22.8	4.7

*MIRV count as separate warheads, but MRV do not. Assumes B-52s carrying four gravity bombs each, Tu-95 and Mi-4 two gravity bombs each. SRAM and AS-3/4 are not counted.

†EMT $= Y^{2/3}$ 1MT
$\quad\quad = Y^{1/2}$ 1MT
where Y = weapon yield

‡Calculations assume maximum weapons load, greatest yield derived from mix of gravity bombs and air-to-surface missiles.

SOURCE: International Institute of Strategic Studies, *The World Military Balance, 1976–1977*, London, 1975, pp. 116–117.

cles. This method, which tabulates missile throw-weight (see Glossary) and bomber payload is presented in sections C and D. The throw-weight/payload comparison does not take varying degrees of technological sophistication into account, i.e., a primitive nuclear weapon weighs more than an advanced one having the same yield, nor does it easily translate pounds of nuclear weapons into destructive potential. The fact that all these various methods exist indicates that there is no single unambiguous way to compare nuclear forces; on the other hand, an appreciation of the overall situation becomes clearer when all the indices are reviewed.

TABLE 3
Other Nuclear Powers

	Nation	Number	Range (miles)	Payload
IRBM	France	18	1,875	150KT
	China	20–30	1,500–1,750	Unknown*
MRBM	China	30–50	600–700	Unknown
SLBM	United Kingdom	64	2,880	3 x 200KT
	France	32	1,500	500KT
		16	1,900	500KT
		16	3,000	1MT
Bombers	United Kingdom	50	4,000	21,000†
		70	2,000	8,000
		40	1,000	8,000
	France	52	2,000	8,000
		75	1,000	8,000
	China	65	4,000	20,000

*Additionally, the PRC is thought to have begun deployment of a 3,000 to 3,500 mile missile and to have begin research and development on an ICBM of 8,000 mile range.

†The payload of bombers is measured in pounds.

SOURCE: International Institute of Strategic Studies, *The World Military Balance 1976–1977*, London, 1976.

Glossary

Antisubmarine Warfare (ASW)—ASW may be either tactical, i.e., concerned with the pursuit and destruction of submarines in a local situation for convoy defense, aircraft carrier defense, etc., or strategic, which is aimed at neutralizing an opponent's ballistic-missile-carrying submarines.

Ballistic Missile—a missile that moves freely along most of its trajectory, under the influence of gravity alone. The missile follows a semiorbital flight path. There are six types of ballistic missiles:

SLBMs   (submarine-launched ballistic missile, such as the U.S. Polaris)

ALBMs   (air-launched ballistic missile, such as the U.S. SRAM)

ICBMs   (intercontinental ballistic missile) 4,000+ miles

IRBMs   (intermediate-range ballistic missile) 1,500–4,000 miles

MRBMs   (medium-range ballistic missile) 500–1,500 miles

SRBMs   (short-range ballistic missile) under 500 miles

Bombers—bomber aircraft are classified according to the distance they may travel without refueling. Thus an intercontinental or long-range bomber is one capable of traveling 6,000+ miles on one load of fuel. Medium-range bombers are those that can travel 3,500 and 6,000 miles without refueling. Bombers may carry either gravity bombs, air-to-surface missiles, or a combination of the two.

Circular Error Probable (CEP)—a measure of missile accuracy. It is the radius of a circle about a target within which 50 percent of the missiles aimed at that target will hit.

Central Offensive Systems—those nuclear delivery systems that constitute a nation's principal strategic retaliatory force; generally this term connotes long-range bombers, ICBMs, and SLBMs.

Command and Control—the communications and decision networks that link the national command authorities with operational units (e.g., missile silos, SSBNs, bombers, and TNW equipped forces) and governs their use of nuclear weapons.

Counterforce—nuclear attacks aimed at an opponent's military facilities, in particular at its strategic weapons.

Countervalue—nuclear attacks aimed at an opponent's population and nonmiltary industrial base.

Damage Limitation—a doctrine designed to protect a nation against nuclear attack by sharply reducing an opponent's ability to inflict damage. Damage limitation has two components: counterforce first strike and homeland defense, the former designed to destroy an opponent's retaliatory forces before they are launched, the latter to intercept and destroy in flight with antiballistic missile and antibomber forces enemy planes and missiles that survive and are launched. Finally, the civilian population would be protected by bomb shelters and other civil defense measures from the effects of those attacking forces not destroyed before launch or in flight.

Equivalent Megatonnage (EMT)—one of various measures of the destructive effect of nuclear weapons on unprotected targets (e.g., cities). Equivalent megatonnage may be expressed as the gross destructive potential of a nation's nuclear arsenal, or as the effect produced by a single weapon. In the latter case, for weapons rated under a yield (Y) of one megaton, it is defined at $Y^{2/3}$. For weapons over one megaton, it is $Y^{1/2}$. See *Yield*.

Forward-Based Systems (FBS)—medium-range U.S. nuclear delivery systems based in Europe and the Far East. These include F-111 and F-4 ground-based aircraft and Navy carrier-based A-6s and A-7s.

Multiple Reentry Vehicle (MRV)—each of a cluster of warheads carried by a single ballistic missile. MRV warheads cannot be individually targeted.

Multiple Independently Targeted Reentry Vehicles (MIRV)—each of a cluster of warheads carried by a single ballistic missile; each warhead may be aimed at a separate target.

Maneuverable Reentry Vehicles (MaRV)—a missile-launched nuclear warhead that is capable of adjusting its course both to evade defending weapons and to "home in" directly on top of its target. The high accuracy of an MaRV makes it a potential first-strike weapon.

Penetration Aid—devices to confuse enemy radars and interceptors and thus ensure that one's nuclear warheads penetrate enemy defenses and reach their targets. Some such devices are designed to clutter and blind enemy warning and air defense radars; these include chaff (small strips of metal which reflect radar energy) and electronic jamming (which may be performed by satellites, support aircraft, or by the delivery vehicles themselves). Others are decoys, such as balloons painted with aluminum that simulate incoming warheads, which are designed to make an enemy exhaust its air defenses on false targets.

Preemptive Strike—a damage-limiting attack launched in the fear that an opponent is preparing to attack.

SSBN—a nuclear-propelled ballistic-missile-bearing submarine.

Tactical Nuclear Weapons (TNWs)—nuclear weapons designed for combat use within designated military operations. Tactical nuclear weapons are usually distinguished from strategic ones primarily by their smaller yield (usually in tens of KT) and short-range delivery systems. Ground combat TNWs include nuclear-tipped surface-to-surface missiles, nuclear artillery shells, nuclear land mines, and nuclear bombs carried by tactical aircraft. Other types of tactical nuclear weapons are nuclear-tipped antiaircraft missiles (both land- and sea-based), nuclear depth charges for ASW, and nuclear antiship missiles, (air-to-surface, surface-to-surface, and subsurface-to-subsurface).

Throw-weight—the combined weight of all warheads, guidance systems, and penetration aids carried by a single missile.

Yield—the amount of energy released by a nuclear explosion. Expressed as an equivalent of the energy produced by a given quantity of TNT, i.e., 1 kiloton (KT) = 1,000 tons of TNT, 1 megaton (MT) = 1,000,000 tons of TNT.

Index

About the Authors

MICHAEL MANDLEBAUM is assistant professor of government and research associate of the Program on Science and International Affairs at Harvard University. He spent the academic year 1976–1977 as a Rockefeller Fellow in the Humanities and a Visiting Scholar at the Research Institute on International Change at Columbia University. Mr. Mandelbaum received a B.A. from Yale University in 1968, an M.A. from King's College, Cambridge, in 1970, and a Ph.D. from Harvard University in 1975. He has written on issues of national security and on American foreign policy.

RICHARD L. GARWIN is IBM Fellow and Science Advisor to the Director of Research at the IBM Thomas J. Watson Research Center in Yorktown Heights, New York. A physicist who has worked extensively in both technology and fundamental science, he served two four-year terms on the President's Science Advisory Committee, 1962–1965 and 1969–1972. During the 1960s he chaired PSAC panels on military aircraft and on antisubmarine warfare, in addition to serving on panels on strategic warfare, intelligence, and chemical and biological weapons. He served on the Defense Science Board in the Department of Defense, 1966–1969.

JOHN H. BARTON is a professor of law at Stanford University, where he received his law degree in 1968. After receiving his B.S. from Marquette in 1958 and spending three years in the Navy, he worked as an engineer, primarily on arms control verification studies. A co-editor with Lawrence Weiler of a forthcoming textbook on arms control, he has also written about issues in energy and international economic law. Barton spent 1976–1977 on leave at the International Institute of Strategic Studies in London, where he studied arms control enforcement and completed a book on the effectiveness of arms control.

DAVID C. GOMPERT contributed to this volume as a senior fellow of the 1980s Project, Council on Foreign Relations, a position he held from 1975 until April 1977. He has since become Director of the Office of International Security Policy, U.S. Department of State. Following his graduation from the U.S. Naval Academy in 1967, he was on active duty in the U.S. Navy until 1971. In 1973 Mr. Gompert was a member of the staff of the National Security Council, and in 1974 and 1975 he served as Special Assistant to Secretary of State Henry A. Kissinger. The views expressed by Mr. Gompert are his own and do not necessarily reflect those of the United States government or any of its agencies or departments.

FRANKLIN C. MILLER is currently a systems analyst in the Office of International Security Policy, U.S. State Department. A 1972 graduate of Williams College, he served as a naval officer for three years before entering Princeton University's Woodrow Wilson School of Public and International Affairs. Mr. Miller, who received his M.P.A. from Princeton with a specialization in international affairs and national security policy, was the rapporteur for the 1980s Project's Working Group on Nuclear Weapons and Other Weapons of Mass Destruction. He is also the co-secretary of a Council on Foreign Relations study group on the future of the U.S. Navy. The views expressed by Mr. Miller are his own and do not necessarily reflect those of the United States government or any of its agencies or departments.

DATE DUE